Vicky Pattison's autobiography, *Nothing but the Truth*, was a Number One *Sunday Times* bestseller in hardback and remained in the Top Ten for seven weeks. Vicky's first novel, *All that Glitters*, received rave reviews from her fans who fell in love with the witty one-liners and snappy comebacks Vicky is renowned for. She also has her own clothing range, jewellery collection and weekly column in *New* magazine. She is one of the original *Geordie Shore* cast and appeared in nine series of the hit MTV show, and is now the star of her own MTV show, *Judge Geordie*. In 2015, Vicky won the nation's hearts and was crowned Queen of the Jungle in *I'm a Celebrity ... Get Me Out of Here*. Vicky is a genuine Geordie Girl, born and bred in Newcastle.

Nothing But the Truth

MY STORY

Vicky Pattison

sphere

SPHERE

First published in Great Britain in 2014 by Sphere
First published in paperback in 2015 by Sphere
This paperback edition published in 2016 by Sphere

3 5 7 9 10 8 6 4 2

A CIP catalogue record for this book
is available from the British Library.

ISBN 978-0-7515-6544-7

Typeset in Baskerville by M Rules
Printed and bound in Great Britain by
Clays Ltd, St Ives plc

Papers used by Sphere are from well-managed forests
and other responsible sources.

MIX
Paper from
responsible sources
FSC® C104740

Sphere
An imprint of
Little, Brown Book Group
Carmelite House
50 Victoria Embankment
London EC4Y 0DZ

An Hachette UK Company
www.hachette.co.uk

www.littlebrown.co.uk

To my friends and family, especially my wonderful parents, Caroll and John, and my sister, Laura

Contents

Nothing
But the Truth

Prologue

I've made a mistake. And it's a big one. I'm sat in a police cell wearing my pyjamas. It's freezing cold and I'm sobbing uncontrollably. This is not how my life was supposed to turn out. I'm miserable, alone, overweight, anxious and terrified I've just totally messed up my career and my life. How the hell can I come back from this?

Chapter One

A Wey-Aye Welcome!

I was born on 16 November 1987 in Rake Lane Hospital, North Shields, weighing-in at 5lbs 11oz. Both my parents, Caroll and John, were twenty-nine and I was their first baby. Dad said I looked like a skinned rabbit, all long and thin and wiry. To be honest, that was probably the last time I was thin until now!

My sister, Laura Jane, arrived three-and-a-half years later, in August 1991. To this day she likes to stay close to my mam – she's much more of a home girl whereas I've always been really independent and done my own thing. I adore my parents – I'm a real family person, but

I stood on my own two feet from a really young age. I've always forged my own way, I think I get that from my mam. She's a very strong, independent woman and has always been inspirational to me. We're all feisty women in my family to be fair, and I wouldn't be surprised if we're descended from Boudica!

I'm like my mam in many ways, but in others I really take after my dad. Some people you can look and instantly see that they're a total amalgamation of their parents, and that's me. My mam is petite with blondey-brown hair, and I definitely look more like her; she's also stubborn and outspoken and those are traits that she's passed on to me. My dad loves a drink and going out and being around people so that's where I get my really sociable side. I've also got his temper. My dad is a right grumpy bastard when he wants to be and there's no point in denying it, I can be too.

The story of how my parents met is so romantic. They're both from Wallsend, which is where I live now. Their parents, my grandparents, were all from there too so it will always be my home. It's four miles from Newcastle city centre and four miles from the coast and is made up of lovely little families, there's a real community feel. Back in the day all the dads worked down the mines or at Swan Hunters, the big shipyard on the River Tyne. Everyone knew each other and looked out for everyone else, and it's still the same today.

My mam and dad went to the same school, The Buddle, when they were eleven years old; which still stands today. My mam said she knew she fancied my dad straight away but he tried to play it cool. He *says* he didn't fall for her until later on, but I don't believe a word of it. It's impossible not fall in love with my mam.

They had their first kiss when they were fourteen and my mam was the one who kissed him apparently. She's a woman after my own heart! You can see where I get it from now, the saucy little minx. My dad is shyer than she is, so I think he was a bit intimidated by her at first, but he soon fell head over heels. My maternal grandparents had turned their garage into a little youth club so all the kids could listen to music and hang out, and that's where my parents cemented their relationship. It's lovely to be able to go back to those places and see where it all began.

Once they got together that was it forever. They got engaged, got married and then along came me and then my sister. My parents are the main reason I want to get married, if it wasn't for them I reckon I would have given up on men by now. Whenever I think: 'I'm happy being single. Do I ever really want to settle down?' I look at them and realise 'that's what life is about'. My grandparents on my mam's side, Mavis and David – or Mave and Dave as we like to call them – celebrated their Blue

Sapphire sixty-fifth wedding anniversary last year and they inspire me as well. I'm so lucky to have such amazing role models. There's never been a divorce in my family, ever.

Everything I am today, and everything I've achieved, is because of my family and I couldn't be happier. I couldn't have done half of it without their constant support of me and belief in me. They're the most amazing family anyone could ask for – they make me so proud and I don't know what I'd do without them. There are so many shit people in this world and so many bad things that can happen – you're really tested at times, and you need those people you can hold up as a beacon of hope.

My grandparents have always loved a party. We'll go round to their house, have a coffee and pretend we're being good, but it's about five minutes before my granddad is dusting off a bottle of Pernod or whatever weird drink people bought him the previous Christmas or holiday abroad. It only takes one person to go into their house for him to see it as a party and, like my dad and I, he loves talking to people: he views all strangers as friends he hasn't met yet. Even though he's in his mid-eighties, granddad still loves being surrounded by people having fun; he'll always have that massive party mentality in him. I think that's filtered through the generations; when I was a teenager our house was always packed to the rafters with mine and Laura's mates and my parents were always so welcoming to them.

My grandparents are quite old-fashioned and I would never swear in front of them or be as opinionated as I usually am, just out of respect to them. My granddad is the sweetest man; he still gives me a fiver every Sunday as he's done since I was a kid. He'll slide it across the table and say: 'You're still not too big to take some money from your granddad.' I'll always be their little granddaughter. I don't think he really understands what I do for a living; I assume he thinks I'm an actress, and I'm happy with that. I'm going to allow him to believe it. Why not? It's not hurting anyone.

My grandma is more savvy, though. She waits for granddad to go to bed and then watches *Geordie Shore*. I know she does, because she drops herself in it by mentioning things that have happened on the show. When Ricci and I were having problems and she saw Charlotte gossiping about me in an episode, she took me aside and said: 'Don't you let that little madam say anything else bad about you.' My grandma Maeve will always want me to go in there and give as good as I get. I get some of my fiery personality from her as well as from my mam, she would never want me to be a doormat. She's always on my side and always has an opinion, but I'm horrified when I know she's been watching the show because it's not for her eyes and ears!

My grandma has also passed down a real sense of pride in looking good just to me. She's just turned eighty-four and is immaculate, she's so well turned out and always has a new blouse or skirt she wants to show me. My cousin got married last year and grandma had been planning her outfits for about six months in advance – she looked amazing on the day. I really love my fashion and dressing smart and I totally get that from her.

My sister Laura is my best friend in the world. On paper she's younger but in every other way she's more mature. She left school at sixteen because, although she's as sharp as a tack, she didn't enjoy the academic side of things. She's got a problem with authority, funnily enough – we're definitely alike in that way! Laura didn't like the idea of college or university, so she went straight into the workplace and worked her way up in HR and finance departments. She has done so well and is an accountant for Fenwicks in Newcastle now. She's got a really old head on her shoulders and is so wise. Laura's level-headed; we'll go to each other for advice and are so protective of each other. There's not a lot I wouldn't do for her. Of course, that's not to say we didn't fight like cat and dog when we were growing up. We had our moments, like all siblings. She's a real softie in some ways, so I'd often win arguments because I don't like backing down. There's not a lot you can do or say to upset me, but because Laura is more sensitive she would

6

often run off to her room while I would be ready for round two.

Though Laura never enjoyed the academic side of school, I loved it. I was confident and a bit of a show off. I was always in the school plays and took any opportunity to be in the spotlight. I played Marty in *Grease* and Dorothy in *The Wizard of Oz*, and every time there were any kind of class performances I'd be right there in the middle of them.

I hung around with a really great group of girls who came from nice families and we all wanted to go to university and do well. I'm competitive and whatever I was doing I had to be the best at, whereas Laura was more laid back and had a group of mates who thought it was cool to be naughty. I just couldn't get my head around that. I saw it as wasting their opportunities – they weren't bothered about getting good marks or ever thinking about life after school.

I wasn't a geek, but I was intelligent to the point where I struggled to pick my options because I liked so many subjects. I loved English literature and really fancied myself as a writer. I also liked Sociology because I'm interested in people, as well as Drama, French and History. However, I couldn't get on with Maths and Sciences, mostly because I can't talk my way out of those subjects. There is only one right answer with them, and if you can't pinpoint that you can't do well. Give me a four-hundred-page script for a play on a Monday and I could learn it by Wednesday, but I find working out an equation a thankless task. I liked essay questions where you could put your opinion across and try and get people on your side. I like people to see what I see and believe what I believe. There's no room for manoeuvre in Maths.

I'm not kidding when I say that I've always wanted to be famous. I knew that I didn't want a nine-to-five job because I would be bored. I loved the Spice Girls as soon as they came out, and I wanted to be like them. Victoria Beckham was my favourite, and I still love her now. I wanted to be fashionable like Posh and cute like Baby. The whole Girl Power message really resonated with me. I adored the idea of five girls being best friends and taking on the world. Even now, every time I go out with my mates for a night out I think we're the Spice Girls and that we deserve loads of attention! We don't by the way – we act like drunken wankers!

I come from a family of attention seekers. When we get the karaoke system out on Christmas day it's like *The Hunger Games*. That mic comes out and the women are almost fighting to the death over it. Not one of us can sing, but you'd think we were Adele the way we act. Give my family a couple of sherries and all of us ladies want to warble while the men sit around shaking their heads and trying to avoid being dragged up for a duet. The exception is my granddad. He's got a lovely little voice, bless him, and I could sit and listen to him all day.

I've always been really driven and ambitious; I think that ambition comes from my mam. My dad always worked hard in the civil service, but as soon as he got the opportunity to retire he took it, whereas my mam is still climbing the ladder. She never wanted to settle for anything and was always looking to find a job that was right for her. Even when my sister and I were young she had three jobs. Not because my parents struggled for money, but because she's so determined and strong. She used to run a slimming club on a Wednesday and my dad would have to look after us. I remember those evenings so well. We'd walk around to the local Somerfield and were all allowed one bottle of pop, one bag of crisps and one bar of chocolate each. Dad would buy us a new Disney film on VHS each week, we'd all sit on the floor together and would have eaten our food and drunk our pop before the credits even started. I was a chubby kid!

Mam also ran a book fair during the day and worked for the RNIB, which is where she got the start in the career she's doing now. She began on the lowest rung possible: putting envelopes through people's letterboxes asking for donations. From there she got into being a telephone canvasser, and then she was promoted to team leader. Before she knew it, mam was their corporate fundraising manager and was planning massive

RNIB events at the Dorchester Hotel in London, which people like Rod Stewart and even the Queen attended. She was this little lass from Wallsend and would go and stay up in London for three days a week and deal with all these amazing VIPs. She was so passionate about it.

Mam never wanted to leave Newcastle completely for the bright lights of London. Geordies are very proud of the region, and very loyal, and her plan was always to find a local charity where she could really help to make a difference in the place where she grew up. These days she's the managing fund director for *The Chronicle* Sunshine Fund. *The Chronicle* is our local paper and the charity raises money for disabled and disadvantaged kids in the North East. She's continuing to make massive changes to people's lives. I wish mam woke up each morning and knew what a difference she was making, but rivers run deep with her and she always thinks she can do more.

Watching her work so hard and do so well has kept me focused. I love strong women generally. I am so pro-women and I see no reason at all that we can't do anything a man can do. I like it when I look at a woman and think 'you do not give a fuck'. My mam has instilled in me that if you work hard you can achieve anything and I'll always be grateful for that.

I had such a lovely upbringing and I know how lucky I am to be able to say that. The only times I ever cried was when I was about eight or nine and the boys at school teased me for being a bit chubby, but it wasn't the end of the world. I realised quite young that we have a fat gene in my family and all of the women struggle a little bit to stay in shape. We're like The Klumps. We're all quite short, so an extra stone shows up on us really easily, whereas someone taller could get away with it. Unfortunately all of the Pattison women also seem to fall for skinny men, which doesn't help.

Growing up I was very tall for my age, and bigger than the other girls. I've always had a real sense of self-awareness, even when I was a kid, so I knew I looked a bit different to them. I was just a bit sturdier and more robust! We're a proper Northern family and we used to sit down to have big meals together. You had to finish what was on your plate, even if you weren't that hungry, because there were 'starving kids in Africa'. As a result I probably overate quite a lot as a kid so I was always on the chubby–fat border.

It was never a problem that I was a bit rounder than my mates until I went to middle school, because then I wanted the boys to fancy me. I didn't want to be the chubby one anymore and it was when I got into sport that things started to change for me. The weight didn't suddenly drop off, but it definitely helped. I initially started being sporty because of my competitive nature, but I was very happy that one of the side effects of that was slimming down a bit.

When you're really young PE just involves running around and having fun, but once I was in middle school I got more into team sports like netball, hockey and even women's rugby for a while, and I pushed myself because, as ever, I wanted to be the best. I felt like there was no point in playing unless you could either win yourself or be on the winning team. I still feel the same way now.

I've never been a lazy person or one to rest on my laurels so if there was a lunchtime netball practice, I'd be there. After school rehearsals for the play? Count me in. Extra French tuition? Definitely. I was constantly busy. Believe it or not there was a time when my mam was worried about me being too academic. In retrospect this was a bit embarrassing – what a helmet! I always had my head in a book and she thought I should be outside having fun. Of course, all of that did come later.

I flourished in my first year of high school. I lost a few pounds and I got a huge fringe, which was the height of sophistication at the time. I used to brush it over a can of hairspray to get the right shape, and then I'd use another can of hairspray to practically glue it in place. Then I'd get my curly brush and roll it around and around underneath it and spray it all over again. Everyone had fringes like that, honestly. The bigger your fringe, the hotter you were. Clothes-wise, I used to wear a lot of hand-me-downs from my older cousin Louise, and I had this pair of gold Dr Martens that I thought were the absolute business, though looking back they were properly disgusting. They even came with a spare can of gold paint in case you scuffed them – those shoes were my pride and joy for a long time. I also tried to dress like my favourite celebrities, so for instance I'd team high-waisted jeans with cropped tops so I looked like a cross between Posh Spice and Kelly Kapowski from *Saved by the Bell*. I see girls wearing similar things nowadays so they can't have been too hideous, can they?!

Because I was always on the go and had my fingers in so many pies I knew loads of different people and was well-liked. It may sound a bit knobby, but I never struggled with anything at school. I didn't get bullied and I was never a bully. I think picking on someone you know is weak or vulnerable is sick. If I'm going to disagree with someone, I would rather disagree with someone bigger and harder than me because they can take it. When people target others because they're smaller or weaker it's horrible.

I often found myself standing up for people who couldn't stand up for themselves. You have to be pretty tough in Newcastle and I always was; I could take care of myself. There were kids at my school from some of the hardest families in the North East, and they could literally smell fear. I knew from the moment I started high school I couldn't let anyone sense any weakness in me because they would go in for the kill, so I was always on alert.

I had a really big group of friends throughout middle school and that carried on into high school. In the beginning we were all really close and we stuck together, but then some people started to splinter off and things changed. When I got to be about thirteen it suddenly became cool to go out and smoke, standing on street corners with your mates, and because I didn't want to do those things, I lost my popular edge a bit. I'd have friends round to mine to watch a DVD instead of going to the park to get drunk and that affected my popularity. The really cool kids were the ones who were a bit rough and I didn't want to be the kind of person who didn't try. I ended up having quite a few run-ins with some of my mates because I didn't want to sneak out of school for a fag or get sent out of class for being an idiot. I didn't think it was cool then and I don't think it's cool now. To this day it really irks me that there are people that thing being cheeky or disrespectful makes you look clever or funny. It just makes you look immature.

It's funny because people often say to me: 'I bet you were a right chav at school' or 'I bet you were well rough', but I was the opposite. I walked my own path and I always looked up to my elders. I still do. I used to cringe when people would answer the teachers back or be rude. It just didn't do it for me – I was never the one throwing chairs about. I got my head down, I did my work and I did well. You're meant to do the best you can with your life and I wanted to make my family proud. For a long time I was one of what we used to call 'flyers'; kids who would do extra classes. So instead of doing one foreign language, I did do two. As a result I was friends with the geeks as well as the trendy girls and boys. My friendship group was far-reaching and I liked that.

When I think back to my school days, though I may not have run with the really so called 'cool' kids, I'm the one having the last laugh now. I bump into some of those people who were too busy acting the idiot to do any work, and they're my age with four kids. Maybe that's what they wanted from life, but it was never going to be enough for me. Fair play to anyone who does what they want to do and is happy – I wouldn't want to judge someone for their decisions, but I *know* there were girls at my school who had so much more potential – they could have done amazing things and they threw it away for boys and booze.

That's not to say I didn't still have my moments of rebellion. When I got to about fourteen or fifteen my mates and I started experimenting with drinking. We used to go this place called 'the rocks', which wasn't a cool bar or anything; it was literally a collection of rocks that was hidden away from the bizzies. I would manage to get six alcopops, and there would also be

Lambrini passed around for us to share. Some utter idiot always bought some 20/20 along, which is like lighter fuel, but only the bravest (and stupidest) amongst us would touch that.

That was around the time I started kissing boys too, usually after a few drinks. My first ever official kiss was with a boy called Stuart when I was away in Fuerteventura on holiday with my family when I was thirteen. It was an all-inclusive resort and the entertainment crew used to come round during the day and ask if you wanted to play games. Of course, competitive Vicky was right in there, so it would end up being just me and all the dads taking part. Then one day there was this young lad who joined in and our eyes met across the water polo court. I was in love. He was fifteen, so a much older man and, in my eyes, well sophisticated.

We started flirting with each other a bit (at least I think I was flirting. I hadn't done much of it before) and then one evening, while all of the parents were watching some terrible band perform in the bar, we sneaked out and sat on a sun lounger outside. I knew he was going to try and kiss me and I remember being so excited but completely mortified because I didn't have a clue what to do. He held my hand and I had the sweatiest palm in the world. I was going through puberty so I was a sweaty mess anyway, and when you heap a load of nerves on top of that I was like a swimming pool. He asked me if I'd kissed anyone before and I was like 'yeah, of *course!*' but inside I was thinking: 'I'm going to be shit and he's going to know this is my first time. He's going to think I'm a freak.'

He went in for the kill, so I cast my mind back to all of the kissing scenes I'd watched in countless episodes of *Sweet Valley High* over the past few years and hoped for the best. I don't think it was what you'd call a good kiss. I thought you just moved your head around a lot so looking back I was probably like a limp noodle darting all over the place. My cousin Louise had told me that the technique was that he sucked your top lip and you sucked his bottom one, so I tried to do that initially but it wasn't the best advice I've ever had. Then, all of a sudden, I felt his tongue in my mouth and I was like 'woah, Louise didn't tell me about this'. I don't think she was as experienced as she made out. Thankfully Stuart was nice enough not to point out that I was absolutely dreadful at kissing.

Stuart was from Coventry so when we got home we spoke on the phone every night for about two weeks and I was smitten. Sadly things soon fizzled out and it wasn't to be. But part of me is hoping that he reads this and gets in touch because I remember him being very cute, like some kind of Ryan Gosling type. Then again, for all I know he's more like Mr Bean these days.

I felt like I returned from Fuerteventura a new, more experienced woman. I had a tan and I was the proud owner of my first tash-on. Now I was ready for more! My first UK-based snog will have happened in a night-club called Ikon, at an under-eighteens night. When I was that age, under-eighteens nights were the best things that ever happened to me. I used to put my glad-rags on and go along and dance to happy hardcore music like Scooter. Some of the clubs had foam parties so you'd leave looking like a drowned rat, feeling like you'd just had it large in Ibiza.

The most fun we had was doing deliberate laps around the club with your mates all huddled in a little pack, where you would try and catch the eye of a young gentleman. If you made eye-contact they would come over with the very creative line 'do you want to score with my mate?' You'd check out the mate and if you didn't fancy them you'd say 'no', and then their answer would always be: 'well, do you want to score with me then?' It was normally a 'yes' because the better-looking one always did the asking.

This will sound terrible but we used to have a points system so that the more people you could neck-on with the more points you got. It sounds a bit slaggy, but we were only young and it was all very innocent. To be bru-tally honest, I can't actually tell you the name of the first lad I kissed back in the UK because it was definitely a total random in a dark corner. I would love to say he was really attractive but he was probably a bit of a troll.

I don't think I got really good at kissing until I was about fifteen and I started to go into *actual* town. Going to the Bigg Market for the first time felt like all of my dreams had come true. It's this area in Newcastle, full of clubs and bars and it's always bouncing. During the day it looks horrendous. It's like a war zone with kebabs thrown everywhere and random stilettoes lying on the floor, but at night it's the place where dreams are made.

When my mates and I were fifteen we couldn't afford to be choosy about where we went out. We couldn't go drinking on the Quayside with all of the footballers because none of us looked old enough – also we couldn't afford to – so we went to the couple of places we knew we would probably get into. They're where I spent some of the best years of my life until I was about seventeen and could get hold of some fake ID and get into the posher places. But I still go back to the Bigg Market now for the nostalgia of it. It also holds a special place in my heart because it was where I met my first proper boyfriend.

Chapter Two

Dean-age Dreams

Every year without fail, we'd have a family summer holiday where my mam, dad, Laura and I would go to Greece, Tenerife or Ibiza and have the best time. But each summer we also used to go to a caravan park called Haggerston Castle near Berwick-upon-Tweed. It was a family tradition and it was like going to a Haven Holiday Park. It had a pool and a bowling alley and a big night-club where they'd have Diana Ross impersonators and discos for the kids. It was horrific – and I loved it!

When I got to about fifteen I was allowed to take a mate along with me, so my friend Sarah came and we went off on our own; horse riding and sunbathing. There were loads of lads there and we felt properly grown-up. One day we were hanging out in the club-house and we met these two lads, Dean and Dennis. I fancied Dean straight away, I thought he was so beauti-ful: he was 6' 3" and tanned with dark hair and the bluest eyes you've ever seen in your life. I loved him instantly, but I didn't think he would be interested because he was seventeen, which made him virtually an adult. He seemed like a proper grown-up and I felt really intimidated because he was so much more worldly than I was. He had a job as an apprentice joiner and *everything*, whereas I was only gearing up to sit my GCSEs.

We all spent a bit of time together over the next few days but no matter how much I tried to use my new and improved flirting skills on Dean, nothing happened between us. I thought he probably saw me as massively young and a bit of a tit. When the holiday came to an end I decided to forget about the summer romance that never was and told myself that the guy of my dreams was probably just around the corner. I wasn't exactly desperate for a boyfriend but my mates were starting to get together with people and it felt like the right time for me to meet someone. I saw a few guys here and there and did a bit of tashing-on, but there was no one I liked as much as I had liked Dean, and I began to wonder if I would be single *forever*.

One night, just before my sixteenth birthday, about nine months after I'd met Dean, I was out in town with a big group of girls. We were all dancing like nutters when all of a sudden my mates Nicola and Emma started staring at someone over my shoulder. I turned around and was faced with the most gorgeous man I had ever seen in my life – again. Guess who? I went bounding up to him like a lunatic and shouted 'Dean!' really loudly at him. He stared at me like I was crazy and seemed to have no idea who I was. I was so breathless and excited I burst out: 'It's me! Vicky! From Haggerston Castle! Do you not remember me? You're Dean, from Dean and Dennis!' He looked really confused and replied: 'I know who *I* am, but I have absolutely no clue who *you* are?' I was gutted. Talk about awkward.

I was totally mugging myself off and my mates were all looking at me as if to say, 'What the hell are you doing? Walk away you utter dick!' But I wasn't about to let him slip away from me again. I was older and wiser now. However, instead of rolling out some smooth chat-up lines, I started digging myself deeper and deeper into a massive hole of shame. 'Don't you remember me? You walked me to my caravan one night? We didn't really speak much?' I bellowed over the strains of Beyoncé's 'Crazy in Love'. Dean stood there with his mouth open with a mixture of abject terror and embarrassment on his face. But he was so gorgeous it was like I'd been

22

hypnotised into being an utter arse. Despite feeling like I wanted the dance floor to turn into a massive sinkhole and swallow me up and transport me back to the non-humiliating safety of my mates, I had this feeling that I never wanted to leave him. It was one of those feelings that you only really get a couple of times in your life, and they're so much more intense when you're younger. I felt like I was in a film. Ok, looking back it was more *Bridget Jones* than *The Notebook*, but at the time I didn't think I'd ever feel like that again. To this day I don't really think I have.

Thankfully, my persistence eventually paid off, and after another agonizing ten minutes of talking he finally admitted that he remembered who I was. That has to be the worst (and cruelest) case of playing it cool I've ever come across. Dean told me he and a couple of his mates were going on to Baha Beach Club, which was a pretty grown-up place to go in those days and you couldn't get in if you were underage. He asked where my mates and I were heading and I had to think on my feet because we were planning on staying where we were, for the simple reason that they'd actually let us in. I said as casually as possible that we hadn't decided yet (like we had options) and he invited us to go with him. I said yes instantly, but inside I was thinking, 'Shit, what if I get knocked back?'

After much persuasion my mates agreed to come

along with me and – it was a miracle! – they let us all in. To me that was a sign that the rest of the night was going to be amazing as well, and I was right. After a few cheeky shots Dean and I had our first kiss – it was everything you want a first kiss to be … and more. There were fireworks going off all over the place and pandas playing violins. I was smitten.

I went back into school on the Monday and I told everyone about this amazing guy I'd met. I was so proud. It didn't ever cross my mind that I might never see him again. I just knew there was something between us and everything was going to be fine. I just *knew*.

I was right. From that night on Dean and I were inseparable. We used to meet up in town each week with our mates and we'd spend the whole night tashing-on with each other all over Newcastle like no one was watching. For my sixteenth birthday he bought me an imitation diamond bracelet from Beaverbrooks jewellers, which back then was the height of luxury. I felt like I was Posh Spice and he was my very own David Beckham. His family were great and he got on really well with mine, and we hated being apart. I think my mam and dad thought I was going to marry him. And back then I think I did as well. We would walk each other to bus stops just so we could spend those extra few minutes together waiting for the bus to come, and we'd be on the phone to each other seconds after we'd said goodbye. He was the sweetest guy you could ever meet and was so nice to me. I felt like life couldn't get any better, even if we were both a bit skint.

I'd always wanted to work and as soon as I could go out and get a job, I did. I wanted my own money that *I'd* earned. My first job was in Shelley's shoes in the Metro Centre, which was a dream come true for me because I got a good discount. I gathered such a brilliant shoe collection. My mates would come in and chat on a Saturday and I used to get told off by the manager constantly, but I felt like I was really grown-up because I was getting wages each week. Dean was still doing his apprenticeship and was paid a pittance so we had virtually no money between us, but we made the best of things. We always managed to have a good time even if we were broke. We loved each other's company so much that we didn't need tons of cash to have fun.

Dean was the first lad I ever had sex with and I didn't sleep with him until I was sixteen-and-a-half, which was a lot later than some of my mates, though a lot earlier than others. I wanted to make sure I was totally ready before I jumped into anything and we'd been going out together for about eight or nine months at that point so he was very patient with me, especially considering he was older. I was so lucky to find someone so lovely. Our relationship reminded me of my parents' in a way. It was very uncomplicated and genuine and we had such a fondness for each other.

I remember trying to set up some of my mates with some of Dean's mates and a few of them had a bit of a tash-on but it wasn't very successful. What I really wanted was one of my friends to get together with his pal Ricky because he had a car and I thought it would make things so much easier, but sadly none of my attempts ever stuck.

This may be a good time to address the whole 'tash-on' thing. Loads of my mates are up in arms about it. Everyone assumes it's a Geordie thing but actually it's my mates and I who made it up years ago. A lot of people in Newcastle say 'neck-on', which never made sense to us because kissing is nothing to do with your neck, it's all about your tash area. I can't even remember where it came from. I think maybe one of our dads said 'aye, have you been out on the razz tashing-on?' so we just rolled with it and have said it ever since. I took it into *Geordie Shore* and used it and all of a sudden everyone assumed it's what Geordies say. We should have got it copyrighted!

When the time came for me to move from high school to sixth form I grew up a lot, quite quickly. I stayed on at the same school and though I still performed well in lessons and joined every club I could, I also started going out more and seeing Dean whenever I got the chance. I guess I got a bit more reckless in some ways and I started challenging authority because I was older and I wanted to have even *more* of a voice than I'd had before. I was getting bored of education and I was ready for new things. I felt like I'd done Newcastle: I'd been at the same school since I was thirteen; I'd been going out in town since I was fifteen; I'd had the same friends for years. As far as I was concerned I'd seen it all and done it all. I was a big fish in a small pond and I couldn't wait to get my teeth into something new.

When I was seventeen I left Shelley's and got a part time job working at Kookai, which at the time was *the* place to work. In fact, while I was working there I met Cheryl Cole. She came up and asked for a top in another size and I didn't realise it was her until someone pointed it out afterwards. I remember her being tiny and polite, and I wish I'd had more of a chat with her because I'm a typical Geordie girl in that I think she's amazing. Everyone in Newcastle does. Charlotte and Sophie were lucky enough to go to her concert last year and meet her, but I couldn't go and I'm still gutted. Cheryl if you're reading this, I love you!

Kookai was so cool and grown-up, and I was hanging out with all of these fabulously cosmopolitan girls. One had done a season in Zante and was studying fashion at university, and another girl had done a season in Malia and was doing a Chemistry degree. Working with those girls opened new doors for me. I started going to better clubs because all of the bar and club promoters would come in and offer us guest lists for all of the best places in town. We would all get really dressed up and go out together which made me feel more mature and also made me hanker after bigger and better things. Once you have a taste of the glamorous life you want more of it, and I wanted as much as I could get.

I felt like I was juggling two lives between sixth form and Kookai and I started to let my standards slip a bit education wise. I was taking A-levels in Sociology, Performing Arts, English Literature, French and General Studies, but my heart wasn't really in it. I know that some of this will come as a shock to people but I'd left high school with really good grades. I got As and A*s in my GCSEs, but A-levels were so much harder because I had a job and boyfriend and an amazing social life. I was flitting about in my gorgeous Kookai clothes with my fabulous new friends and in my head I was already at university. I felt like there was nothing my teachers could tell me because I already knew it all. I got a real teenage godlike complex around that time. Most people get theirs when they're a bit younger but for some reason mine kicked in at seventeen and that feeling hung around for quite a while.

I started to really get into a lot of trouble when I stopped going to my classes. For the first time, I was rebelling. I think that was the time when I lived my *proper* teenage years. I was going out five nights a week and selling shots in the evening in a club called Mood. I had a twenty-year-old boyfriend who owned a car who used to pick me up from college – I thought I was the bee's-knees.

When I turned eighteen I became worse because I was officially an adult. I wanted the independence to be able to do whatever I wanted, when I wanted. I thought it was the coolest thing in the world that I had a thumbprint to get into a club in town called Blue Bambu. It was the height of technology at the time and everyone in Newcastle wanted to be a part of it. The manager of the club's mam and dad lived on my street so I knew him, which is how I got my 'in'. I used to rock up and see all of my friends from sixth form standing queuing up, hoping and praying they'd get in, and I'd waltz up to the front, kiss the manager and put my thumb onto this machine so it could read my print. I felt like I was James Bond. I'd be escorted straight through to the VIP area and I'm sure that's when my 'VIP edge' first started. I knew I was destined for better things when I got thumbprint access.

I gave my poor mam a lot of trouble and my sixth form teachers were constantly on the phone saying: 'Vicky isn't attending. She's got a forty-five per cent attendance rate for her classes and if she carries on like this she'll have to pay for her own exams.' They weren't willing to put me up for the exams because they didn't think I was going to pass. I must have put my mam through hell because she constantly had to answer the phone to these ranting teachers, but she dealt with it brilliantly and even though she gave me a good kick up the backside a few times, she had faith in me.

My sixth form's lack of belief turned out to be a bit of a blessing in disguise to be honest. It made me determined to prove them wrong – I knew I could do it. So when it came to the exams I managed to convince them to let me sit them, despite having done the minimum amount of work possible. I was a bright girl and knew I could get good grades if I put my mind to it. In the run up to the exams I really focused, and then crossed my fingers that I'd done enough.

Dean and I were both young and a bit daft in some ways, but we ended up staying together on and off for two-and-a-half years. It wasn't all plain sailing. In 2005 we went on holiday to Malia at the same time with our mates and both ended up kissing someone else, which was a nightmare. One of his friends just happened to see me tashing-on with some lad in a bar, and then another of his friends told me he'd done the same thing. We were both as much to blame, but I was completely inconsolable and our relationship suffered so much as a result that I wondered how we could ever come back from it.

We rowed about it for weeks and were on the brink of splitting up so many times. One minute we couldn't be around each other, the next we couldn't live without each other. In the end we accepted that we were both on holiday with our friends, we were drunk and it wasn't the end of the world. But it did change things for both of us, even though we carried on pretending it didn't.

Looking back now I wasn't old enough to deal with my feelings and the intensity of the relationship. If I had met Dean when I was twenty-four we would be married now without a doubt. He is *that* man; he's that perfect person. I still know him now and I see him around town sometimes. He's got a new girlfriend who is absolutely beautiful and I'm so glad he's happy. But to this day he will always be the one that got away.

My problem – if it is a problem – is that whatever I have I've always wanted more out of life. I've never been content with what I've got and always want to do better. I have such a fierce drive that I want it all. At that time, I wanted an amazing career and getting married young wasn't a part of my plan. I think there have been times in the past where I've overlooked guys who may have been right for me because I wonder if there's something else out there. Not romantically, but professionally.

When I finished my A-level exams I wanted to go and do a season in Magaluf, then after that I had always planned on going to university. Ultimately, that's what led to Dean and I breaking up. I wanted to do all of those things so I did them without much thought for whether our love could survive it. There was no blazing row or big drama, I just knew that I had plans and those plans wouldn't have worked if I'd been with someone. I guess looking back I did the breaking-up for those reasons, but I think of it as a mutual decision. We both knew our relationship couldn't work unless I was content to stay in Newcastle for the rest of my life, get a job locally and settle down. That was never going to happen.

I was eighteen and ready to take on the world, and so I was very matter-of-fact and almost callous about our break-up. Of course within a matter of weeks I regretted my decision and I missed him like *crazy*. I wanted him back so badly because he was the most decent and gorgeous bloke I'd ever met, but by then he'd already moved on. A lad like him wasn't going to stay on the market for long. He had been snapped up and I'd missed my chance. Even now I feel bitter towards the girl that 'stole' him from me, even though it was my choice to split up and he was a free agent. I know it's irrational but when I see her in Newcastle I feel angry about it – there is no love lost between me and her. Husband thief! And she was a stripper. *And* not a very attractive one in my opinion.

I'd well and truly lost Dean and I was heartbroken. It

was only when I saw him with someone else that it really hit me how much I loved him, but I had no right to try and get him back. I'd burned that bridge to the ground. But a part of me will always love him. You never forget your first love and I think it's almost impossible to cut off all of your feelings entirely because you'll always think 'what if?' Even now when we bump into each other I'm transported back to being sixteen and head over heels in love with him. There's nothing I can do about that and we've tried to be friends, but can you ever really be friends with an ex? We'll get to that later!

Having said all of that, I genuinely hope that Dean and his current girlfriend have loads of happy years ahead of them. I had my chance and I walked away and hopefully there is someone else incredible out there for me. When I look back it's hard to imagine how different my life would have been if we'd never broken up. I could be married with kids now, living in a semi-detached in Newcastle and working in M&S. I'd probably be really settled and fat!

The lovely thing about my relationship with Dean is that he gave me such a great attitude towards men and because of him I really trusted them for a long time after we split up. Even though I'd been hurt by our relationship ending I wasn't afraid of falling in love again. Back then I believed that any person I bumped into could have been the love of my life and I always kept that hope alive. I didn't think there were bad lads. I felt like I was Superwoman and that any man could be my Superman. That's what your first love should do for you. Sadly, I'm more distrustful of men now, but I will never stop wanting to fall in love and find the right person.

Thankfully I had Magaluf to focus my energies on after Dean and I broke up. As soon as my exams were done I fucked off without a second thought, and I ended up having one of the best summers of my life. Magaluf was like Newcastle with sun and the best laugh ever. I went away to try and forget about home for a while, but of course my A-level results were always in the back of my mind. If I didn't get the grades I needed I wouldn't be going to university, and that would have been a disaster for me. It was a huge part of my life plan.

The day the results came out my mam was straight on the phone to me and my heart was racing. She sounded upbeat which I saw as a good sign, and when she said 'you've got four As' the relief was incredible. Mam said that when she went to get my results my Sociology teacher – the one who had been making all of the calls to my mam saying I wasn't going to pass – came shuffling over with his tail between his legs and said to my mam: 'Oh, she managed to pull it out of the bag!' Mam just smiled at him, but I like to think that moment made up for all of the shit I put her through that year.

From that moment on I felt like there wasn't anything

I couldn't do. I've always wanted to prove people wrong and show that I can do whatever I set my mind to and that proved it to me. I'd managed to get four As without letting my social life drop and I felt invincible. I'd had it all and still achieved what I needed to. That's my aim in life; to have everything I want. I want my social life, my family, my friends and an amazing career – and I don't see any reason why I can't.

Now I knew I had the results I needed to get into my university course I felt like I could really relax and enjoy the rest of my summer. I was working behind the bar at a club called Boomerangs six nights a week and living just off the main strip. I'd originally gone out there with a girl called Nikki and we were planning to get a place together, I had really liked the idea of having someone I could share the experience with. But she met a lad during our first week there, fell head over heels in love with him and ended up going back to England, leaving me on my own. They didn't last and still to this day I wonder if she regrets being so hasty because she ended up spending those months back in Newcastle when she could have been having the time of her life.

I didn't think twice about staying out there once Nikki had left. I'd gone there to do an entire summer and that's what I was going to do, even if it meant going it alone. I have so many brilliant memories from those months. It was the first time I'd ever lived on my own and I think that helped me to get over Dean because I had to properly stand on my own two feet. I did a hell of a lot of growing-up because I had to be totally self-sufficient. I was the only one paying for my rent and bills and buying myself food so I had to get myself up and get to work each day no matter how hungover I was. No one else was going to be buying my dinner if I couldn't. I honestly think that if I'd stayed in Newcastle that summer and seen Dean around a lot I would have ended up *begging* him to take me back.

I made so many friends I thought I'd have for life in Magaluf, but I couldn't even tell you their names now. But if they're reading this, thanks for making my summer so memorable! I did stay in touch with one guy called Liam because purely by chance he was also going to Liverpool John Moore's University, which I had been accepted to. He was a lovely lad from Manchester and it was purely friendship but we ended up staying friends throughout our entire time at university, and he played a massive part in my life over those three years.

It was so hard to leave Magaluf when the summer ended, but knowing that I was coming back to start an amazing course in Liverpool really softened the blow. My mam still had to drag me back kicking and screaming though, and in the end she booked my flight for me. I think she was worried I wouldn't come home if she didn't. I arrived back a week before I was due to move into my halls for Fresher's Week so things were a bit of a rush, and I had no idea what I was in for.

I chose to do a course in Drama, Media and Cultural Studies because they all formed a part of my life plan. My aim was still the same as it always had been: to be famous or work in the media in some way. I had this notion that I would become the British equivalent of Carrie Bradshaw. I wanted a glamorous life working for a top magazine or newspaper, or in radio or TV. Obviously I would live in a gorgeous apartment in London and have a very famous boyfriend to boot. I couldn't quite decide exactly how I was going to make a name for myself and I'd change my mind daily about exactly what I wanted to do. One day I'd want to be a newsreader, the next I'd want to be a TV presenter, and then I'd decide I was going to be a high-flying journalist. All I was totally clear about was that I wanted a fabulous, glossy life and I couldn't think of anything worse than never achieving anything.

I wanted to get out into the big wide world and constantly be meeting interesting people. I used to read these terrible chick-lit books about a poor girl from Sheffield who moved to London and lived in a crap flat and fought to make it. I craved all of that. Money and fame have always been my goals and I've always been very upfront about that.

Some of my friends and I laugh about how different

we are because they've never made any secret of the fact that all they wanted from life was a lovely husband, some kids and a nice house. That's a very normal ambition in Newcastle and none of us judge each other. They don't think I'm ruthless and ambitious for wanting so much, and I don't think they're settling. We're just different. The most important thing in life is to wake up each morning and feel fulfilled, whether you're working in a call centre or presenting the biggest TV show in the country. You have to find what's going to make you happy and have the courage of your convictions.

Don't get me wrong, one day I would love to settle down with someone amazing and have a nice house, but the kids I can take or leave. I'm not putting myself under any pressure because at the moment children aren't on my radar, and I don't know how I'm going to feel in a few years. Maybe it will never feel like the right time? And if that's the case, that's okay. At the moment I'm living my life like a man and it's all about work and money, and I'm embracing it. (Just for the record I do NOT have a penis!)

I know for a fact that I won't be able to be someone's wife or have children before I've achieved everything else I want to. I'll know the time is right when I feel like I've been successful enough on my terms, and really worked hard for the things I want. I've never been able to stomach people who sit around moaning about their lives being crap. If you want something, you have to go out and get it. No one is going to hand anything to you on a plate. That's not how life works.

When I left my first school my headteacher said to my mam: 'Vicky will achieve whatever she wants to in life.' That never left my mam and it's only now that I understand the gravity of it. Whatever you set your mind to, you can get. Look at me now. I'm right where I planned to be (give or take a few little slips ups along the way . . .).

Chapter Three

Box Fresh

Moving to Liverpool was a total revelation to me, but also a massive shock to my system. I'd gone from knowing absolutely everyone at my sixth form and in Newcastle to being totally on my own. It was the first time in my life I experienced true fear and loneliness. I felt like I didn't belong and I was so out of place. I'd expected it to be like *Hollyoaks*. I thought I'd walk into the SU bar, order my first drink and a gorgeous group of boys and girls would invite me to go and sit with them and then that would be it for the next three years. We'd get into crazy capers and drink all the time and we'd be the coolest group going.

Funnily enough, it wasn't like that at all. I remember my parents driving me down and walking me into my halls at Grand Central, right next to Liverpool Lime Street train station. As I went into my bedroom for the first time I thought, 'what the hell? This isn't a room. I'm going to be living in a fucking box.' I felt I was going to be like Harry Potter when he lived in the cupboard under the stairs – I kept looking around for the rest of the space. It was about four foot wide and ten foot long with a single bed, a desk and bugger all else. I instantly felt depressed about the thought of that being my new 'home'.

There were six of these 'bedrooms' side by side, all inhabited by girls. There was one Scouser who had her boyfriend there the whole time so she was constantly locked away eating Domino's; the girl next to her kept herself very much to herself; the girl along from her was a mature student from Stockport who ran home at every opportunity, and *her* next door neighbour was very religious and used to turn her nose up at me. The only girl I really got on with was a girl called Kelly, who was from Staffordshire and was stunning with long blonde hair. The only problem was that, even though we got on really well, she was doing a PE course so she was really into her health and fitness. As a result she didn't want to go out drinking every single night, which I was desperate to do. I think at uni you either luck out with your flatmates and you're out in the infamous Bar Revs on the first night having the best time ever, or you're really bloody unlucky like me.

My mam and dad stayed in a hotel nearby on that first night to make sure I settled in okay and both of them admitted to me some time later that they really didn't want to leave me there because they thought my dorms were depressing. They could see how upset I was feeling and though they came close to offering to take me back home, they knew I'd find my feet eventually.

There was such a massive, eclectic mixture of people at John Moore's and of course not everyone is going to get on and like each other. It was a bit of a minefield. When you're growing up you've got all of your mates around you so you're not terribly bothered if not everyone wants to be your best friend. But at uni, where you know no one, you suddenly become desperate to be liked because the idea of spending the next few years of your life sat in your bedroom cut off from the world is pretty daunting.

It was such a scary prospect for me to be completely alone. I felt like everyone else there knew people; either their sister was there, or they'd come with their best mate, or their cousin was in the year above. I felt like everyone had links to other people and I was flying solo.

For the first couple of months I was really in two minds

about whether or not I'd stay. Because my course was joint honours, it meant that I was spending half of my time with the media and cultural studies students and half of my time with the drama students, so I was totally split and was missing out on things. On top of this, I didn't feel like I really connected with either group. The people on my media and cultural studies course were geeky and not like me at all, and the people on my drama course were really in your face and over the top. I struggled to see where I fitted in.

Other students were bonding and friendships were being formed and I wasn't a part of it. I couldn't get my head around the fact that I was doing these different courses on two different sides of the uni. I didn't feel like I belonged in either of them and there was no crossover so I really struggled to form any lasting friendships. I'd meet someone and we'd get on well, then I'd have to go and work on my other course. I was flitting back and forth and never in one place for long enough to really get to know people. I was used to being the popular kid, and suddenly I wasn't. At all.

I remember going home for my reading week in October. I'd only been at uni for three or four weeks, but it felt like I'd been away for a lifetime. I went out with my mates to all of the old places we'd hang out and I remember thinking 'it would be so easy to just come back here'. But I had to have a strong word with myself and remember that nothing in life worth having comes easily. I would have dropped out, loved being back home for a couple of months, probably have tried to get back with Dean, and gone back to working in Kookai. Then once the novelty had worn off I'd have got bored and massively regretted my decision.

At the end of my reading week I picked myself up and did the six-hour journey on the National Express Coach back to Liverpool with the screaming kids and snoring men (the words 'National Express' still fill me with absolute horror). Something clicked on that journey back and I thought: 'You've just got to do this Vicky. Throw yourself into it even if you don't feel like you've got much in common with your fellow students. Suck it up.' I knew that if I didn't start really living and breathing uni I would regret it later. Yes, it's about learning and getting a degree, but it's also about living away from home, putting off growing up for a little while longer, and ultimately having fun.

Funnily enough, Liam, the guy I'd met in Magaluf, turned out to be my saving grace. Because he was from Manchester he knew loads of people. He was outgoing and funny and was on the football team so had become really well connected really quickly. He was living opposite me in Grand Central and before I knew it he'd made friends with the whole block and was introducing me to new people. Through him I became mates with a group of girls who lived upstairs from me – Lucie, Helen and Kelly – and I also met the guy who would become my next boyfriend.

The lad was called Ross and in retrospect he was a total and utter bell-end. But a very cute one. He was a bit taller than me with dark hair and a really good body – he played for the university rugby team and lived in my building. We had our first kiss while we were all out at Medication, the Wednesday student night at a club called Nation. Four vodka Red Bulls were a tenner, there was sweat dripping from the roof and the last song of the night was always 'Zombie Nation'. It was a top night out. After that first kiss, Ross and me spent loads of time together. We'd hang out in each other's rooms (well, cupboards), go clubbing and to the cinema and live on Chinese food. It was the height of romance.

Ross and I used to joke that we ate his student loan. We lived right around the corner from Chinatown and for the first time in my life I could get a takeaway every night if I wanted to without anyone telling me off, so I did. As a result I absolutely ballooned. I look back at photos now and I've got this round chubby pie face that was created by noodles, but at the time I didn't think too much about it. I probably went from a size ten to a twelve–fourteen and I was skint so I was still trying to squeeze myself into my smaller clothes because I couldn't afford new ones. It was muffin-top central. I basically put on the 'Fresher

Fifteen', as everyone used to call it, in the space of about six weeks.

I finally started to really enjoy life in Liverpool and Ross and I had a real laugh together. The only fly in the ointment was that he'd had a serious girlfriend before he'd come to uni and he'd had to defer for a year because she fell pregnant. It was a giant leap into the unknown for me because I'd gone from my sweet and simple relationship with Dean to this grown-up scenario where another woman and a child were involved. At first I kind of liked it because it made me feel quite mature having a complicated love life. That rapidly got old when he kept having to go back home to Pontefract every other weekend to visit the baby, but I really liked him so tried to be as understanding as possible.

Things became pretty serious between us and he came to stay with my family in Newcastle, and then I went to meet his family just before Christmas. While I was there I also got introduced to the mother of Ross's baby. I was trying to be super friendly, but she was incredibly hostile towards me. I put it down to her being protective over Ross, but something didn't feel right. When we got back to uni I heard something that would explain why things were so strained – friends told me that it seemed Ross had still been seeing his ex when he went back to visit the baby, and had only 'officially' broken up with her the week before I went. If that was right, it would completely explain why his ex wasn't air kissing me and throwing high fives – she was furious and heartbroken. Needless to say that was the end of mine and Ross's love bubble.

Despite the break-up I felt like I'd really got into my stride at uni and there was no stopping me. I started to come out of my shell and get more into the drama side of things. My media course became something that I just 'did' rather than enjoyed, so I put all of my energy into doing the thing that I liked most, which was acting. I met a lot of like-minded people there and when I came back after the Christmas holidays I felt like I was flying. I got a job in Kookai in Liverpool and made friends with the girls I worked with, and it wasn't long before I started selling shots in local bars in the evenings again. I was single, I was going out and having fun with a great group of girls, and it was amazing.

Before I knew it, it was like I'd recreated my old life in Newcastle in Liverpool. They're not very different really. Everyone loves going out, the girls love dressing up and looking glamorous and wouldn't dare ruin their outfit with a coat. They save all week to spend all day Saturday getting ready before they go out and piss all of their money up the wall. It felt like a second home in a way. It still killed me when I went back to Newcastle though, and I used to dread Sunday nights when I had to go and get on the bloody National Express back to my tiny box room.

But being at uni did me so many favours and completely opened up my world. As well as being self-sufficient it forced me to think outside the box and make friends with people from different walks of life from all over the country. It was really tough being away from my family sometimes because I knew things were never going to be the same again. I wasn't a kid any more.

My first year at uni ended up being a massive learning curve and probably one of the most life-changing periods I've ever had. It was a nice feeling going back home to Newcastle for the summer and knowing that I had a lot to look forward to in my second year. I had a great group of friends and it was going to be even more fun now I was properly settled in. But there was going to be one big difference; I would be heading into year two with a *gorgeous* new boyfriend.

When the first year was over I arrived back in Newcastle with several bags of washing and a grown-up attitude, and I immediately went out to try and get a job so I could save up some money to go on holiday with my mates. I applied to a shop called G-Star and was so pleased when they offered me the job. That's where I met Kailee, who is still one of my best friends. She is first like me: fun, loud and loves a good night out – we hit it off instantly! It was such a laid back place to work, it was non-stop banter, and I totally landed on my feet.

My life was amazing. I was living with my parents and

they weren't making me pay board, I was getting on dead well with my sister, going out with my mates, working in G-Star with a load of really cool people and making good money. I had no complaints at all, I couldn't have been happier. The only thing missing was a significant other. But then the second big love of my life made an appearance.

I had always been a bit of a face around town because, though a lot of people don't realise it, Newcastle is really small and everyone knows each other. Having worked in some of Newcastle's coolest clothes shops and bars and been a big fan of going out, everyone knew who I was. People who look a certain way and are the same age will drink in the same bars, and that summer we were always out at a leisure complex called The Gate. It's massive and has got bars on the bottom floor, restaurants in the middle and a cinema at the top. It's always freezing in Newcastle and no one wears coats – hence our saying 'coats are for c**ts' – so the fact it was indoors was a godsend. The Gate and Blue Bambu were the places to be seen so I spent my entire summer flitting between the two.

I met a few lads out and about and had a few tash-ons in the early summer, but I've never been one to settle easily and I have to have proper banter with a guy to like him. I've realised that I need someone who can keep me interested and entertained for any relationship to work.

I don't just mean a bit of a dickhead who keeps me on my toes by acting like an arse, but someone who can mentally stimulate me. I don't want to sound conceited, but because I'm intelligent whenever I've been out with thick lads in the past they drive me up the fucking wall. It can't be all style and no substance. If you're with someone who isn't very bright even the most basic conversation can turn into an argument because they can't grasp what you're trying to say. I don't have the patience for that, so I get frustrated. I'm not the most patient of people sometimes, I'll hold my hands up and say I'm not, and something as simple as that can mean make or break. Thankfully I soon found someone who was gorgeous *and* funny.

One of my best mates is a gay guy called Paul who used to be the front of house greeter at TGIs in The Gate, which is how we met. Paul is one of the most flamboyant and charismatic people you'll ever meet and one Sunday night I'd been at home getting ready to go on a date with a lad and I was *so* excited. I was all dressed up but just as I was about to leave this lad texted to cancel using a really ridiculous, shit excuse. I was getting a custard pie in the face and I knew it, but there was no way I was going to sit there all dressed up with nowhere to go. I got straight onto the phone to Paul and arranged to meet him for several large drinks.

As soon as Paul saw me he said: 'Fuck that guy, he

doesn't know what he's missing. Let's go and get mortal. You've got to meet this lad I'm in love with. I met him last week in Tiger Tiger and he's gorgeous.' We headed to a bar called Players in The Gate and as soon as we walked in I clapped eyes on one of the barmen who looked like he'd been carved by angels. He was this beautiful Adonis of a man. He was about 5' 10" with a shaved head, a strong jawline, tanned skin, bluey-green eyes and the most amazing smile. He was wearing a roll-neck as part of his uniform which wasn't really doing it for me, but the rest was *perfect*. I was speechless for a bit and had to stop myself from staring at him like a freak.

Paul introduced me to him and as my heart fell when I realised that this was the lad he fancied. Paul turned to me and said: 'This is Anthony. How fabulous are his eyebrows?' and as soon as I could find my voice I was like: 'Yeah, they're wicked!' though really I was thinking 'great, this is the first time I've ever talked to this incredible man and I'm complimenting his eyebrows. Why am I saying this to my future husband? And hold on, Paul's flirting with him so surely he must be gay?' I was gutted.

Anthony was staring straight at me and there was a real spark between us, so I wondered (and prayed) that I'd got the wrong end of the stick. Several parts of my body were very clearly telling me that he was straight, but maybe that was just wishful thinking? Paul quickly spotted that there was an attraction between me and Anthony, and his eyes were darting back and forth between the two of us as if he was watching a tennis match. Paul is absolutely hilarious, but he can be very catty when he wants to be and he suddenly blurted out: 'She's just been stood up you know?'

I got all flustered after that so I ordered my drink and walked off as soon as possible. I thought then if there had been a chance that anything was going to happen, it wasn't going to now I'd been completely mugged off. Paul thought it was all most hilarious – which I have to admit it was – so we both proceeded to get really drunk and jokingly bitch at each other about it. When he finished his shift Anthony ended up coming clubbing with us both because we were all keen to make the night last. We went to a place called Cosmic Ballroom that played tech house and got stuck into the shots. Everyone in there used to get really drunk and dance like wankers, and we were no different. I was trying every trick in the book to try and get Anthony to notice me. I was dancing with his mates and acting like I was the most amazing person in the room. The night was probably a six out of ten on the fun scale but I was acting like it was a ten and I was in fucking Vegas. I was flirting with everyone and laughing at things that weren't funny just to try and get his attention. I was giving him every signal possible – I was already head over heels in love with him.

Every now and again he'd throw a few glances my way and would give me a bit of attention, but it suddenly hit me that most guys who were that gorgeous were total players, and I didn't want to be used and then tossed aside as if it was nothing.

I was still pretty inexperienced when it came to relationships and sex. I'd had one great experience with Dean, one not so great one with Ross, and I'd kissed a lot of guys, but that was about it. I was confident, but I'd never had a one-night stand and I certainly didn't want Anthony to be my first. It's not in my character to sleep around – I was already in this for the long haul. I love a tash-on but I really only want to have sex with people I really care and who care about me. My heart was beating out of my chest every time I looked at Anthony and I knew I wanted so much more than a quick drunken fumble.

The rest of the night is a bit hazy but I know that I drank absolutely loads, acted like a bit of an idiot and yet somehow at the end of the night I found myself in a car with Anthony heading back to my house. I was worried that if I let him go I might not get him back, so against my better judgment I invited him in. My parents were away so we went up to my room and started tashing-on and I got so swept away with everything I found myself having sex with him. I was horrified because this was a lad I'd just met, but at the same time if felt right, if that doesn't sound too cheesy.

We woke up the next morning and it should have been awkward and weird but it just wasn't. Anthony stayed at mine until he had to go to work that night, and I remember my mates and I went in to see him at Players a few hours later. I was really worried that he'd act like he wasn't interested and then I'd know he'd only been after one thing, but he was lovely and we arranged to meet up the next night with all of our mates.

The following evening we went to Players and Tiger Tiger and had an unreal night. Anthony came back to my house again, and ended up staying for three days. That was it. Love. That pretty much set the tone for the rest of our relationship. It was passionate and it was intense, and it stayed that way for the entire time we were together. We were best friends and had the same sense of humour, so we had a real laugh together as well as massively fancying each other. We liked the same films and TV shows and our friends all got on well. Paul wasn't all that impressed at first, but he's the type of person who doesn't take anything to heart, and once he knew Anthony and I were onto something good and in it for the long haul he forgave me for stealing this god away from him.

I genuinely thought Anthony was the man for me. I was nineteen and completely swept away. I felt so comfortable with him. When I was going out with Dean I only liked him to see me when I was looking good with my hair and make-up done because I was so young and quite naive, but now I was slightly older and living away from home for half the year I felt like I was an adult. So Anthony and I used to go the gym together and I didn't mind that I looked all sweaty and horrible, or I'd wake up after a party with mascara running down my face looking a total mess, but I was fine with looking a state. Anthony had his own house, so that bought another dynamic to our relationship because it meant we could have loads of time to ourselves, and sometimes I did sit there and imagine what it would be like if we lived together, and if maybe – because I was so in love with him – that could be enough for me?

Anthony was hugely into fitness so I followed his lead and found that I started to really enjoy training. As a result I managed to lose all of the weight I'd put on in my first year, and then some. I got down to about nine-and-a-half stone and felt incredible. As well as fitness, we also shared a love of partying, so often we would go out on a Friday night and still be going on Monday morning. We used to call it the 'Smonday' club. It was a great time of my life because I had no responsibilities and a gorgeous boyfriend. I also had regular money from my student loan that my mam had taken off me and sensibly drip-fed me, and I was working to top it up. I was on top of the world.

Chapter Four

Orange Is The New Black

When I went back to university for my second year it was so bloody hard to leave Anthony because we'd had such a brilliant summer together. There was no way we were going to split up and we knew we could find a way to make things work, even though we were so far away from each other. Thankfully I'd moved out of halls and into a place above a bar called The Flute with some friends, so I was no longer living in a rabbit hutch.

My new digs were right next to the uni, the student union and loads of bars and it was *the* place to live.

There were only thirty-five flats in the block and to get one you had to go and queue up for ages when they all became available. I went along with Kelly, Lucie and Helen and we managed to score one, and it felt like we were living in Buckingham Palace. It had laminate floors and a leather sofa and I could actually move in my bedroom. Looking back it was pretty grim, but it was ours and we loved it.

There were five floors and loads of drama students and dancers moved in at the same time we did, so living there was like being in *Fame*. I'd be walking down the stairs and there would be a girl in pink tights limbering up, or someone learning a script very loudly. I became quite artsy and seeing how ambitious everyone was made me even more determined to work in media. Maybe I wasn't ready for the quiet life with Anthony after all? I had this ridiculous idea that I could decide later on because once I left uni with a degree there would be an amazing job waiting for me. I was sure people would be beating my door down to offer me brilliant opportunities, so I could wait and see how I felt when the time came.

It felt like so much was different in my second year. I had a new home and a new boyfriend and I wasn't the frightened girl I had been at the start of my first year. I was more worldly-wise, but at the same time I was gutted that I'd had to leave this godlike man back home to go back to studying. However it wasn't long before he came to visit. Along with thirty of his mates.

I'd been back at uni a few weeks when Anthony decided to come and stay for one of his friend's birthdays. I arranged for all of my mates to come out as well so there were about twenty girls. We all got properly dolled up and went to The Comedy Store at Liverpool Docks before they arrived. I was so excited about seeing Anthony that I didn't even concentrate on the show because I knew he'd be arriving in Liverpool any minute and I couldn't wait to see him. Eventually he rang and we all met at a bar called Modo on Concert Square.

I was so happy when we finally met up – we couldn't stop hugging each other. The lads had been drinking all day so they were mortal, and as we left to go on to the next bar this guy started on Anthony for no reason. Anthony always had a bad temper so before you could say 'Jaegerbomb' it all kicked off. Then his mates started getting involved and the next thing I knew it had turned into this massive street fight. I was panicking and didn't know what to do, when all of a sudden I saw the girlfriend of the guy Anthony was fighting with run in and start hitting him, so without thinking I dived in. It was like something out of a film and the next thing I knew the police turned up and started dragging us all apart. Everyone calmed down and it looked like it was all going to be resolved. The police weren't going to arrest anyone because no one had got hurt and we were all going to be sent off with a stern warning. It wasn't like anyone needed to go to hospital or anything. But Anthony would not bloody calm down. He was shouting and screaming and lashing out, so in the end the police had to put the cuffs on him. I was pleading with the police – begging this policewoman to let him go – but she looked at me, shook her head and said: 'No, he's going to have to spend a night in the cells.' I wasn't having any of that, I'd been looking forward to seeing Anthony so much and I knew that if he got arrested that our happy reunion would be over. In my head I was having a really rational conversation with the police officer and appeared really together and sensible, but in reality I was probably coming across as pretty full of myself and really drunk. Either way, I just wouldn't let it go, and before I knew it I ended up getting arrested along with Anthony. Brilliant. The first time my boyfriend had ever come to visit me at uni and we both got 'cuffed and put in a police van. It was probably the worst date ever – I was planning a romantic visit to Albert Docks and instead all he got to see was the inside of Liverpool Police Station.

The reality of the situation properly hit me once we got to the police station. I was in a police cell, shitting myself, and although I was only in there for a couple of hours, they were two of the worst hours of my life. At first when I was sat in there in the silence I was still pretty wasted and full of nervous energy – for some reason I thought I was 50 Cent and I started doing press-ups and running around and all sorts. Then all of a sudden I sobered up and all of this stuff began to go through my head about how I was going to get chucked out of uni, and how disappointed my parents were going to be in me. I felt like hell, and I was also so worried about what had happened to Anthony because the police were refusing to tell me anything.

At the end of the two hours a policewoman opened the cell door and told me I had to go and be interviewed. She looked me up and down, stopped dead in her tracks and asked me where my trousers were. Of course, being a Geordie, I hadn't been wearing any – I believe what I was wearing as a dress was actually supposed to be a top, so it barely covered my bum. It was a brown, sleeveless, thin-knit number with gold thread running through it and an open back, so it barely covered anything to be fair. I'd worn it with gold stilettoes, gold bangles and big gold earrings, all of which they'd taken off me in case I'd harmed myself with them. They even took my hair extensions so I looked like a right bloody mess. I don't know if they thought I'd try and hang myself with my hair extensions or something, but to be fair they were longer than my dress, so maybe ...

When I explained to the policewoman that I was

wearing my entire outfit she was not impressed. I felt like saying to her: 'Look, it's nothing without the gold ear-rings and shoes. You really need them for the full effect,' but I didn't think she'd appreciate it. The upshot was that, because I was going to be interviewed by a male police officer, she didn't think what I was wearing was appropriate so she disappeared off and came back with a bright orange convict jumpsuit for me to put on. It was made out of the itchiest material known to man; it felt like it had been crafted from bees and nettles. I looked and felt like I was an extra in an Akon video.

I went in to be interviewed and I was expecting a really tough time of it but thankfully the police officer was really sweet. I think he could tell from talking to me that I was a nice girl from a nice family and I'd never been in trouble before. I was a young student, I'd acted like an idiot and I was being punished for it. He said that they weren't going to take it any further, though they still cautioned me, meaning that I got my first criminal record at the grand old age of nineteen. But the law is the law and the good thing was that it gave me a proper scare. Everything happens for a reason.

I don't want to make light of the situation as it was really tough but what happened next was the only glim-mer of humour in a pretty serious situation. I was told that one of my friends had come to collect me so out I walked in my lurid jumpsuit thinking 'this will give them a good laugh', but just as I was about to step into the waiting area I saw that it was Anthony sitting there waiting for me. He'd been released before me, so he and my mate Paul, who had also come down for the weekend, had come to take me home. I totally panicked. It was one thing your boyfriend seeing you look rough after a night on the town, it was quite another for him to see you in an orange jumpsuit. I handed the police officer my bag of hair, which I'd just had returned along with my shoes and jewellery, and quickly whipped off the jumpsuit and put my heels back on. When I eventually walked out Anthony looked at me, laughed and said: 'I clocked you through the window and I saw the jumpsuit. Good look.' The utter shame.

Anthony felt so guilty about everything. He gave me a massive hug and said: 'I'm so sorry. If I hadn't been fighting none of this would ever have happened.' But it was my stupid mistake. The ridiculous thing was he hadn't even realised I'd been arrested. He was so drunk he thought I'd come along to the police station to keep him company. It was only when he was released and went back to his hotel that his mates asked him how I was and he realised what had happened. Even though it was really traumatising for us both, it ended up bringing us closer together in a strange way. Obviously we'd been seeing each other for a while by then but it was that weekend when he asked me officially if I would be his proper girlfriend. I just thought 'why not? You're gorgeous and funny and we're both utter fuck-ups. We belong together.'

Even though Anthony and I got on brilliantly, like all relationships it wasn't perfect. We're both very strong-willed so when it was good it was amazing, but when it wasn't it was shit. We could argue for hours on end and then afterwards we'd ignore each other's calls and texts for days. We were so stubborn. That was when I went from being fiery and strong to being quite angry and maybe even a little aggressive, because I would get so wound up by him. I think the arrest episode in the end became a bit of a sticking point and I veered between thinking it wasn't really his fault to feeling really angry about it.

Our lifestyles were totally different too. He was still working in Players while I was going out every night. I'd call him at four in the morning drunk and would cry because I missed him but he had to be up for work the next day, so that caused problems. We were both jealous people and towards the end of my second year we found the distance between us hard to handle. Somehow we managed to make things work for us that whole year I was away. I would go home or he would come and see me and we stayed in touch as much as possible. When we were actually speaking, that is.

At the end of the second year I moved back to Newcastle for the summer holidays. I was working back in G-Star and in various clubs and bars again. On the surface things were good, but my relationship with Anthony was completely crumbling. We were trying to pretend it was okay but it's not healthy when you can't talk without shouting, and even though we loved each other we also drove each other mad. It all came to a head one day and after a huge blazing row we decided to go our separate ways. We had to admit defeat.

It was a total contrast to the way Dean and I had split up. There was a lot of anger and swearing from both sides. We were both bitter to the point where we almost hated each other. We didn't speak to each other for a long, long time after we broke up, which was really sad. I was devastated because I loved him so much, but I knew it was for the best because we were ripping each other to shreds.

It was soon time to head back to uni for my final year and when I got there I literally partied my way through it to try and forget about Anthony. I missed him so much and looking back on it now I don't think we were ready to break-up, but the distance (and the arguing!) forced us to. Even though I kissed other people and flirted a lot at uni, Anthony was always in my head. I used to drunk-dial him sometimes and often he wouldn't answer; on the rare occasions he did he was so stoic about things that it made me worse. I would get so wound up and either send him furious texts or really soppy ones saying how much I still loved him. He ignored most of them, so I found myself feeling even angrier towards him. It was clear that I still had very deep feelings for him and I was really hurting, but being single meant that I could concentrate more on my life in Liverpool, which had been difficult to do when I was seeing him.

I steamed through that year and I was out all the time. My favourite night was Wednesday when we'd go to Medication at Nation. All of the sports teams would go and we'd all tash-on and then go on to a big house party. I must have made about three Thursday morning lectures in my third year. I also used to go to all the gay venues like G-Bar and Garlands, and I bloody loved it. After three years of partying and some seriously hard work towards the end – it was like my A-levels all over again – I eventually left uni with loads of new friends, tons of amazing memories – as well as a 2:1 degree. But I also had absolutely *no* idea about where my life was going.

Chapter Five

The Birth of VIP Vicky

After finishing university I had some kind of weird ambition meltdown. I moved back home and lost all my drive. My dissertation had been really full on and I'd put everything into my exams and enjoying my last year, so I felt like I needed a bit of a break before I went about trying to conquer the world. I don't think it helped that the job offers weren't exactly flowing. As I said, I thought people would be fighting each other to get me to go and work for them, but the reality is that you need to be looking for a job halfway through your third year to have any chance of heading straight into decent employment.

I left Liverpool on a real high but when I crash-landed in Newcastle absolutely skint, jobless and living back with my parents, it wasn't long until a real sense of doom set in. I still wanted to move to London and be famous but the stark reality hit me; it's just not that easy.

I decided to give myself a break for a couple of months while I got a plan and some money together. I got my old job back in G-Star, but this time working full-time, and I also started working as a cocktail waitress in a bar called Florita's in the evenings. Before you could say 'Bigg Market' I became a real girl about town again. I really enjoyed it for the first couple of months because it was a bit of a novelty after three years away, but when the end of summer arrived anxiety kicked in because I was completely directionless. Of course, I wasn't going back to university come September so when I looked ahead all I saw was a massive expanse of nothingness. I told myself that I'd save up all of my money and move to London. I'd stop going out, buying clothes and going on holiday, and I'd be the new Cheryl Cole in no time. I've always had delusions of grandeur. But – shocker – things didn't quite work out as I planned. I couldn't even stay off the Jaegerbombs or out of Topshop for two days. I was, and always have been, rubbish with money.

As I've said before, Newcastle is small so it wasn't long before I started bumping into Anthony all the time. We started having the odd conversation when we were drunk, and because my mate Lindsey was seeing his friend Mick we started to move in similar circles again. We properly started speaking to each other in December 2008, the Christmas after I graduated. Things progressed and we started seeing each other again. Anthony officially asked me to be his girlfriend – for the second time – on St Patrick's Day the following year while we were out on the piss. I still had all of those feelings for him so I jumped at the chance. We slipped back into how we had been before and it was all so easy I totally lost my way and all thoughts of London went out of my head.

I don't know what happened to me but I wasn't at all fussed about working towards a proper career any longer. I was back in love with Anthony, I could walk to the front of the queue of every club and bar in town, I got free drinks all night and I still had a VIP thumbprint for Blue Bambu. I thought this was enough for me.

I never had to worry about getting in anywhere and to me queuing would have been social suicide. If I got any hassle I could get the lasses who were giving me trouble thrown out – I was treated like a queen. At that particular time I thought that was all there was to life and I didn't need anything else. My friends and I thought we were invincible.

So there I was, settled, comfy and in a routine and drifting happily long. I felt like I was living the high life because I was hanging out with footballers like Andy Carroll and Steven Taylor and I got totally sucked in. I was basically living my university life without the lectures. I'd work in G-Star, rush home to have my tea and get changed, then go back out and either work or go out on the lash. I thought I was meeting new and interesting people and expanding my mind, but looking back most of them were probably quite vapid. I used to tell people when I was drunk that I was just saving up to go and work in London in radio or fashion or whatever it was I fancied that night, but I wasn't doing anything to make it happen. I was having fun so nothing else mattered.

At that time my mate Lindsey was working as the manageress of Tiger Tiger and she came to me one day and said that they were going to relaunch it and make it the best venue in Newcastle. They wanted me to apply to run the VIP area and I honestly thought I'd made it. My job would entail running the all-new 'white room', which was going to be hugely exclusive. People would need a VIP card just to get through the door and it was all table service. I would have my own private doorman and I could decide who I did and didn't want to let in.

Before I'd even got the job I was thinking about who I *wasn't* going to let in. We all had this running joke that if you were prettier than me you weren't getting in, and if you were prettier than me *and* you had an attitude you *definitely* weren't getting in.

I went along to the interview, got offered the job and I felt like someone had given me an Oscar or said I could get off with David Beckham. I had a great degree, but all I wanted to do with it was be a VIP host in Tiger Tiger. If ever there was a nail in the coffin of me moving to London, that was it. I was the least ambitious I'd ever been. The most I pushed myself during that time was picking up a couple of shifts in other bars hosting their VIP areas. I was doing Tiger Tiger on a Monday, Wednesday and Friday, Madame Koos on a Tuesday, Ohso on a Thursday and Riverside on a Saturday. Any nights I had off I was going out abusing my VIP status. That was when I officially became VIP Vicky.

You've got to learn to watch your back more than ever when you become a door whore like I was, and I think doing that job changed me. You meet some proper scumbags, and you have to be able to stand up for yourself. You get pushed around so much that if you don't show that you're in control you really get the piss taken out of you and people will bully you.

I also got the second God-complex of my life. I had proper power and I knew it. If you can get someone into a club without them having to pay or queue they think you're amazing. All of my mates worked in bars and clubs as well, so together we were a force to be reckoned with. If you wanted to get into anywhere in Newcastle you had to be nice to us. Other people knew it and we knew it. I was only twenty-one and I went power mad. I was the Mussolini of the Newcastle VIP world. I behaved like a total arsehole. If I could sum that period up I would call it 'The Utter Twat Year' because that's how I behaved.

When you're on a massive up, you will always be heading for a massive down and after a few months, getting footballers' BBM pins and free drinks wasn't really doing it for me anymore, especially coupled with all of the abuse I was getting when I was working. I definitely brought some of it upon myself because of the way I acted, but people were also generally vile and they took it so personally if you didn't let them in. The pressure started to really get to me.

On a Monday, Tiger Tiger's student night, three thousand people would come through the door, and each and every one of them wanted to be in my VIP area that only really sat around seventy-five. I could sometimes managed to squeeze double that in and though no one was comfortable everyone would have the best time ever. But imagine having to say no to all of those other people – not everyone was going to take it well. The Freshers were the worst. They had a real sense of entitlement and would get wasted on £1 vodka Red Bulls then try and shove their way into the VIP area where people were paying thousands for tables. My nights consisted of constant debates and arguing with tons of drunken people.

Then there were the footballers. They had to be treated well because they spent big. Danny Simpson and Andy Carroll used to come in, and they wanted to drink all night and have a bit of privacy and I had to make that happen. Groups of girls would come in and claim their mate was in the VIP area and point to a footballer. I'd turn and give the footballer a look and they would indicate whether or not they wanted me to let them in. Most of the time he'd have new girls in so I'd say to them: 'Sorry lasses, not this week.' Of course they would be furious and say things like: 'What do you fucking mean? We were here last week. Who do you think you are?' I had to keep my composure and stay calm with these girls who were, for want of another phrase, football slags. All they wanted was to buck a footballer and drink his Grey Goose vodka and that would be the highlight of their week.

There was one footballer who came in, bringing a big group of girls with him. They were having a laugh and drinking his champagne, when he spotted another girl he liked the look of, so he came over and asked me to throw the other girls out and let the girl he fancied and her mates in. It was so bloody awkward. Another time a friend of Dean's new girlfriend rolled up wanting to get into the VIP lounge. She'd given me some real attitude in the past so I didn't even give a courtesy glance to see if the area was full or not; I just turned her down flat and went back to my clipboard. She started kicking off so I got her ejected from the club and she was threatening to do all sorts to me. It's little wonder I wasn't always that popular around town back then.

Everyone who went out in Newcastle knew who I was, and a lot of them were people I'd knocked back from getting into clubs or got thrown out at one time or another. It sounds like nothing but people took it so personally. I've never been the kind of person who needs everyone in the world to like me but it wasn't ideal because this was the time when I started getting into fights. I became feistier than ever because I'd had to. I couldn't take any shit.

There were other issues too. For instance if I was in a bar and Dean's ex-girlfriend was in there that would cause agg. All it took was for one of her mates to look at one of my mates the wrong way and suddenly it was all going sky high. Geordies are friendly and amiable and up for a laugh, but the flip side of that is that as friends they are fiercely loyal and protective of each other, and my mates and I were no different. There was always some kind of drama, and I think we liked it that way if I'm being honest. We wouldn't let anyone disrespect us.

It got so bad that we ended up getting into fights most

weeks. We're not talking a little slap; it was brutal. We'd be rolling around on the floor punching and kicking each other. The fear goes when you're drunk, which is both good and bad. I've never walked up to someone and started a fight, but I was a target because of what I did so I was always on red alert.

One of the worst moments of my life was when I was hosting in Madame Koos and a load of my mates and my sister were in the VIP area. This lad and two lasses came stumbling up and demanded to go in but it was packed and they didn't have the required wristbands to get in so I had to turn them away. They started abusing me so I said: 'I'm sorry, I don't speak drunken twat. Can you please fuck off?' They careered off so I didn't think any more of it, but when I came back from the toilet about ten minutes later I could see that there was something kicking off as I walked down the stairs. It looked like one of those cartoon strips where someone is beating up a baddie and all you see is a cloud of smoke with arms and legs coming out of it. It was a full-on punch up involving several people. When I looked closer I realised that my sister, Laura, was in the middle of it.

I panicked like mad and ran over to try and help her. It turned out that the trio of idiots had come back, seen I wasn't there and tried to push their way in. My Laura is no mug, so she really politely told them they couldn't come in and one of the girls threw a drink on her. Laura pushed the girl and before she knew it all three of them went for her, including the lad. It turned out that because he's gay he'd thought it was all right to hit a woman. They were stamping on her face and punching her and all sorts. Christ, they picked on the wrong person that night. My mates and I were straight in there dragging the girls off, and then thankfully the doormen arrived and threw them all out. Luckily Laura was fine, but I was beginning to see the dark side of life as a VIP host.

Another night that was memorable for all the wrong reasons was when a group of guys walked up asking for a table. I had none left but the doorman gave me a heads-up and told me to make one available ASAP. It turned out the guys were some of the biggest gangsters in the area, and not the kind of people you leave waiting around. I cleared a table for them and as soon as they walked in I knew something was going to kick off. They weren't out to have fun; they were out to cause trouble. They were massive blokes and they instantly created an atmosphere. They were almost daring guys to give them any reason to start a fight.

This local lad, who is a personal trainer, walked in and obviously knew them because he went over and started chatting. But things went from friendly to nasty in a matter of minutes and all of a sudden my clean white VIP area was sprayed with blood. It's one of the most horrific things I've ever seen. Even the doorman wouldn't step in, even though they were almost killing this guy. Adrenalin kicked in and I ended up throwing myself into the middle of it to try and stop it, which was so stupid. I could have got really badly hurt. Thankfully I was fine and in the end they all left, but it was a horrible experience.

I saw that night just how nasty my job could get. It wasn't just about getting dressed up and serving Veuve Clicquot to rich people, it's also the nasty bastards who are drunk and can't take no for an answer. There were several times I had bald patches on my head from where girls had ripped my hair out. Once I was even bottled in a toilet and was quite badly injured. It was ludicrous. Sometimes we'd have nights out that were so brilliant you couldn't top them no matter where you were in the world, but the danger was the flipside of that lifestyle and you have to take the rough with the smooth.

After several months of working on the doors I fancied a change of scene and Anthony and some of my mates were feeling the same. So we all decided to move to Ibiza. Well, why the hell not? I was starting to feel a bit guilty about drinking my life away so I decided that I would have one last mad six months and then I really *would* start saving up for the next stage of my life. I'd done nothing with my degree and I saw my other friends from university getting good jobs or scoring more qualifications and I was still running around town getting mortal every night.

I saved up my money and we all moved to Ibiza in May 2010 – me, my friend Kailee, two girls I went to university with, and Anthony and his mates Jordan and Mick. In my heart I've always been an Ibiza girl. I love dance and house and tech and I love drinking, so it's my perfect place. I thought I was going to land there and it would instantly be like starring in a music video, going to all of these amazing clubs and meeting really cool people. Though I'd planned to stay there for six months, before I'd even arrived I'd decided that I would probably never want to come home.

The four of us girls lived in San Antonio, which was two minutes walk from West End, the main party area, and to start with we had a brilliant time. But Anthony couldn't find his feet out there and couldn't get a job, which was a real knock to his ego. He also didn't feel very settled where he was living with the lads so he ended up moving in with me temporarily and sharing my single bed. Only the arrangement turned out to be more permanent and after he'd been there for a couple of weeks it caused a real rift with me and the other girls, which in turn caused problems between me and Anthony.

Needless to say, things didn't turn out to be quite as glam as I had hoped generally. Half a year is a hell of a long time to be somewhere when you don't have a proper job. I thought it would be easy to land something in a bar with all of my experience, but it's so competitive it took me a while before I got offered my first hosting job, in a bar called Savannah. It was on the strip where everyone went to watch the sun set and I thought I would be standing at the door wearing a gorgeous floaty white maxi dress and being fabulous, while coaxing in beautiful, tanned tourists. I was *so* wrong. The hostess job turned out to be a waitressing role and you have never known what being manic is until you've worked the sunset shift on the sunset strip in Ibiza. I'd never carried a tray before in my life and I was expected to carry six plates and drinks at once, all of these super-fast waiters would be rushing past me while I walked at a delicate snail's pace. They used to shout insults at me in Spanish – I've since Googled some of them and they weren't pleasant. One night, one of the chefs even threw a plate at me when I got an order slightly wrong. He thought he was bloody Gordon Ramsey.

Every single person wants to be sat on that decking with a drink in their hand, and heaven forbid if they're without an Amaretto Sour when the sun sets. You don't hear the end of it, and tips were a rarity. The hostessing part was a total joke, it never happened for me. That role was reserved for some gorgeous Spanish bird while I was sweating my tits off wearing a shit 'Savannah' T-shirt and earning bugger all money. I was expected to work fourteen nights on and then I'd get one night off. It was hardly what I'd signed up for.

I wasn't seeing Anthony or my mates and they were all going to fabulous clubs and dancing to Swedish House Mafia while I slaved for minimum wage delivering tourists patatas bravas. I didn't get paid for six weeks and when I got my first pay slip I decided enough was enough. It was such a paltry amount that I refused to go back there.

My luck totally changed when I stumbled across Zoo Project. That place is a slice of heaven of earth. It's held in this abandoned zoo ten minutes outside of San Antonio where everyone goes to get massively off their face. There are all of these different sections to hang out in and everyone is gorgeous and quite often dressed up as animals! It's the best place to go out in Ibiza and I somehow managed to get a job working there. To this day it's one of the best jobs I've ever had. I used to go round all of the clubbing hotels and sell tickets to people who looked like they were up for a party. I was my own boss and I only had to work for three hours a day, all while drinking Kopparberg and chatting to people around the pool. I lived on Burger King, toasted cheese sandwiches and Kopparberg that summer. It wasn't the healthiest, but I was dancing it all off most nights.

While my work life was flourishing, my living and relationship situations were turning into something of a disaster. I always say that you never know people until you live with them and as a result of living with these two girls I'd met at university I found out what they were really like, and it turned out they weren't all that nice. We all ended up arguing so much they moved out and I stayed living in the apartment with Kailee and Anthony.

As well as this, Anthony and I had hit another massively rocky patch. We'd gone from being in love and happy to being under each other's feet all the time, and of course, working at Zoo Project I was meeting and getting to know everyone in the area. We'd walk down the strip and people would be shouting out to me and stopping me to chat and he really didn't like it. We'd always been quite possessive of each other but this was a whole new level. I was starting to see a different side of him. Anthony became really moody and aggressive – though he was never aggressive towards me, he was lashing out at other blokes. He was getting paranoid from too much drinking and not enough sleep and he was even getting jealous when I talked to his mates, which was ridiculous.

I think we put too much pressure on ourselves moving to Ibiza *and* living with each other. We'd never lived together before, and being with each other 24/7 proved too much, so it all fell apart. We still cared about each other so much but we'd row and I'd kick him out, and then he'd be back a week later feeling sheepish after sleeping on his mate's sofa. It was a classic case of can't live with each other, can't live without each other. In the end I made the decision to make a clean break but because he was so angry about everything there was no chance of us staying friends. His attitude was 'if you don't want me, fuck you'. I really struggled with that because I still cared about him so much, and for the second time I was faced with a life without him in it. I was coming up for twenty-two and we'd been together on and off since I was eighteen so it was a massive chapter of my life coming to an end. It took me ages to adapt to not having him around and for a long time I felt really disloyal for splitting up with him.

I lost Anthony forever in Ibiza. He hasn't spoken to me since and it's like I don't exist to him. I saw him last Christmas in a bar in Newcastle and I tried to smile at him but he just looked at me and then turned away. He obviously hates me which is sad as I'd really like to still count him as a friend because we spent so much time together. He's a lovely lad. I wish him well in whatever he is doing and does in the future.

I may have lost Anthony in Ibiza but Kailee and I cemented our friendship for life. After he moved out we had the final months together partying and it was absolutely unreal. I danced my way through the break-up. I threw myself into drinking and clubbing and made the best of the situation. I spent every single penny I had having a good time, and definitely wasn't thinking about what the hell I'd do when I got back home to Newcastle!

Chapter Six

Shore Thing

Leaving Ibiza was so hard. I could have stayed forever but when it came to the end of the season it was impossible to get a job anywhere and I knew I had to face reality at some point. I came back so skint I couldn't even get a mobile phone contract. I went into town to get one with some cash my mam had lent me but they told me I had to have at least a pound in my bank account to qualify, and incredibly I didn't even have that. Ridiculously, I'd spent the last of my funds on travel because I managed to miss three flights home due to my extensive partying. Then of course I had to have a big

'welcome back' night out with my mates so I was massively overdrawn.

I had no job, no boyfriend and nowhere to live apart
from back home with my parents. I sat down one day
in my childhood bedroom and looked around and thought
'you idiot, you've pissed everything you had up the wall'.
Looking back I wouldn't have changed it for the world,
but it was a real wake-up call at the time. I'd just come
back from partying with the likes of Faithless and Richie
Hawtin in these amazing clubs and then crashed down
to earth with a bang so big I'm surprised my arse isn't
still bruised. I was the older sister, but Laura was the
one who was settled with a boyfriend and a job and a
car. Thank god for my mam and dad because they, and
Kailee, helped me get back on my feet.

Kailee had got a job in a call centre and asked me
if I wanted to apply for a position there as well. I can
honestly say that it sounded like my worst nightmare. It was the one thing I said I'd never do because
I didn't want to be nine-to-five in an office doing something I hated. The repetitiveness of it and the idea of
having to deal with the public horrified me. I couldn't
think of anything more mundane. But I was in a bind
and beggars can't be choosers, so I had to suck it up
and take what I could get. I applied, got the job, and
prepared myself for dealing with a lot of arseholes.

Sadly the job was every bit as awful as I expected. I'm

not cut out for being told what to do or moaned at constantly. People were phoning up and shouting at me because their Sky TV wasn't working and I literally didn't give a shit. To be able to do something well I have to be passionate about it and I didn't care about HD and broadband in any way, shape or form. It destroyed my soul working there. Kailee was so good at it, and she's still there now doing brilliantly. Her attitude is that if she can't solve your problem she'll find someone who can; she genuinely cares, but I'm too much of a bitch. The bottom line is that I'm far too moody to work in a call centre. I wanted to be back in Bora Bora raving it up not listening to Brian from Kent telling me he couldn't find the Geography Channel.

I used to get so irate but I was lucky enough to have a lovely manager. She was called Leigh and she had to listen in to our calls sometimes, and afterwards she'd take me aside really subtly and say: 'Vicky, what did you forget to do on that call? You didn't read your five golden broadband rules.' Or she'd tell me off for being snappy, but in the gentlest way possible. As much as I didn't want to be there I needed the job so I was incredible grateful to her. She could easily have sacked me for being crap.

The other issue was my office attire. I'd never worked in an office before so I didn't own any suits or anything and I had to try and make the best of what I already

My mam and dad aged twenty-one in Benidorm – they are still that in love today!

My first birthday –
looking stylish already.

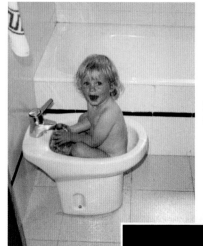

Not sure that's what it's for, Vic!

My grandma and grandpa at Butlins in Ayr – we loved caravan holidays.

Meeting my baby sister Laura for the first time, 19 August 1991.

Sisterly love through the years. I'm the original Miley Cyrus!

EuroDisney with my mam and sister – I was always very regal.

Displaying my flair for accessorising at an early age, rocking that HORRENDOUS fucking hat!

Ibiza with the family.

Ready for the prom with all my mates.

Me and my first love Dean on my eighteenth birthday.

The Drama crew at Uni – my extensions are a SHOW!

My twentieth birthday in Liverpool, with my boyfriend Anthony (front and centre).

Standard Thursday morning at Uni – hungover after a night out in Medication. I should have been in lectures but instead I lay in bed with my flatmate Charlotte . . .

Me and my Kookai girls – Alex and Steph. I'm wearing the infamous top/dress from my arrest in Liverpool.

Me and my sister Laura when we were both blonde!

My twenty-first birthday with my mam and grandma – three generations of Birdsey/Pattison women.

My wonderful family on my twenty-first.

Living it up in Zante in 2008 (should have gone to Specsavers).

Hanging out with the lads, the year I worked in Magaluf.

Me and the girls in 2010 when I was working in Ibiza.

had. Some of the other employees used to try and get me sent home because I wasn't wearing the correct clothes. No one could bloody see me on the phone! One day I made a real effort to be smart and I wore these black high-waisted trousers and a shirt, but because the trousers were too long for me I wore some high heels with them, so these two women in the office complained about the height of my shoes. I mean, seriously? Did they have nothing better to do?

It was a proper effort to go in there every day. The only thing that kept me going was knowing that I was making money I could spend on a night out with my mates when Friday night finally rolled around. I went back to doing some work in clubs and bars here and there to make some extra money too. It was during one of those nights when one of my mates handed me a flyer and said: 'They're looking for some people for a new reality TV show in Newcastle.' My first thought was: 'Are they fuck!'

The flyer said something along the lines of 'Have You Got What It Takes?' They were handing them out to literally everyone and so I didn't think much of it. *The Only Way is Essex* has just started and it had taken off in a massive way and everyone was talking about reality shows. The word on the street was that this was going to be the Geordie version of *TOWIE*. I thought about it over the course the evening and jokingly said to my friends: 'We'd be perfect for this. Can you imagine them filming us on a night out? They probably wouldn't be able to show half of it.' Little did I know . . .

A couple of weeks later I was working a shift in Tiger Tiger and a group of people from MTV came in. I showed them to their table and I watched them all night as they checked out everyone in the bar. I started chatting to them and found out that two of them, a girl called Lauren and a guy called Eddie, were casting directors and they were looking for people to join the new show. After that I kept seeing them around when I was working and I got to know them pretty well. They kept asking me about various people they were considering and I'd give them really honest feedback. The funny thing is that I'd say things like: 'Oh no, you don't want him. He's an utter nob and he's always mortal.' Back then I didn't know that was exactly what they were looking for.

One night in October 2010 Lauren and Eddie asked me if I'd ever consider auditioning. By this point I'd seen the kind of people they were looking for and I'd clocked on to what sort of qualities they were after. They were hunting for brash, in your face, loud, jack the lads and lasses, and that wasn't for me, even if I did act that way at times.

When I told my mates I'd turned down the opportunity to try out they were horrified and told me I *had* to give it a go. The more I thought about it the more I decided I had nothing to lose. I couldn't work in the fucking call centre for the rest of my life, and I could always say no if I really didn't want to do it, so the next time I saw them I said I'd changed my mind. I got invited along to my first audition at the Malmaison on the Quayside, and they told me to come as if I was going for a night out. I wore a black jumpsuit with the sides cut out and I piled on the fake lashes, make up and hair extensions for good measure.

I walked in to this meeting room and two guys were sat there behind a table. Unbeknown to me one of them was the head of casting for MTV USA, and the other guy was Steve Regan, who is the head commissioner for MTV UK. After a bit of small talk they asked me why I wanted to be in the show and what being a Geordie meant to me. I wasn't at all prepared so I said the first thing that came into my head: 'Being a Geordie is being proud of where you're from. It's going out every night. It's not wearing a coat no matter how cold it is. It's knowing every doorman on the Diamond Strip. It's bleeding black and white. It's loving Cheryl Cole. It's loving a Greggs pasty. It's loving and caring for your family. It's thinking all Southerners are soft.' When I finished they smiled and thanked me, and I walked out feeling like I'd just been Punk'd or something. It was such a strange experience.

I felt quite positive but obviously I had no clue if they liked me or not. I'd gone from being in two minds about the show to really bloody wanting to do it. I was on a total high thinking that this could be my big break. I wanted to go out with my mates and get pissed and talk about it, but I couldn't tell anyone about the audition because it was made very clear that if I did tell people I would have no chance of getting picked. We had to be one hundred per cent discreet because the show was going to be all about the element of surprise.

I barely heard anything from MTV for about two months after that and it was absolute torture. I had a couple of phone calls here and there but there was no point where I was told I was definitely in so I was constantly on tenterhooks. I knew loads of other people that were going for auditions and that made me feel even more nervous. None of my friends auditioned because I've always been the loudmouth show-off in my group. I'm the attention-seeking drama queen and although it may sound terrible (actually, it really does) it's like I'm the star and they're the supporting roles. I couldn't do anything I do without them though, and they're content for things to be that way. Being on *Geordie Shore* would be their worst nightmare, but for me it signified a way out. For the first time in years I was becoming really excited about the future. The fame flame inside of me had been relit and I knew this could be the start of something big. There was potential for this TV show to be the springboard I'd always hoped for, and it could even mean I never had to talk to anyone about HD and broadband again.

In my head no one would be better for the show than me. I'd worked the doors, I was VIP Vicky and I was strong and feisty. *Geordie Shore* was meant for me and the longer things dragged on, the more I wanted it. The annoying thing was that even though no one was supposed to talk about it, I was hearing reports about other people who had been for castings and been called back for their third or fourth audition. I couldn't understand why I wasn't being asked to do another one. I saw it as a really negative thing and I felt like it was slowly slipping away from me. In the meantime I was getting my head down and trying to concentrate on my call centre job, while wishing I was anywhere else in the universe. For some ridiculous reason I got promoted so I started training people. God knows how when I could barely do the job myself.

One day some lad called Gary Beadle walked in. I knew Gary from around town because he was a bit of a face and went to a lot of the same nights to me. He'd also slept with a couple of my mates. I think he's slept with most people in the North East to be fair. Nothing's ever happened between me and Gaz, and I think that's probably because I've always known what he's like, but I've always liked him as a person.

Gaz walked straight over to my desk to say hello and told me he'd just got a job at the call centre. Hilariously I then got put in charge of training him and the first thing he said to me was: 'To be honest Vicky, I'm hoping I won't have to do this for very long. I've had a couple of auditions for that *Geordie Shore*.' So much for being discreet! He was telling absolutely everything about the whole process and I replied: 'Oh yeah, it sounds really exciting. I wish I'd auditioned now, Gaz.' But inside I immediately panicked because from what he was saying it was clear that he was much further along in the process than I was. I thought my dream was over.

For a couple of days I couldn't get it out of my head and I was completely inconsolable. I had been totally myself when I'd gone into my audition and now I was beginning to wonder it if wasn't enough. Maybe they wanted someone more serious? Maybe they wanted a tart? Maybe I wasn't funny enough? I was going over and over it in my head wondering what I'd done wrong. Gaz had been for three interviews and I'd only been for one. He even told me he'd been showing the casting director pictures of his cock. How was I supposed to compete with that? I couldn't send people pictures of my tits, they were crap! I saw my mates that night and I was so upset I told them outright I was fucked and that the show didn't want me. Bollocks to being discreet about everything. I'd gone into proper panic mode and if they didn't want me what was the point in going through that on my own.

The following Saturday night the lasses and I went to Riverside en masse and I had it in my head that I was going to get fucked. The show wasn't happening for me and I was gutted – I needed to let loose. We walked into the VIP area and got given a couple of terrible bottles of cheap Cava on the house so we swiftly got stuck in. After a couple of hours of being in there I spotted Eddie, one of the original casting directors, in the bar. He looked like he was on his own so I invited him over to join us and we all proceeded to get absolutely mortal. I was running around, cracking on to lads, having a tash-on, falling over, having dance-offs – you name it. I was having what I considered to be a completely normal night. Unbeknown to me Eddie was watching everything.

Just as we were about to leave Riverside I knocked over a drink by mistake and it fell onto this girl sitting nearby. She had been aggy all night and she was clearly looking for trouble. She stood up and had a right go at me, saying that I'd thrown it over her on purpose. Even though it was a complete mistake, and I apologised, she wasn't having it, so at that point my mates started wading in. Being Southern and absolutely petrified Eddie was trying to calm us all down and I didn't want to make things worse so I walked away. As I did the girl shouted to me: 'Oh yeah, run off!' Well, that was like a red rag to a bull. I stormed back over, picked up the nearest drink and said to her: 'I didn't throw a drink on you, but if I had you'd had known about it because I would have done this,' and I chucked it straight in her face. I calmly put the glass down, turned around and walked out before I was escorted from the premises.

We ended up going on to this gay club called Power-house where we danced all night. I didn't really think anything of the night because it was pretty tame by our standards, but I woke up with a cracking hangover to the phone ringing at eleven a.m. It was Lime Pictures saying they needed to see me again. I'd only had three hours sleep but I was over the bloody moon, so although I was very obviously still drunk I got myself together and went down to meet them. From that meeting on I seemed to get fast-tracked. I had a screen test and saw the show's psychiatrist, Stephen, who asked if I'd been bullied or had depressive thoughts, so they could make sure I was emotionally stable. I still didn't know if I was I was defi-nitely in the show or not, and because by this point Christmas was looming I reasoned they probably wouldn't make any big decisions until that was out of the way.

I cannot tell you how desperate I was to get a phone call to say I was in *Geordie Shore*. I hated my life at that point. I was single, I was working in a shitty call centre and getting bullied by the other women who worked there. I had barely any money and the only things keeping me going were my family and my mates and this little glimmer of hope that I could be about to do something massive. I was praying for a 'yes'.

I heard from MTV about a week later when they called and asked me to go in and film some of the green screen interviews that would later feature on the show. They're basically the bits people see where we're talking straight to camera in the show – usually about each other.

That's when I told them for the first time I was 'VIP Vicky – A Geordie girl with a VIP edge', which will haunt me forever. When I finished, the producer, Guy, said to me: 'What would you say if we told you that you were one of the housemates going into *Geordie Shore*?' and I replied: 'I'd tell you to fuck off!' There was a pause, and then he said: 'Well you are. You're in.' I could not believe it. That's the bit you see at the start of the credits where I'm doing this ludicrous dance move with this crazy grin on my face. I'm over the fucking moon because I've just been told I don't have to work in the call centre anymore and I'm going to be on TV! Every time I see that clip I should cringe, but I love it because I know that was the moment I found out I could quit my horrible job and would never have to say the five fucking golden broadband rules ever again.

I don't know if that night out with Eddie was a turning point or if they'd already made their decision about me, but Steve told me some time later that he knew from the moment I did my speech about Newcastle in my first audition that he'd found what he was looking for and they had to have me in the show. I just wish they'd told me a bit bloody sooner.

I was absolutely buzzing, but I had no idea what I was letting myself in for. I was so wet behind the ears. I initially thought it would be the new *TOWIE* as everyone had been saying, but I'd also started to hear rumours that it was going to be more like the American MTV show *Jersey Shore*. I was really excited about that rumour because I was a huge fan and I loved Snooki and JWoww. Once I got my head around that, I was even more up for it. I knew what they were looking for and I was going to give it to them; I wasn't going to hold anything back. They were going to get VIP Vicky, psycho Vicky and volcano Vicky. They were going to get the real, trustworthy, fun me. I was willing to go into this and give it my all because I felt like I had nothing to lose.

When someone's just told you you're going to be in a potentially really big TV series you don't care about anything. I would have jumped off a cliff or given them my first-born child if they'd asked me to. I finally felt like my dreams were coming true. I didn't have the knowledge that I have now that there will be some people that will go in there and play a game, and some people will bitch behind your back, and there will be a lot of editing. I was just excited. How naive was I. I would never go back and play anything differently in terms of how I got into the show, but hindsight is a beautiful thing and I would like to have known then what I know now about reality TV.

The first people I told I was in the show were my family, and then I had to go into work the next day to tell them I was leaving. Filming was due to start on the Monday so I didn't give them much notice. Or, indeed, any. My manager Leigh was amazing about it. I had about twenty-five lates and ten unauthorised absences to my name and really I should have been sacked a long time before, so when I told her about getting into the show she turned around and said: 'Vicky, I'm so glad because I really can't keep you in this job any longer. I was going to have to sack you at some point.'

That weekend went so quickly because I was busy packing everything up and preparing to go in. I'd pulled together every penny I had to get together a new wardrobe of clothes and new hair extensions so I was back to being totally broke. My mam also took me shopping and bought me some bits and pieces, bless her. We weren't being paid a penny when *Geordie Shore* first started, so I was taking a big chance. The show would be paying for our food and drink but apart from that we got zip and

Topshop had just sucked up the last small amount of savings I had.

When Sunday night arrived I was totally shitting myself, and on top of that I'd been told that I was going into the house first. The producers said it was a good thing because it showed that they had faith in me as a character, so that was comforting. I was getting all psyched up and then someone from the show called me on Sunday night and said they were going to have to push things back and I wasn't needed until Tuesday now. I tried to sound really casual so I was like 'oh sure, no problem!' but this massive knot was building in my stomach and a little voice in my head was saying 'they've changed their minds and they don't want you'.

The same thing happened on Monday. Just as I was unpacking and repacking for the twentieth time they called me and said there was a plumbing problem in the house and they couldn't get us in for another couple of days. I thought it was game over. I'd quit my job and now they were giving me the brush off – even though I hated the call centre it was the only money I had coming in, and I'd burned my bridges there now. I was devastated. I was constantly waiting for the phone to ring to give me good news, and just when I started to think it was all some kind of elaborate hoax I finally I got the call saying that it was full steam ahead and I was officially going into the house on the Thursday. Thank Goooooooood!

It later transpired that there was no plumbing problem; it was more of a casting problem. They had this guy who was supposed to be going into the show called Jay McKray. You may remember him because he went on to do *Big Brother* and married another housemate from that series called Louise Cliffe. Lime Pictures and MTV UK were fighting tooth and nail to get him in because he's brilliant and such a character, but MTV America said no because he'd had, ahem, a few runs in with the law. So that was what held everything up. The poor guy had his bags packed and everything but in the end America put their foot down and that was that, he was out.

To this day I still think Gaz was lucky MTV didn't put Jay McKray in there because he would have been the main man and Gaz would have been in his shadow. In the end James Tindale went in as a last minute reserve. Exactly the same thing happened with Greg Lake. Another guy was supposed to be part of the original line up but the rumour was that he was deemed to be too much of a troublemaker, so Greg took his place. There were a lot of last minute changes and the house could have been a very different place if that hadn't happened.

Aside from rumours, all we'd really been told about the show is that eight people were going to be living in a house together and we would be filmed 24/7. I didn't know anything about the house or what to expect. We could have been in a luxury mansion or a total shithole. At that point I also had no idea who I was going to be living with. Apart from assuming that Gaz would be there, obviously. The girls could have been anyone. Dean's new girlfriend could have walked through the door for all I knew.

I'd spent the night before getting ready and putting on my fake tan and curling my hair extensions, and I was ready for it. I was wearing a black backless Vicky Martin dress that I'd been given for my birthday the year before. I was really body confident back then. I was about nine-and-a-half stone and a nice size ten with boobs and a bum.

I strutted down to Premiere Apartments in Newcastle and Lauren the casting girl – who little did I know then would end up turning into a good friend – greeted me and took me to a huge room. She told me they were running a bit behind so I could chill out and relax for a bit, and she also said they had to check my bags for any contraband I may have been trying to smuggle in. Books, phones, magazines, iPods or any device you can use the internet on were all considered contraband and I should have seen that as a bit of a warning flag that we were going to be very controlled.

I'd been up since four a.m. so by this point because I'd had to get there for six a.m. I was starting to flag a bit. Lauren said to me: 'Come on Vicky, we need you to be really big for this. You need to liven up,' and she fixed me a gin and Berocca. It was actually really good because I got the hit of the gin and the zing of the Berocca and it totally woke me up. It was like me but on a really, *really* good day.

I was strutting around this apartment talking non-stop in a tiny mini-dress at eight a.m. The last time I'd been so dressed up that early was when I was still going from the night before. I was doing a lot of deep breathing and holding my stomach to calm my nerves and everything was buzzing around in my head like a swarm of bloody bees. Then suddenly Lauren told me it was my time to go in. This was it!

Chapter Seven

House. Mates?

Just before entering the *Geordie Shore* house I was a nervous wreck. I had sweaty palms, a sweaty upper lip, sweaty everything. I was *so* scared. The house was amazing. It was a million pound, five-storey mansion in the posh Jesmond area of Newcastle and as soon as I was through the door I started running around like a lunatic looking in all the rooms. It was so much pressure being the first person in there because I was trying to be entertaining but I had no one to bounce off. I was almost considering conversations with the toaster and kettle after an hour and a half on my own, just to make myself look interesting. It was such a relief when the second housemate, Jay Gardner, walked in.

As everyone knows, Jay and I ended up getting together and I think everyone assumes I was instantly attracted to him, but if truth be told I wasn't. I just thought that's what was expected of me. I thought I was meant to find him attractive. I've always been a massive flirt – my friends call me a wine taster because I like to go out, have a tash-on with a lad and then bin him. I suppose that's what I was put in the house for, and as soon as Jay walked in I thought 'yeah, tall, good looking, we'll have fun flirting' but I never anticipated it becoming as serious as it did. He was a good crack and we had good banter but I wasn't blown away by him to the extent they made out. They had me and Jay down as the next Kate and Wills but I don't think we were ever really each other's type.

James was the next person to enter the house and I was really shocked to see him because I knew him from around town. He worked as a topless host in one of the bars and he'd also been seeing my mate Kailee for a while. Charlotte was the next girl in after me and she was so sweet and squeaky; I thought she was endearing, but not up my street at all. It was nice to see some friendly faces, and when Gaz walked in after her I started to think that I was going to enjoy being in there because at least I knew people. It was a real relief.

The only thing I was worried about were the lasses because I knew loads of bitchy girls from town who I suspected may be coming in. I expected some of the other VIP hosts to swan in loving themselves off and hating me instantly. That was the real shocker of the day for me. I'd been so worried that the other girls were going to look like models and I would be the least attractive. I thought they'd all be perfect and I'd be the fattest and ugliest.

I still didn't really know what the producers had been looking for so when the other girls walked in I was taken aback. I was expecting these vain, arrogant, stuck-up bitches and that's not what I got at all. It was funny because they'd gone for a real stereotype with the guys. They were all from Newcastle or really close by, and apart from Greg they were all of a similar age and into the gym. But with the girls it was different.

The definition of a Geordie is someone who lives three miles from the bank of the River Tyne, and that's me. Charlotte Crosby is from Sunderland so she's a Mackem; Holly Hagan is a Smoggie, someone from Middlesborough; and Sophie Kasaei is a Sanddancer, someone from South Shields. They're not Geordies in the slightest so I didn't know them from Adam.

Sophie was the next of the girls to come in and on first sight I wasn't keen. She was brash and loud to the point of being chavvy, she was like a tornado whirling about the place. Greg, the last of the lads, came in after Sophie; we moved in similar circles so I knew him from the clubs. Greg was always a bit of an odd choice for the show because he was quite reserved. He was definitely no Gaz.

Poor, poor Holly was last in and in my opinion MTV led her like a lamb to the slaughter. She'd just turned eighteen and she was too young to be there. I was twenty-three and she seemed like a proper child to me. Holly may have looked older, but she'd never really been out of Middlesborough so she wasn't in any way worldly. Where Holly came from she was a big fish in a small pond, and now she was in a TV show with people who were older and had more life experience. She seemed so naive and lost.

That first day was so surreal. I got into the house at eight in the morning, and Holly was the last person to enter at eight that night. I was trying to keep it real while at the same time pushing myself – being the most enter-taining and over the top version of 'Vicky' I could be. I found myself becoming a bit of a caricature because there was so much pressure. Sophie and Charlotte were sloshing around in the hot tub and they kept getting drunker and drunker and my opinion of them was dip-ping lower and lower. I ended up having to put them to bed on the first night and I remember thinking, 'I've got four weeks of this. This is going to be hell on earth.

What the fuck have I let myself in for?' Not that I wasn't smashed myself, mind. I'd been drinking all day; we all had. I was drinking away my nerves.

I'll happily admit that if the producers had said I could walk out there and then I would definitely have considered it having seen who I was going to be spending the next month of my life with. I was used to hanging out with people who were my age or older and I was thrust into this environment with girls who seemed so much younger and dafter than me.

If you'd told me that day that in the future I would consider Sophie, Charlotte and Holly to be some of my best friends I would have laughed in your face. On that first night, all of them got on my tits. Every time another one of them walked in I thought 'fucking hell, how am I going to do this?' We were in this contrived environment and were going to have to start false friendships, but I do think that the programme makers were hoping for fireworks between us. And they got them.

The other three girls clicked instantly because they were young and excited and a bit stupid, but I remember crying and kicking off on my second day and asking the production crew why they'd put me in a house with those people. I thought they were a bunch of nobs and there was no way I would be able to get on with them. I felt like I had nothing in common with the girls at all and it suddenly hit me that I was away from my friends and family, stuck with a bunch of people who were predominantly total strangers. The thought of not being able to just pick up the phone to my mam and ask for her advice was so upsetting. We weren't allowed to use the phone as and when we wanted to but I really wanted to call her and ask 'have I done the right thing?'

Actually, in the long run it turned out to be a real eye opener. I thought those girls couldn't teach me anything because I'd done so much more in my life but actually I ended up learning loads. Holly taught me how strong a person can be when they're faced with some really tough opposition from everyone around them. People think she's a bit ditzy and probably quite thick, but she's strong and compassionate. I loved Charlotte's spirit and how excited she got about everything. Sophie has such a zest for life and it was infectious and uplifting when I was down. There were times when they ended up really propping me up. I'm quick to judge and that first series taught me to take a step back and get to know someone properly because what you see isn't always what you get and all of the girls surprised me.

Before any of us even set foot over the threshold of that house I'm sure MTV had a clear idea of what roles they wanted us to play and I believe Holly was brought in to be the one no one really liked. Gaz was the ultimate lad, shagging around and breaking hearts; Charlotte was the ditzy tart; Sophie was the ladette; James was the loveable dope; Greg was the sophisticated older man; Jay was the alpha male and the dad of the house. And I was supposed to be the bitch. I was the voice of reason with cutting wit and I didn't hold back.

Everything was intensified in the house. On the first day I wasn't even sure anything was going to happen between Jay and I, but by the second or third day I was acting like his girlfriend, and that's just not me at all. It usually takes me months to get to that stage but it was like everything was speeded up. I clung to anything and anyone I could to give me a bit of support and stability.

It's hard to understand what being in somewhere like the *Geordie Shore* house is like unless you've been through it. All of those things that usually keep you sane; your phone or books, are taken away from you. There were times when I cried in there and I'm sure people watching it were thinking 'what are you crying for? You get paid to get pissed for a living', but it can be really tough. I was so used to being able to call someone if I felt down, but there was no way of conversing with anyone apart from the seven other housemates and some of the crew. I've experienced some of the loneliest times of my life on the show over the years. On the positive side having no outside contact meant that we were forced to interact with each other, and we came out with some great one-liners because we weren't constantly distracted by

Twitter or Instagram, we were having proper conversations.

It sounds callous but I'd always thought that to survive a reality show you either had to be really thick, really ignorant, or a massive game player, and I'm none of those things. I had assumed that if you're stupid or arrogant you can breeze through it and not care what's going on, or if you go in there with a game plan you can see the light at the end of the tunnel. But it was hard for me because I'm hypersensitive and incredibly self-aware. I'm a worrier and I'm neurotic and in that environment I started to drive myself insane.

For the first five days I couldn't sleep at all. We didn't have clocks so I never knew what the time was. I'd wake up when it was light with no idea if it was seven in the morning or three in the afternoon, and having been pissed the night before I would get instant beer fear about what I'd done and what I'd said and want to hide underneath the duvet. I kept waking up next to Jay and I'd have to crawl out of his bed feeling completely shaky. I'd gone from being a strong woman who was playing the field to an utter melt. It wasn't a case of just phoning a mate to apologise for being a dick the previous night, I couldn't escape from these people. I had put myself in a position of abject pain and anxiety.

The green screen room was my saviour. I didn't edit or screen myself at all in there, and that meant it was where I could really let rip away from everyone else. I saw it as a form of therapy. No one in the house ever asks you how you are or if you're okay because they're all so caught up in what they're doing. It's the most self-involved environment in the world and you find yourself with no one to talk to and nowhere to turn, so I needed that space to get everything off my chest. I knew that the others were talking about me behind my back and it made me so paranoid. I wasn't used to that kind of thing because my friends and I are so upfront with each other and everything is said loud and proud. If I've got a problem with someone I tell them, but people were sneaking around and bitching and I hated it.

In short, the first series was such a rollercoaster. One minute I would feel like I was involved in this amazing show that over eight thousand people had auditioned for, and the next I desperately wanted to be back at home eating a pizza and watching crappy TV with my family. I wanted to be with the people that I loved when the other housemates were grating on me. Holly was the worst. It wasn't her fault, but she was continually annoying to be around. She was eighteen and had no clue about who she was and because of that she acted like an idiot, and I had no patience with it. I ended up avoiding her as much as possible. She was young and unprepared – everything she went through had such a massive effect on her, and I didn't want to be the one who had to pick up the pieces when I was trying hard to keep my own head together.

When I look back at how Holly acted in series one, I really respect her because there were times when literally no one in the house wanted to be around her, and she sucked it up and just kept coming back. She was very resilient and she proved how strong she is and I admire that about her. I would have felt like walking away but she battled through.

Against all of the odds, I did start to bond with the girls about a week after we all went into the house. I developed a real motherly instinct towards them, but I got lured into a false sense of security that we were mates, and of course we were all still secretly looking after number one. That was made very clear to me one night after we'd been out on a girls' night. We were all mortal drunk and Charlotte and Sophie wanted to stay up until the boys got back. I told them they'd be better off going to bed because the lads were out pulling so they wouldn't be bothered either way. When the guys came back Charlotte and Sophie went into their room and winged: 'Vicky says you don't care about us at all. You do, don't you?' The lads took it completely the wrong way and flew off the handle. Next thing I knew everyone in the house was talking about me behind my back and I became *Geordie Shore* enemy number one.

All I'd been doing was trying to look after the girls

and it had been totally taken out of context. Because Charlotte and Sophie were desperate for the lads' attention they'd made it into something it wasn't. They'd made me sound really mean. I was pretty oblivious to it at first and it wasn't until we were out in a club called Tup Tup Palace a couple of days later that one of the producers told me what had been going on. Looking back now she was obviously stirring things up and giving me that little push I needed to storm in and have a go at everyone, but I thought she was being kind. She was basically the organ grinder and like the good little monkey that I was, I did what was expected of me. I stormed over to Charlotte and Sophie and had such a massive go at them. I was genuinely hurt. I wasn't used to backbiting and I hadn't done anything wrong. I couldn't fathom the way they were going about things. I'd never needed male approval the way they did so I couldn't understand why they'd used me to try and get the lads on side.

I fell out with practically everyone that night and no one cared. What hurt the most was that I thought they were my friends. It was the shittest I felt in series one. Jay was the only one who was there for me when I was crying and saying I wanted to leave. He cuddled me and comforted me and I'll never forget that. He didn't have to be that caring because we had a pretty tempestuous relationship, but he showed his true colours that night.

There was also a lot of tension between the boys in the house, which was hard to deal with. Greg felt really different to Gaz, James and Jay, and there were always rows bubbling away so it was a really stressful environment. We should all have pulled together and been there for each other in such a bizarre situation, but sadly it ended being the opposite most of the time. The other upsetting thing is that we were met with such opposition every time we went out. People in Newcastle did *not* like the fact we were doing the show. People used to openly say to me: 'What are you thinking? Why on earth are you on it? Walk away. You're mugs.' It was probably because half of them had auditioned and not got in so there was a lot of bitterness, jealousy and resentment there.

I came close to walking out a few times when things got *really* rough but the producers begged me to stay and convinced me I should be there. At the time I didn't know what I would be walking away from because for all I knew the show could have been a massive flop. In my down moments I started to question if I was doing the right thing being in the show at all. In the end I got so low and upset over my fallout with Charlotte and Sophie the producers let me phone my mam and she was there like a shot. They gave me special dispensation to see her and to paraphrase, she said to me: 'Fuck them. Don't let them win. Go back in there and smash it.' Ever since then she's been fiercely protective when it comes to the show. She's the lioness and I'm her little cub. She won't let them take the piss out of me.

Eventually I did decide to stay because I wasn't going to let some silly little girls and bullish boys get the better of me. I made up with Charlotte and Sophie and carried on with the series – and it's probably the best decision I've ever made. But there have been moments like that in every series. The only one I haven't wanted to walk out of was Australia because that was just incredible. But it's like anything; you're always going to have your ups and downs wherever you are and whatever you're doing.

One of my other low points in series one was spit-gate. As I've mentioned, I wasn't Holly's biggest fan, but I had started to get on with her a little better as the series progressed. She was still rubbing everyone else up the wrong way and one night she got really drunk and started causing trouble and did something stupid like throw a bottle. Everyone was having a go at her at the same time and I think all the shitty things she'd been through in the house up until that moment hit her all at once and so she started crying. I looked at her and it hit me that she could be my younger sister Laura, and what was happening to her wasn't fair, so I went over and gave her a cuddle.

Just to add to the misery of that night Jay and I had been arguing because I felt like he was playing a game with me and at that point we weren't speaking. He'd also been tashing-on with some horror from Whitley Bay right in front of me when we'd been out earlier that day which didn't put me in the best mood. Then all of a sudden he decided to tell Holly exactly what he thought of her. His timing could not have been any worse, while she was sat there sobbing. We were all mortal drunk and when Jay said to Holly that he had thought she was all right at first but since she'd come back after leaving she'd done his head in, I totally flipped. Jay was a grown man saying those awful things to a young girl so I told him he was out of order and he called me a c**t. Don't get me wrong I'm not shy about the c-word and sometimes I use it as a term of endearment, but I knew he really meant it and that's what got me.

I'd been pretty well behaved up until this point. I'd rowed with a couple of girls in clubs and thrown some chairs in a rage, but what Jay said was a step too far and I exploded. I got so mad that I ended up screaming at him and then, awfully, I spat in his face. My emotions were running incredibly high and I had been needled until I snapped in spectacular fashion. We ended up being separated by the rest of the cast and I was so upset. I'd just burnt my bridges with the one person in the house I had been relying on to have my back, and now I had no one. I was also *so* ashamed about spitting at him. Who does that? It just goes to show how magnified everything is in there.

It's when things like that happen that I wish I could say the show is scripted so I could pretend I've been told to do really awful things, but it's simply not true. We are never told what to say or do. The producers would have had a real job trying to get us to follow any kind of script considering we were drunk eighty per cent of the time. Occasionally there is a bit of stirring done by the producers but nothing is set up in terms of our reactions or anything, so unfortunately what you see is all us.

Not surprisingly, after 'spitgate' Jay and I kind of drifted apart relationship-wise. I didn't see a future with him and I think he knew that. I still loved him as a friend and he'd been such an amazing support, but spitgate did drive a big wedge between us. The minute we knew we weren't going to work we pretty much cut ties and things were never really the same again. Jay had also been worried that he was going to look like a melt following me around like a lovesick puppy, and he wanted to be seen as more of a fanny rat. He wanted to be more like Gaz basically, and he just isn't. I think his plan was to look more like a lad so he became louder and brasher.

Having said *all* of that about series one, which obviously sounds pretty negative, some of my best memories of the show to date are from that first series and I still look back on it really fondly despite everything. We were going to clubs five nights a week and the pantry was constantly stocked with booze so we could drink whatever and whenever we wanted to.

Also, we were all naive about the TV process and that's a good thing. We had no clue what we were doing. Holly had only taken four weeks off her job in a call centre because she thought she would have to go back afterwards, and she actually did for a while! Sophie had also been working in a call centre, Charlotte had only been working fifteen hours a week in a bar, James was working for his dad, Jay had been on the dole, Greg had left his job as a gas fitter and Gaz and I were all prepared to go and get another rubbish job if the show bombed. None of us had any clue about what might happen. But one thing was for sure, we were all bloody skint.

We weren't paid for the show until some time after it had been filmed, and then we started getting a grand a month as an ambassador's fee. People assume that if you go into a TV show you get paid loads and walk onto chat shows and magazine shoots, but it wasn't like that at all at this point. There was no monetary gain to be had from joining *Geordie Shore*. I remember having to try and get a sixth wear out of a pair of false eyelashes in the house because I couldn't afford to buy any new ones.

My final, tearful scene in series one involved me saying goodbye to Jay, getting into a taxi, putting a pair of sunglasses on my face and being really melancholy. But I'll let you into a secret – that wasn't how everything ended between me and Jay that season. In actual fact, once the cameras had stopped, he got into a taxi and I ran after him and banged on the window to make the cab stop. Then I got in and hugged him and said: 'I'm so, so sorry things didn't work out. I'm sorry I spat in your face and I care so much about you.' We made our peace and it was so sweet, I really didn't want to end that first series with any anger between us. As it happened, I didn't need to bother because Jay and I kept our distance from each other for the duration of the second series.

After we wrapped on series one none of us had any idea if there would even be a second series. I'd invested everything in the show – my heart and soul – and to think we may never have that experience again was unimaginable so of course we were all praying it would be recommissioned. But the viewing figures would be the decider, and all we could do was cross our fingers and hope for the best.

Chapter Eight

Green Scream

Once we left the house things changed hugely and the friendship dynamics shifted. Even though we all lived pretty close to each other it had felt really final when the cameras stopped rolling – we had no real reason to spend time together any more. We hadn't been friends before the show and I wasn't convinced we would be after, even though we knew we had to do some promotion for the show as a group. But actually, I stayed in touch with people way more than I expected.

I remember Sophie and Charlotte calling me post-*Geordie Shore* and saying: 'We're going out in Jesmond.

Come along!' The three of us met up and then bumped into Gaz and James. That's when I realised that actually we were going to stay friends. We had all shared this amazing experience and it felt like we had this brilliant secret that no one else knew about.

The eight of us ended up meeting up quite a bit over the next couple of months while we were doing press for the show, which meant we were going up to London and doing interviews and photo shoots and staying in posh hotels. At last it all felt really glamorous and exciting and we all become closer than ever as a result. Even Jay and I were getting on well again. But those friendships soon evaporated when they started airing *Geordie Shore*.

We all gathered to watch the very first episode at Aspers Casino in Newcastle with the MTV crew and some of our friends and family. All of these bigwigs from MTV were asking me if I was excited about seeing myself on screen for the first time, but I was shitting myself. You have an idea of how you look in your head that doesn't always translate to how you are in photos or on camera so I was terrified I would look a right state.

The first thing I thought when my face came on screen was that I pull some of the most ridiculous faces in the world. My friends have renamed me Vicky Funnyface. I scowl even when I'm happy which is ludicrous. I also talk like a man when I'm angry which everyone couldn't wait to point out. It was awful watching myself and I've probably only watched about forty-five per cent of the shows to date because I find it so cringey. It's like going on a night out, getting pissed with your mates while some dickhead follows you around with a video camera and then them making you watch it back the next day. I look like an utter bell-end on TV and I don't want to see that. I can watch the other cast members falling over and acting like tossers until the cows come home, but not me.

One of the most awkward things about the screening was that we were seeing all of the things that other people on the show had been saying about us. We were getting that first glimpse of what it's like to watch people slag you off behind your back. I'll hold my hands up; when I get in that green screen room I'm acid-tongued and take no prisoners, but I was never malicious, and some other people were. For instance, I saw a really nasty side to James. He can be really cruel and nothing scuppers a friendship like seeing what someone *really* thinks about you.

Everyone slags each other off in green screens because it's your time to vent, and because more of my green screens got shown it looked like I was slagging everyone off more. That honestly wasn't the case at all, because everyone else was doing the same thing, they just didn't get as much airtime as I did. Sometimes you're in there for hours and you get into the zone so you can get totally carried away. At the end of the day if I'm going to say something that's controversial, punchy and humorous I know it's getting shown, and it was. I came out looking like I was the most opinionated and bitchy member of the cast but it was only because I was funnier so a lot of my pieces were used. James has become much better at green screen over the years so he's being shown loads more on the show now. It's just the way it works.

There was one awful moment during the first episode where they showed me calling Sophie a gobshite and my heart dropped, I couldn't even look at her. I did mean it at the time because I thought she was brash and awful but I didn't know her at all then, and now I love her. Luckily she's such a good sport she took it on the chin and laughed, but she could have gone completely the other way and totally blanked me.

It's got to the point now where we take everything that's said in green screen with a pinch of salt, but back then we were still quite sensitive because we didn't know any better. These days people can call me whatever they want in that room. I know what they're doing – they're getting their airtime and the attention they want – so they can go for it. But it's taken me a long time to get to that point and not feel hurt.

The show came out in May 2011 and did brilliantly from the word go. It got the highest ratings MTV had ever had for a homegrown entertainment show. As soon as it aired, everything changed overnight. I know it sounds ridiculous but that was when I properly realised that we weren't just a group of people having a laugh and being filmed; we were now being watched by thousands and thousands of people. All of sudden people were using our catchphrases and we were being recognised in the street. It was an amazing feeling to be a bit famous, but it also meant it was open season when it came to slagging us off. Thankfully, Charlotte, Sophie, Holly and I were really supportive and we leaned on each other when we found it hard to hear what the public was saying about us.

We came in for a *lot* of criticism and we got a really hard time. People didn't know how to take us. The public were used to seeing these gorgeous, glamorous girls in *TOWIE* and *Made in Chelsea* who had hours to get ready before they went on set, then there were us girls, who had a camera thrust in our faces at eight in the morning after a night out. I'd have eyelashes hanging off and lipstick smeared across my cheek – it was an honest, warts and all version of us, and of life. We effectively faced a big backlash because we were normal and a bit of a mess. We know we're not supermodels and I've always thought that the girls in the show were picked because of our personalities not our looks, and I'm fine with that, but some people watching the show didn't seem to be.

We were never going to be like the girls in *TOWIE* or *Made in Chelsea* and look flawless, but the problem is that if you're in the public eye and you're above a size ten you're fat, and if you're below a size eight you're anorexic. If you sleep with someone you're a slag and if you don't you're frigid. We were judged so severely and we had so many awful things said about us, so us *Geordie Shore* girls made sure we were there for each other if anyone needed a bit of a boost.

Annoyingly the boys seemed to get off scott-free – despite all of their shagging around and twatty behaviour they were held up as 'proper lads'. They would get high-fived by guys in clubs because they slept around, but people turned their noses up at Charlotte because she'd had sex with Gaz on camera. We couldn't win.

Compared to some of the other lasses I did pretty all right during the first series. I was considered the best-looking, even though I didn't for one minute think I was, so I didn't get as much shit as some of them. I was asked to do the lads' mags and getting a lot of attention from the press – it was what I'd been dreaming of since I was a kid. Also, I didn't sleep with anyone during the show, despite Jay's best efforts. I remained true to myself and I was strong. I also showed emotion, which people liked. I was bloody lucky. Despite shagging Gaz, Charlotte did all right too because she's so cute, she's like a little bunny. But Holly and Sophie got ripped apart, and they weren't prepared for it. Holly took it particularly badly and I felt so sorry for her. That was when I first realised how vile Twitter can be. It's a great tool for self-promotion and I'm really grateful to it in lots of ways, but it can be brutal. Some of it was so personal and no girl should ever have to hear that kind of thing about herself. Holly can laugh about it now but at the time it was horrendous.

There were some times on the show when we came across pretty badly and maybe we deserved a bit of a battering, but you have to remember that a hundred hours of filming go into just forty-two minutes of the show so the most extreme things are shown. I could have been sat chatting to the other girls with a cup of tea and having a laugh for ninety-nine of those hours, but of course what's shown is me rampaging around throwing drinks at people.

What people see for forty-two minutes a week is not the full person. Yes, Charlotte is ditzy, but she's also very shrewd at times. And, yes, Gaz is a top shagger, but he can also be really sweet and he has a sensitive side. You don't necessarily see those other aspects of us and maybe if people did they would think twice before calling us out on Twitter. We're just the same as everyone else and we do feel hurt and confused that people don't realise that when they slag us off.

As a result of the show doing so well the producers were soon planning the next installment – a summer special called 'Magaluf Madness'. I was over the moon that the show was definitely carrying on and we were going to be doing more filming, but I was secretly still feeling quite hurt about all the things the other cast members had said about me. When I found out about Magaluf I'd only seen up to episode three and had just witnessed James slagging me off like there was no tomorrow. I didn't know he had it in him as he seemed so amiable in the house most of the time, but he definitely found his balls in green screen. I'm very confrontational and believe in getting everything out there, so it felt alien that people would rather bottle things up and winge about it behind my back rather than say something directly to me. By the time we were due to fly out to Magaluf I'd seen most of the series. I was so pissed off about what some people said I had a real bee in my bonnet and didn't want to go. In episode four or five James had called me a 'fucking chav' and a 'Bigg Market slag' and I was livid about it.

The day we were all due to fly out to Magaluf *This Morning* wanted someone from the show to appear live to defend the show. We'd been getting some negative press and they wanted to give us a right to reply. The show's agony aunt, Denise Robertson, was also going to be sitting in on the interview – because she's from the area she was disgusted with how we were acting. Of course, as I was the most articulate member of the cast by a country mile, I got chosen to go on alongside Kerry Taylor, who is the head commissioner for MTV.

Holly Willoughby was off on maternity leave and Jenny Falconer was standing in for her and I found her a bit patronising, but Phillip Schofield was lovely and I asked him to come out on the lash. Sadly it hasn't happened yet. By that point I was sick of people moaning on about *Geordie Shore*. I'm still sick of it to this day. People always say that Newcastle isn't really like we portray it to be and we're a bad representation, but we're not just a representation of Newcastle, we're a representation of the youth in Britain. If you don't like it or don't agree with it turn off and stop being so naive. I'm passionate about this because I think people are ignorant and closed-minded. If someone really doesn't think people in Newcastle party as much as we do they need to go down to the Bigg Market or the Diamond Strip. They'll be in for a shock.

Denise was on the attack from the minute I sat down on the sofa. She was a total battle-axe. One of her main issues was the fact the show was called *Geordie Shore* when some of the people on it weren't from Newcastle. She really didn't hold back in criticising us for giving a bad impression of the region, and some of her insults were quite upsetting. I was furious and even though I was nervous, once I found my voice I really held my own. I'm argumentative anyway, but I was really raring to go that day and pointed out to Denise that she wasn't exactly our key demographic. It was my first national

TV appearance but I stood up for myself as well as being articulate and getting my point across.

When I'd finished filming *This Morning* I jumped straight on a plane to Spain. I finally arrived in Magaluf to a totally empty house and immediately felt excluded from everything. I walked around and when counted all of the beds and there weren't enough for us all I felt like such an outsider. It was a terrible way to start things off when I was already feeling apprehensive. I went to sleep in what I guessed was the shag pad, to be woken up hours later by Jay bringing two girls back. The greedy bastard's only got one nob for Christ's sake. That was the first time anyone had seen Jay and I on camera together since series one and the scene showed him kicking me out of the bed so he could get it on with these girls while I went and slept on the camp bed. Brilliant.

When I saw everyone else the following day, it soon became really apparent that the goalposts had shifted and some people had come back with an agenda. They'd had a taste of fame and now they wanted more. The boys became very competitive with each other and had cottoned-on to the fact that the more you slag people off in green screen, the more of it gets shown. People were starting to realise that they could make a proper career off the back of the show so they were fighting for camera time. Not all of us were going to become breakout stars, but everyone was determined to give it a bloody good go. Obviously I've always wanted it to lead to bigger things and I've been really vocal about it. It's very obvious Gaz does too, but some of the others like Holly were surprised about the attention we were getting and they all lapped it up. We had the potential to make money and forge a really good career if we wanted it. As a result the backbiting reached a whole new level in Magaluf and afterwards.

It was the first time we'd seen each other since we'd all watched the first episode together and things were really, really tense. There was a massive divide between the girls and boys. A huge, bloody great big rift. Charlotte had seen all of these awful, insensitive things Gaz had been saying about her behind her back and of course she'd really liked him. It was cruel.

I have and always will be team Charlotte when it comes to her and Gaz. I never for one moment felt sorry for Gaz throughout everything that went on between them. He may have said he loves her on the show but I don't think he ever did. Sadly she was so besotted she would have done anything for him. I don't think he's callous and unfeeling and he does care about her and thinks she's a top girl, but he didn't treat her kindly. It's going to take a hell of a lot for Gaz to settle down. Maybe a Victoria's Secret model with the sex drive of a rabbit would be able to keep him on his toes and make him commit. Charlotte is amazing, but she was never going to be the girl to pin him down. She always made it too easy for him. He hurt her so many times and it was horrible to see.

The positive thing about Magaluf was that we were away from Newcastle so we weren't getting hassle from people back home. But the negative thing was that the tension was palpable. Things got so bad some of the crew even started taking sides. A few members of the female crew didn't want to work with the lads because there were saying such vile things about us. All in all it was a bloody disaster.

I hugely admired Holly for coming to Magaluf after seeing what we'd all said about her. I'm so surprised she didn't crack. I'm sure if you asked her now she would say that the first series was one of the hardest times of her life, and you've got to be pretty resilient to push on through something like that. Holly had to live what were effectively her university years in that house and when I look back to how I feel when I first landed in Liverpool I don't know if I could have stuck it out. But she did, and she came back looking like a totally new person. She went to London and had her hair dyed bright red, and toughened up a lot, but also became nicer to be around.

The time in Magaluf was also a bit weird for me because just after series one finished filming I'd started seeing a guy called Dan. He was a big face around town because he managed clubs and bars and was a right handsome bastard. He'd been trying to put a shift in with me for years, but I'd always been with someone. I'm very rarely single to be honest. Some of my mates had got off with Dan in the past, but that's par for the course in Newcastle. It is like a goldfish bowl and it's pretty much impossible to find someone your mates haven't got off with at some point! It wasn't anything serious but we had been going on dates and having a lot of fun and I thought it might lead somewhere.

I knew it could easily get to the point where it could become much more serious, but I deliberately avoided seeing him too much so it didn't progress. I felt bad about it, but I had to be so careful. Though I really quite liked him, there was no way I wanted to go into the new series properly attached to someone. I'd seen what happened to Holly when she had a boyfriend in series one, and I didn't want to follow in her footsteps. It was part of the reason she got so much stick; because she cheated on him on the first day. She'd barely put her suitcase down before she was sucking Gaz off.

There are a few things that the public won't forgive and being unfaithful is one of them. It took Holly the whole of Magaluf to turn viewer's perception of her around. I knew that if I went in there with a lad I wasn't sure about it would have been a disaster, there was no way I could say I wasn't going out on the pull without giving the real reason why. On the flipside if I did start properly seeing someone and then got off with another lad I would have been in all kinds of shit. So in the end I'd had to nip it in the bud and end the relationship before it even started – and I was feeling pretty annoyed about it.

Another thing that really fucked me off in Magaluf was tall, gorgeous and incredibly annoying. What a lot of people don't know is that a new cast member was brought in in the shape of a Scottish girl called Marie. She had long blonde hair, a great body and no personality. She was about as much fun as earache. I don't know what the producers thought Marie was going to do. I suspect they thought she may ruffle a few feathers, but she failed to cause even a ripple because she was so dull she was totally edited out. I actually felt quite bad for her because she probably sat down to watch it all excited and only realised then that she wasn't in it. She must have been trying to catch the odd glimpse of her hand or leg to show her mates. It was pretty harsh.

In the end I knew I had to make the best of the situation in Magaluf and it did turn out to be a good laugh after a very bad beginning. The girls and I cemented our friendships and became a really strong team. We had this amazing night out with this group of Manc lads one evening. We'd seen them on the beach earlier in the day and thought they were fit so we'd arranged to meet up and have some fun. We were sick of the boys bringing back all of these nameless, faceless girls and we decided to play them at their own game. We brought all the Manc lads back to the house after we'd been clubbing and Gaz and the other guys were fuming. They couldn't hack the competition. Especially when Charlotte and I started tashing-on with a couple of them.

Things started to get really nasty because Gaz, Jay, James and Greg weren't getting all of the attention from us. At one point they all stormed upstairs while we had a pool party. We heard later from some of the production crew that Gaz and Jay were saying such vile things about us they actually had to cut some of it out of the show. That was when certain female members of the crew started to avoid them. Some of the crew had worked on *Embarrassing Bodies* and yet they were more disgusted by what the lads said about us than the things they'd seen on there.

After that night the rift between the girls and the boys grew and grew and I think we were all really ready to go home by the time filming finished. I wanted to go and chill out away from the lads and the cameras – both of them end up doing your head in sometimes. Generally I used to pass out most nights, but if you're lying in bed trying to sleep and you're sober you can hear the cameras moving around and following you. Because most of the time we're drunk we totally forget there are cameras and that's why they catch us in such awkward situations. When we're on *Geordie Shore* we're filmed 24/7, and it does start to have a weird effect on your psyche. For a couple of weeks after I finish a series I can still hear the sound of the cameras in my head, even if I'm just in my bed at home. It gives you a really uneasy feeling.

People compare *Geordie Shore* to *TOWIE* but we're much more like *Big Brother*. *TOWIE* is more like *Hollyoaks* because they have scripts and things and we don't have any of that. Along with *The Valleys* we're considered to be the most realistic of all the reality shows and I totally agree with that. On *TOWIE* they have time away from the cameras when they're not filming, but for us there's no escape. I may be biased but I think the girls give more than the guys on our show, probably because we're more emotional. Charlotte and I will be in tears about an argument and the guys will sit there being stoic and acting like cavemen. But I would rather be emotional and honest. The minute you start editing yourself is the minute things start to go really wrong; that's when you stop being a reality star and start being a bad actor.

When we came back from Magaluf, Dan got in touch straight away and asked me if I'd got off with anyone. I had to be upfront with him and say yes, I'd kissed two people. I'm a really honest person anyway, but it's not like I could lie even if I wasn't because I knew it would be going into the show.

I hadn't done anything wrong, because I'd always made the situation very clear but he was angry because he thought he was going to look like a mug in front of his mates. They were already taking the mickey out of him because the episodes where Jay and I got together had been shown while we'd been dating. People obviously forget they'd been filmed months before. It all got a bit messy with Dan and it did leave me wondering if I'd ever be able to have a 'normal' relationship again, or I was destined to have a life of tashing-on on TV for the nation's entertainment!

Chapter Nine

Mad Dan and Ridiculous Ricci

Things really started to take off for me work wise after we finished filming 'Magaluf Madness' in late July. I got signed up by an agent, started getting asked to do loads of photo shoots and PAs and I was beginning to adjust to life in the spotlight. I fucking loved it.

PAs are hilarious things. I've done so many now that a lot of them blur into one. You basically get paid to go along to a nightclub, get drunk, say a few words on stage and have your photo taken with people. They can be really funny events but you do have to watch your back a bit. Some people take real pleasure in going along just so they can tell you how unimpressed they are about meeting you. It's sad, really.

It's much more fun if you do them with other cast members. During one mad night with Charlotte I went into the toilet to find her passed out on the floor with her knickers around her ankles and her head against the sanitary bin. She's always such a laugh to go along with. If you go with the boys they're generally too busy tashing-on with girls to want to hang out with you, so it's nice if some of us girls can go together.

One of my most memorable PAs – not that I can actually remember that much of it, mind – was in St Helens last New Year's Eve. I was so drunk by midnight I totally fucked up the countdown. I started out okay saying: 'Ten, nine, eight . . . ' but then I got distracted by something and stopped. The manager was shouting: 'Vicky, just say "one"!' so I shouted: 'Happy New Year!' a few seconds too late. Everyone looked at me like I was a total imbecile. I ruined New Year for everyone in St Helens and then I had to be put to bed by Chidgey from *The Valley*s. You know you're in real trouble when someone from *The Valleys* has to put *you* to bed.

Don't get me wrong, after series one I wasn't exactly thrust into superstardom overnight, but I started to get recognised more and I get offered loads of fun things. I did the cover of *Loaded* with Jess Wright from *TOWIE* and Binky from *Made in Chelsea* and was getting all these offers to do interviews and go on TV shows. It was a whole new, very exciting world. I'm a massive fan of reality TV and have always watched it. I think it's a natural thing to want to see what's going on in other people's lives and I get so passionate and involved. I followed all of the other shows and when I saw people landing hosting jobs or getting their own clothing ranges I wanted a big slice of that.

I'm sure people would like to think that there's big rivalry between us and the other shows but I watch and love them all, from *TOWIE* to *The Valleys*. I know a lot of people from our 'rivals' now, like Amy Childs, Jess Wright, Jasmin Walia and some of the *Made in Chelsea* boys. It's funny because we don't have to sit down and chat when we first meet. It's like we all know each other really well already and we're all in this reality TV show gang because we all understand what each other is going though.

I feel like I have a real affinity with *Made in Chelsea* and *TOWIE*. When I first met Jess Wright I was asking her to put in a good word with her cousin Elliot within about five minutes. We didn't know each other but because I follow her on Twitter and watch the show I felt like I was her best mate! That's what reality TV does. You see the trials, tribulations and the tears and you feel like you're a part of it. I bloody love it.

After the stress of 'Magaluf Madness' it was good to

be back home with my family and have something to focus on. Work was flowing and I started seeing Dan again and we went on a lovely holiday to Ibiza together. We weren't due to start filming series two until October 2011 so I had some proper breathing space to see if the relationship could work without the pressure of *Geordie Shore* putting a strain on things. Dan was a real gentleman and he spoilt me rotten, but there were warning signs that he liked the fact I was well known. He made sure everyone knew we were together by putting it on his Twitter profile, and he was always very happy to jump into pictures with me if a fan asked for one. Something didn't feel quite right.

Dan's brother managed a bar in Jesmond called Berlise and one night we were in there watching a David Haye boxing match. When I went to the bar I bumped into a mutual friend who told me Dan had sent him a direct message on Twitter saying: 'Come down to Berlise tonight. I'm with my lass Vicky from *Geordie Shore*.' That was the first huge red flag and I remember thinking, 'hold on, I'm a lot of things before I'm 'Vicky from *Geordie Shore*'. I'm Vicky, Caroll's daughter, I'm Vicky, Laura's sister, I'm Vicky who did the VIP door in Tiger Tiger. It really bugged me.

I've always said that I will never let *Geordie Shore* define who I am. I want to be Vicky Pattison first and foremost; I want to be known for who I am not what I do. I don't want to allow the show to put me in a box (I had enough of living in a box during my first year of university!) There is so much more to me. If you allow a TV show to consume your life it's dangerous because you lose who you are, also if you then lose your place on the show you have nothing left. I was so angry with Dan about that message and him seeming to use me and when I confronted him we had a huge row. I said to him that I thought he was only into me because of the *Geordie Shore* connection and the attention that came with it. He insisted he'd always liked me and while I did believe him, I was well aware that he'd made it his mission to get together with me following the success of series one.

As time went on there were more and more warning signs that he was basking in the glory of me being on TV. I was on holiday with the girls later that summer and he called me saying: 'Vicky, you'll never believe what's just happened to me. I've just had *The Sun* on the phone wanting to write a piece on me.' That instantly got my back up. Dan's done a couple of bits of modelling around Newcastle, but he's hardly a fucking celebrity. As if *The Sun* would want to write a feature about him when he was totally unknown! If anything they would be trying to get dirt on me and I wasn't about to let him steam on it and talk shit about me. He got really defensive and said it was a brilliant opportunity for him and he wanted to do it, so I hung up. He was so obviously keen to capitalise on going out with me, the twat, but either it didn't work or else he changed his mind and listened to me as no piece ever came out.

A week before series two officially started filming the producers invited us all down to the Thistle hotel in Newcastle. We were under the impression we were going to sign our new contracts and have a chat so we could tell the producers about the latest goings on in our lives. We were called in to see them one by one and as I was waiting for Greg to come back out one of the crew came down and told me he wanted to see me. Greg and I were the two eldest cast members and we were from the same area so we'd always had a bit of a bond. I went upstairs and he was in floods of tears. He was totally distraught and told me that he'd been told by the producers that there was no place for him in the second series because he hadn't forged any relationships within the group. He was only twenty-seven but when you think that Holly was just nineteen at that point there was a massive age difference.

I really felt for him. We'd been plucked from total obscurity and what we'd had so far was just a taste of this life we could have. We were being paid to go to nightclubs and being given nice free things and Greg was one of the people who was enjoying himself the most. It was in that moment that I realised how quickly everything can get taken away from you. It had been all fun and games when Marie had been cut because I didn't care about her, and she hadn't been in there from the start, but I was so upset for Greg.

I took Greg home to his mam's house and looked after him. I sat with him while he cried and it was heart-breaking because he really wanted to be a part of *Geordie Shore*, but he simply wasn't enough of a prick. He also become too aware of the cameras and how he was being portrayed, and when you do that you become one-dimensional. Greg is such a top lad but he just wasn't good enough TV. He's too nice. If you're not making a splash and creating good stories you're dis-posable, and his time had come. You have to be vocal and opinionated and that just wasn't Greg. I did under-stand the producers' decision to some extent, but I still thought it was cruel to take his dream away. I guess it's the nature of the beast and it was a big wake up call for all of us because any one of us could have been next to be cut.

By the time series two rolled around I'd decided to give Dan another chance, despite his previous actions. I was pretty smitten with him and I'd accepted his whole-hearted apology for being such an idiot. I had to tell the producers upfront that I was seeing someone and they were really happy because they said it would bring a new dimension to me being in the show. They filmed some green screen of me banging on about how gorgeous he was and how no one was going to turn my head that series. If only I'd known . . .

When Greg got cut we knew that they would be bringing a new boy in to replace him and I had an idea of the type of guy he would be – fit, good looking, a bit laddy – but I had no idea it would be Ricci bloody Guarnaccio. I already knew him slightly and to be blunt, I thought he was a bit of a prick. Like James, Ricci used to work as a topless host in Tup Tup Palace, which was one of my regular haunts. One night after I'd been hostessing in Tiger Tiger I went for a takeaway with my sister and as I was stood outside this café while they waited for their food these three lads walked past. They were topless, but wearing jackets over their bare torsos. I thought they looked like utter tossers.

They all stopped and started chatting to us and it soon became apparent that all three of them were trying to put a shift in with me. There was no way I was letting any of those wankers get my phone number. They were all making jokes and trying to be charming, when Ricci shoved his phone under my nose and said: 'Are you going to put your BBM pin in there then?' I was so taken aback at how confident he was I did it. Afterwards I stood there in shock looking him up and down and wondering why the hell I'd given my number to such an utter bell-end. The next day he sent me a BBM request, which I declined. I wasn't going to make the mistake of making contact with him.

We were all moved to a new house in series two because we had totally trashed the house in Jesmond. The houses in that road had been worth a million pounds each pre-*Geordie Shore*, and by the time we moved out we'd managed to devalue them by around two hundred grand! The association with *Geordie Shore* had sent prices plummeting. We must have been very popular around there.

So instead of our beautiful mansion we were put into a glorified warehouse down on Davy Bank, which is on the banks of the River Tyne. It's about two minutes from my parent's house in Wallsend and was pretty rough because it was on an industrial estate. But of course, on the plus side there were no neighbours to complain about the noise, and no one knew where we were. The producers were trying to be respectful to the people in Newcastle who hated the show by keeping us as far away from them as possible.

On camera the house looks amazing to live in but it's fucking horrendous. It's basically a tin warehouse that was freezing cold in the winter and boiling hot in summer. There were rats running all over and loud lorries driving around at six in the morning. It was disgusting, and was our punishment for living like complete animals in the old place. We probably deserved it to be fair.

It was a total shock when Ricci walked in for the first time. The first thing that went through my head was 'great, it's the topless tit'. I literally rolled my eyes at the thought of having to spend ages locked away with him loving himself off. Of course he was bloody good looking, but I couldn't get past the fact that he was such a nob-end. In a way it was a relief because at least I wouldn't be tempted to cheat on Dan with him. Or so I thought.

I honestly don't know what the *Geordie Shore* house does to you. I can't tell if it's because you know you're trapped in there and are starved of any other contact, but within an hour of us being in our shitty tin house I felt attracted to Ricci. I cannot explain why but I felt this really strong connection. We went from politely saying 'hello' to being into each other in a big way almost immediately. The only way to describe it is love at first sight. Or first hour. It's so hard for me to look back on it now because I fucking hate him, and it feels so alien to be talking about him in such a positive way. But as I've said before, I'm always honest. I have to dig really deep to think of Ricci's good qualities because right now it doesn't feel like he has any, but there must have been things that made me fall for him.

I think a huge part of it was that we were totally each other's type. I even said to him: 'You're going to be trouble for me!' Understatement of the fucking century. I still wonder if the production crew put Ricci in there because they knew I'd probably like him and it may break Dan and I up, but I've asked them about it since and they've totally denied it. Still, if they were hoping to create entertainment by bringing Ricci in, job done.

I straight away felt like I didn't want to be apart from him, which is handy when you're in a situation like that. It wasn't like when I'd got together with Jay because as much as I'd liked him at the time, I felt like I could take or leave Jay and we were actually better off as friends. But with me and Ricci it was all or nothing from the word go. I really didn't see it coming. I thought we may have a bit of a flirt and a bit of fun but the more time we spent together the more and more we fell for each other. He totally loved himself, but he also seemed to care about me a lot too and that made me feel amazing.

As with every series, I got completely pissed on that first night in the house, and that's when Ricci and I had our first (very innocent) kiss. He kissed me on the lips but it was only a peck so there were no tongues or anything. There is TV evidence to back that up if anyone doesn't believe me!

While everyone was expecting a new boy to join the cast we had absolutely no idea that another girl was also going to be shoehorned in. Enter Rebecca. I didn't make any secret of the fact that I didn't like them bringing her in. I was really defensive, but it wasn't about her as such, I was furious at the production crew. At that point I'd known some of the crew for a year and I trusted them and considered them to be friends, and they'd bought this random in for no good reason.

I was worried. After Magaluf all of the girls had finally got to a point where we could call each other friends, and to bring an outside element into that group seemed unfair. We'd finally bonded and I had only just started to feel comfortable and happy around everyone, and now there was this big dark-haired spanner being thrown into the works. It worked with four girls and four lads, so why bring in a fifth wheel? Was it just to wind us all up? Probably. That's when I realised that as much as I could have a laugh and joke with the crew, at the end of the day we're all there to do a job. Their job isn't to make you like them; it's to make an entertaining show that gets good ratings. The lines had blurred with me and I had to have a bit of a word with myself.

MTV could have bought the nicest girl in the world into the house and I still would have been mad. But the fact Rebecca came in with a bad attitude didn't help matters and it was clear there was no way we were going to get on. She had what we call a 'twisty face' in Newcastle. I thought she was rude, arrogant and ultimately, wasn't a very nice person. Hence we managed to have a falling out pretty much *straight* away. It started mainly because I hated the fact she swanned in and felt like she owned the place and didn't make much of an effort to be friendly. I admit that us girls had been moaning about her a bit on the sly, but when she came up to me and asked me if I had a problem with her I was livid. How dare she. This was my bloody house. Sort of!

Things erupted and we had a huge row that very first night. I said some pretty harsh things but she didn't hold back either. I ended up looking like the biggest bitch in the world but what MTV didn't show was that sweet, innocent Charlotte and lovely Sophie were also slagging her off and didn't want her in the house, so it all came crashing down on me. It was only Holly who didn't mind her to start off with.

I think by that point I'd decided that I'd been painted as a bitch so I may as well own it. With reality TV you get pigeonholed and so you have to play your part and do what's expected of you. There are times when I'm understanding of the process, but there are also times when I watch the show and think: 'Oh, fuck off, that's not how that happened. I spent an hour that day consoling Charlotte but all you want to show is me shouting at Gaz. You don't want to show my nice side, you just want to show my bad one.' The thing is, you can't expect everyone in life to like you because they won't. Someone once said to me: 'So what if people hate you. It proves that you stood up for yourself some-where along the line and at least you've evoked an opinion.' I totally agree with that. I'm never going to be universally loved because I can't keep my mouth shut!

I would much rather divide the nation and have half of them love me and half of them hate me than nobody know who I am. The only thing that does annoy me is when people think they know *everything* about me. They think they've got me pegged and that I'm just an opinionated, angry bitch with no heart and no feelings, but I'm far from it. Sometimes I'll scream at the TV or I'll vent on Twitter if I watch something where I'm portrayed badly, but you've got to take the rough with the smooth. I did feel resentful towards Rebecca and I was vocal about it and I don't regret anything I said to her. Us girls were slightly thrown under the bus with the situation, but that's the way the game works.

Even though things did calm down between me and Rebecca, she was still slagging me off behind my back the entire time. My issues with her ended as soon as I realised she wasn't a threat to me, but for her they continued. I had my own problems with my love life and I didn't have time to worry about some silly little girl, but she had nothing better to do than concentrate on disliking me, which is pretty sad.

Series two was hard for me romance-wise because I was in a genuine love triangle. Though I was seeing Dan outside of *Geordie Shore* I was falling for Ricci more every day in the house. I wanted to be with Ricci every single second and I felt physical pain when he walked out of the room. I wanted to come clean to Dan about liking Ricci as soon as possible, so I asked the producers if I could call him, but they said a flat no. They wanted to do a big reveal on the show where I told Dan about liking Ricci, and they somehow managed to convince me that it was a good idea. They wanted Dan to come into the show, see Ricci and I together, realise what was going on and then get the fallout on camera.

All I'd done was kiss Ricci on the lips and have a cuddle, and though it was all very innocent I still felt completely torn because I still liked Dan. Anyone who thinks Bella from *Twilight* has got it made is *so* wrong. It's really hard liking two guys. I changed from being Team Ricci one day to Team Dan the next. Usually if you're in that situation you've got the luxury of being able to deal with it on your terms, and at the very least in private, but not me.

When Dan came into the house and I did eventually see him again I realised that I still had *really* strong feelings for him. Just having that glimpse of normality and the outside world was so refreshing. In the back of my head I was also slightly worried that Ricci could just be playing a game for the show and using me to get more airtime. You get really irrational thoughts when you're in an environment like that; you start to wonder if everyone's got a massive game plan and if anyone's feelings are true.

This is a bit of insider gossip but we got given a little break about five weeks into series two and it was the best thing that could have happened. It was doing my head in being in the house with Ricci when I still had a relationship going on with Dan. I was told categorically that I wasn't allowed to see Dan or Ricci during that time and that everything that happened between us had to be done on camera. All I wanted to do was see my parents and have a hug, and have some girl time with my mates and get their opinions on it all.

I got together with a big group of my mates at my parents' house on my first night out of the house and had a takeaway and I explained the situation. They all started to look really shifty. The girls and I never keep things from each other and I knew there was something they weren't telling me. To start with I thought it was to do with Ricci, but once I dug a bit deeper it all came tumbling out. My mate Lyndsey told me that just before we started filming series two Dan had been trying to sell stories on me behind my back, the sneaky git. He claimed to my sister and my agent that loads of people were approaching him and offering him money to talk about me, but I thought he was talking bollocks. It wasn't like we were on the front page of *The Sun* every day so how the hell would the magazines and newspapers even know we were together? We were hardly Brad and Ange. I can't imagine he was being hounded by the nation's press. I felt he was trying to betray me again and I felt so stupid.

I'd been in the *Geordie Shore* house crying and getting stressed because I was worried about hurting Dan and the whole time he'd been trying to stitch me up. I was really upset so I picked up my phone and texted him saying: 'WE ARE FUCKING DONE.' He messaged straight back saying: 'Is this about Ricci? I know what you've been up to.' But I had only had that peck and some cuddles with Ricci at that point and I hadn't seen him outside of the house. I was so angry about Dan trying to push his bad behaviour back on me. I told him in no uncertain terms that I knew he'd been trying to sell stories on me. That night it became so obvious that he loved the celebrity lifestyle more than he loved me. I think he grew to *like* me but because the lifestyle and me were so intrinsically linked he got confused about what it was he really wanted, and I'm pretty damn sure it wasn't me.

It was like the floodgates had opening with my friends. They all admitted they thought Dan was slimy and untrustworthy after all of the things they'd heard about him. He was a fame hungry twat and he was trying to use me to climb up the ladder, and from that point on I wasn't having it. There was no way I was going back into that house if he was and now I'd dumped him there was no reason for him to be a part of the show.

Embarrassingly to this day Dan mentions the fact that

he was in *Geordie Shore*. It's so tragic. He was on the show for about five minutes, and I doubt the public even remember who he is, but he's still trying to use it to get exposure. Thankfully it's not fucking working.

Even though I was obviously under *very* strict instructions not to see Ricci outside of the house I messaged him straight away after all this happened and said I needed to see him. He came over and sat and had some drinks with me and my mates and he was polite and personable and all my mates thought he was great. He seemed to be everything Dan wasn't.

I had done everything the big bosses of *Geordie Shore* had told me not to do but I didn't give a fuck. I knew they would go mad at me for dumping Dan off-air and seeing Ricci, but this was my life and I had to do things my way. There were some things they weren't entitled to, and this was one of them. I told myself the show would be able to explain the situation in green screen. Maybe they could show me leaving a voicemail for Dan saying it was over? No chance. I'd disobeyed them and I was going to be made to pay.

When we all reentered the house I told the producers straight away what I'd done. I made an excuse and said that I thought Dan had been put through enough and I didn't want to have a public break-up on the show. I also told them I wanted to make a proper go of things with Ricci. They weren't pleased because of course they had wanted me to save those dramatic moments for when the cameras were rolling. When the series aired it became clear that without the break-up being shown on TV, I'd left myself wide open to the impression that Dan and I were still together. Sure enough when the show aired everyone thought that I'd two-timed Dan with Ricci and I was having my cake *and* eating it. With two giant spoons.

I knew I'd caused the producers problems but I wasn't aware of how much I was going to be taught a lesson. On a human decency level I still think I did the right thing and if I went back now and had to do it all again I wouldn't change anything. No matter how much of a shit Dan had been I didn't think anyone deserved to be ditched and humiliated on television.

Ricci and I ended up properly getting together and series two was the first time I ever had sex on camera. I hated it *so* much. It was always going to be the element that I loathed the most. The bitching and backbiting is nasty but I'm actually a bit of a prude and an ice-Queen when it comes to that side of things. I think some things are personal and they should be kept that way. I despised the fact that someone was watching me with a camera and that my parents could potentially see it.

I was, of course, mortal drunk the first time it happened. It was something Ricci really pushed for and because I was pissed I caved in. He hadn't come into the house and been the top shagger he'd expected to be, and

I think he felt like he'd lost some man points in that respect. I guess Ricci thought that having sex with me would help macho him up a bit. I liked him so much and understood where he was coming from so I stupidly went with it. I was sure we were going to be together for a while, if not the rest of our lives, so I knew I wasn't going to be nailed and bailed.

The worst thing was that my mam stopped speaking to me for ages when she found out what I'd done. Until that point I hadn't done anything too humiliating on the show. Yes, sometimes my language is appalling, I can be violent and I can say some really bad things in the heat of the moment, but those are things my mam can overlook. She's a strong woman too so understands my outbursts, but having sex on TV is very different. I think that really changed the public's opinion of me, and it also changed my opinion of the show because it had taken everything from me.

The whole series proved to be pretty eventful and I felt like I'd played my part well and provided the producers with some bloody good footage. I didn't have anything more to give, so when we had a big party on the last night I wanted to get mortal and enjoy myself. Then I discovered the bosses had suggested that me and Rebecca should talk. Just what I needed, that would only turn into a full-on showdown and I really wasn't up for any more drama.

I was never going to love Rebecca, but I was over it. Some of the crew were winding my up, saying: 'Come on, don't you want to be the Queen of the series? Don't you want to go out with a bang?' and I'm sure they were planting the seeds of an argument in Rebecca's mind as well. But I honestly didn't want to go out that way. I just wanted to have a laugh and see the series out on a high – I wasn't about to start a massive argument for entertainment purposes. Unfortunately some people are more easily led.

I tried to do some damage limitation so I pulled Rebecca to one side and said: 'Look. It's been "suggested" that I start a row with you but I'm not going to do it. I've got no problem with you. It's water under the bridge and we're mates. Yeah?'

I hoped that would do the trick and carried on with my night, had a few drinks and I was having a great time when all of a sudden Rebecca walked up to me with a stinking look on her face. I could tell by the way the cameras had been set up that they were expecting something to kick off. Rebecca said to me really stroppily: 'Vicky, can I have a word with you?' I looked at her and thought 'you're trying to drag up an old argument for more camera time you fucking idiot'. She had become a fame hungry little tit and I wasn't going to give her the satisfaction so I walked away. She tried to kick off an argument with me twice more that night and she wouldn't even let it lie, even when I went to bed. I was in the Fuck

Hut with Ricci so I could not believe her audacity when she walked in and started on me again. Yes, we were on a TV show and we could all be a bit dramatic, but we were also there to be ourselves and I hated the fact that she was trying to set up a row. I only did something when it was real to me and I would never have created a big dramatic finale out of nothing. I had been right about her all along. She wasn't like me, she wasn't nice, and I didn't like her. I felt drained and slightly broken by that point. I was exhausted and was losing trust in everyone.

I don't want to sound all doom and gloom because, as always with *Geordie Shore*, there were some bloody funny moments. When Gary, Charlotte, Ricci and I went to visit Ricci's parents at their house it was my chance to impress them. Though I smashed a glass and was mortified, it was nothing compared to what Charlotte and Gaz did. They both went to bed in the spare room, and despite promising that they weren't going to have sex they were soon at it. Only Charlotte got really bad giggles and farted. Gary smelt it, and when he asked her about it and she laughed so much she pissed the bed. I wasn't exactly welcomed into the family with open arms after that, but God it was funny.

The producers knew what had bought in the ratings in series one and they wanted more of it. They needed to push things that bit further so they wanted more drama, more fighting and more fucking. It scared me a bit because

I didn't know where it would end. I always had to have a better one-liner, Charlotte had to be more outrageous and naked and Gaz had to shag more women. I was feeling like I had given everything but nothing was ever enough.

When series two aired I was in for a rude awakening. When I first went into the show I was really strong and feisty and I was exactly who I'd been for the past twenty-two years. I had a great group of friends and a fantastic family and I knew people liked me, so why did I need to change? I knew that if I was myself the public would 'get' me. I have no issue with how I was shown or perceived in series one. I was me – a bit of loudmouth who thinks with her heart before engageing her brain, but also very loyal and protective. I may have been a little *too* feisty at times but that's who I am. Little did I know that my realdownfall would come just one series later.

I believe in life you have to have the courage of your convictions and if you believe what you're doing is right then go with it and fuck everyone else. At the end of the day, you're the only person who wakes up with you every morning and has to live with the decisions you make. If you make decisions for yourself and the people you care about you can't go far wrong. There was a time when I worried too much about what people thought about me and that's when I lost who I was. Even though I can't place all of the blame on his head, it all started when I got together with Ricci.

Chapter Ten

An Indecent Proposal

I was hated by the public after series two and it was a long way to fall having been on such a high pedestal in series one. I had been a hero who was a real champion for women everywhere. I didn't sleep around and I stood up to the guys. Then the second series aired, everyone decided I was a massive two-timing cow and people were slagging me off for something I hadn't done. That's when I made the decision to stop giving the show so much. I no longer wanted them to take the worst parts of my personality and mug me off. They expected me to walk blindly into series three and do it all again, and there was no way that was going to happen.

I'd stopped being the golden girl and had turned into 'Ricci's girlfriend' and a bit of a drip. Ricci was desperate to be popular but he really fell out with Gaz, which is never a good thing to do with such an established character.

People had also seen Ricci make me cry and he'd himself got a reputation as a nasty drunk (funny that). When he was sober he was selfish and spoilt and ignorant, but he wasn't nasty in the same way he was when he was drunk, and that did come over on the show. He's only nice when he's getting his own way. All in all the two of us were not well liked.

I went back home to live with my parents again but I spent pretty much all my time in early 2012, between series two and three, in with Ricci. We were in a love bubble and it was nice to have him there to turn to if I got down about the abuse I was getting off the back of the second series. The things people were saying were making me feel so low about myself. And the worst thing was, some of what they were saying is true – especially when it came to my looks.

After a couple of series of *Geordie Shore* I had become fat. I was a big tubby mess. I'd never had the time to lose the weight I'd put on during a series before the next one started so I was getting bigger and bigger and it was all booze and pizza weight. I had put on an average of half a stone to a stone in each series.

The drinks of choice in the *Geordie Shore* house are vodka Red Bull or Jaegerbombs. I was probably drinking about two or three thousand calories a night, and then there were crisps and chocolate on top of that. No wonder I'd bloated, and being with Ricci didn't help matters.

Ricci is a naturally slim guy with a fast metabolism and a six-pack. He could wake up in the morning after a massive Domino's and still look amazing, and when you're going out with someone you kind of adapt to their lifestyle. Only my metabolism isn't quite as good as his. The weight was piling on as nights out dancing with my mates, which I saw as cheeky cardio, turned into evenings on the sofa with Ricci, or meals out together. Food was a huge part of our relationship. Ricci and I would have a big night out on a Saturday and then spend all of Sunday sitting on the sofa with crisps, wine, Haribo, chocolate and a Chinese takeaway on top.

It wasn't until series three in Cancun that I was able to take a step back and I realised just how much weight I'd put on over this time. People were putting comments on Twitter like: 'You can see Vicky's comfortable with Ricci. #fatty' and 'She's gone from being the fit one to the fat one.' I was being called a fat slag and all sorts. No one would ever walk up to you in the middle of the street and say something like that, but they're happy to do it when they're hiding behind a laptop and the insults came flying at me via the internet. The weird thing was that Ricci actively encouraged me to eat, but he was a feeder. He also started to become incredibly controlling. Had I known what I know now and if I knew how to spot the early signs of an unhealthy and emotionally damaging relationship, I would have seen they were all there.

Ricci seemed really in love with me. I was his world and he didn't want me going anywhere without him because he was so obsessed with me. That could only be a good thing, couldn't it? I liked him so much that in the beginning I let things slide when I shouldn't have done.

We'd lived together in *Geordie Shore* and when we came out we were in each other's pockets so we barely spent any time apart. We were doing press for the show together and I even arranged for Ricci to get signed by my agent. The lines between our home and work life were so blurred and he even got annoyed because I didn't have a photo of both of us together on my Twitter profile, so I had changed my picture to keep him happy.

I've always been really independent and I do like time on my own sometimes, but Ricci didn't like that at all. I could have been going out with Tom Hardy and I would still have wanted a couple of hours on my own to do my

Sudoku and have a bath, but Ricci made me feel guilty about wanting to spend a second alone. That became a running theme of our relationship.

At first things were just a bit intense between us, and then slowly but surely I found myself getting cut off from the rest of the world. He came to all of my PAs with me because there was no way he'd let me go on my own, even though he wasn't being paid to be there. It was like a *Geordie Shore* BOGOF – he wasn't getting booked for any PAs so he was hanging off my coattails. It felt a bit like Dan all over again. He loved the attention being on the show afforded him and he had wanted to be the new Gaz, but things didn't quite work out how he hoped. He thought he was going to have this instant popularity but it simply didn't happen.

Ricci was an only child and he was his mam's pride and joy. As a result he was spoilt rotten. He trained at Toni & Guy as a hairdresser and when he qualified his parents opened a salon for him to work in. Five weeks later he got a call asking him to go into *Geordie Shore* so he totally left them in the lurch, which says a lot. He got whatever he wanted, but one thing his parents couldn't buy him was popularity.

Ricci wasn't making any money of his own so where do you think he decided to get it from? I was paying for pretty much everything. Because I was more established I was making good money and he had nothing, so I was being drained. He used to owe me fortunes but every time he earned any money he would go on a shopping trip or to the bookies. I stupidly put up with it because I wanted to make him happy. When he was happy my life was easier.

We did have some really good times together but as the months went on they became less and less frequent. He was always so jealous and I felt so trapped, but I was desperate to try and make things work because I was in love with him. I was paying for us to go to nice hotels and have lavish nights out and it's not as if he was ever grateful. I became more and more cut off from friends and family. It was the beginning of a really bad time.

Because I hated how I had come across in series two a huge part of me really didn't want to be involved with series three. The Dan and Ricci situation had made me look really bad and I remember being on the phone to my agent, crying and saying I couldn't go through with it. He advised me to suck it up and get on with things for the sake of my career so in the end, with a heavy heart, I went to Cancun for series three in early March.

The whole series was horrendous. Lime Pictures had decided I was difficult to work with, so I was the last one to fly out along with Jay, five days after Ricci had left. I was so worried Ricci would have cheated on me on one of the lads' nights out and I wondered if that's what the producers were hoping would happen so it would create more drama. I also suspect they thought something may reignite between Jay and I again, even though he had a girlfriend by then.

Jay had got together with a girl called Chloe in between series one and two and he thought they were for life. I don't know the ins and outs and of what happened between them but I know that Jay stopped acting like '*Geordie Shore* Jay' when he got with her. He stopped rowing with me, he wasn't bringing back random lasses and he was no longer Gaz's wingman. His heart hadn't really been in series two so I was worried about him in series three.

Jay and I arrived mortal after the ridiculously long flight and Ricci was furious with me in private. Though we acted all loved up for the cameras, he barely spoke to me when we were alone. Not a great start. Because I was really conscious about coming across badly and paranoid about upsetting Ricci I started to filter myself from day one which was such a massive mistake. I'd been one of the main characters and let *Geordie Shore* into every aspect of my life – I'd been laid bare and it was taking a huge emotional toll on me. I wanted to have a break from it all and for the focus to be on the other girls.

Holly was certainly having a good time. A lot of people don't know this, but she'd always had her eye on

James, even way back in series one, but he wasn't keen. All through series two James had moaned about the fact he wanted a sunbed to top up his tan, but we managed to nab them first. Towards the end of the series he was told: 'If you want a sunbed you've got to sleep with Holly tonight.' That evening when Holly put the moves on him as usual, before you could say 'twelve minutes on a flat bed, please,' James was shagging her. But there was certainly no need to barter a sunbed in Cancun! Holly and James were carrying on with each other all series so there was obviously a bit more between them than James was letting on.

I soon learned that pulling back and trying to be something I wasn't was stupid, stupid, stupid. I knew my role in the show and what is expected of us, but I just wasn't able to give them what they wanted. Because I had deliberately withdrawn myself, the producers had to try and find interesting situations for me, which is probably why I ended up spending the night in the middle of nowhere getting pissed with Holly.

But the other reason I'd become withdrawn was because I was trying to protect myself. People only saw the tip of the iceberg of how awful Ricci was to me in Cancun. They saw him get drunk and mean every now and again and argue with people, but he was clever and he'd wait until we were in a taxi away from the cameras and then start on me verbally. He could also say a thousand words with just one look and would call me horrible names really quietly so no one else could hear. Ricci should have been my support system in there but instead he became the enemy. It's not like I could talk to the other girls because I knew they weren't happy about Ricci and I being together – I knew they'd been slagging me off behind my back. I was so lonely, even though I was glued to my boyfriend.

I felt like I was constantly walking on eggshells and running around after Ricci trying to keep him happy. I couldn't even show how unhappy I was because I wanted the outside world to think our relationship was perfect. I put on a show. The more unhappy Ricci was, the more unhappy he made me. I felt really isolated and separate from the other cast mates, it didn't feel like I was close to any of them anymore; it was all about Ricci. If I tried to have a laugh with them he would give me filthy looks or stop speaking to me. We were out in a bar drinking tequila one night and I clinked glasses with Jay. When I looked over Jay's shoulder Ricci was giving me this vile look as if he wanted to kill me.

Ricci didn't even like me getting drunk, but that's what the entire show is about. I was really struggling to keep my head above water. The one person I was relying on was emotionally bullying me. He can't have genuinely been in love with me, because if he was he wouldn't have treated me like that. He was making me into the worst version of myself and I was losing all of the aspects I liked about myself. My anger and bitchiness was becoming a permanent fixture and I started to feel out of control. My relationship with Ricci was making me scared, miserable, anxious and fat.

After a hell of a lot of tension things came to a head on Sophie's last night when she'd decided to go home. I was steaming drunk and so frustrated with everything that I let rip. A drunk person's words are a sober person's thoughts, and everything I'd been feeling up until that point came out. I'm open about the fact that I have a bad temper and I lashed out at Ricci in spectacular fashion.

Of course, Ricci had been so cunning no one had seen what had been going on behind the scenes. They didn't know how controlled I felt and I was at breaking point. Our row was so bad we both got taken out of the house and put in separate hotels and it was devastating. I was so ashamed of how I'd acted and I knew in my heart that we should break up.

The following morning the producers came to see me and said they were really torn about what to do for the best. They wanted to protect me because they could see I was broken, but they also wanted me to stay until the end of the series. I should have run to the airport as fast as Usain Bolt but instead I allowed myself to get talked round. I was hungover and fragile and I wanted to keep everyone happy, so – incredibly – I agreed to stay. Ricci and

I made up and I told myself that if I could get through the next few days I could go home and see my family and sort my head out.

A few days later I found myself sitting in this beautiful restaurant with Ricci. I thought we were there to talk about our relationship and see if there was any way we could make it work, which needless to say I was very skeptical about. The whole set up was very ostentatious and after a bit of going back and forth I looked up and there was a fucking airplane with a banner saying 'Vicky will you marry me?' I nearly threw up there and then. I was in total and utter shock.

It certainly wasn't how I would ever want someone to propose, in front of a load of crew I didn't even know, thousands of miles away from the people I loved. But what the hell was I supposed to do? Say no? I was on autopilot. I bet the producers were glad I'd stayed. Ricci proposing to me would make incredible TV, and provide a triumphant end to series three. I. Was. A. Mug.

I showed all the right emotions – elation, joy, surprise – but I didn't *feel* any of them inside at that moment. Saying yes felt like the *right* thing to do, not what I *wanted* to do. I felt like I didn't have a right to a say. Everyone had been running around behind my back organising everything and how could I turn him down? The ring was beautiful but as soon as it was on my finger that was it; I was trapped. That ring may as well have been shaped like a pair of handcuffs. I had become the sort of person who does things because they're easier than not doing them.

However, I won't lie, there was definitely a small part of me that was happy Ricci had asked me. Just the fact that someone loved me enough to want to be with me forever felt amazing – I was truly excited about the prospect of a wedding. I was twenty-four but suddenly I felt really grown-up and I was looking towards my future. At the end of the day I'm a girl and I think we all want a big wedding and to be the centre of attention for a day. I got so caught up in the idea I blocked out the fact I was doing it with completely the wrong person.

The end of series three couldn't have come quick enough for me, and when I got back to Newcastle I broke the news to my friends and family and got some very mixed responses. My parents said they just wanted me to be happy, because that's all they ever want for me. Ricci and I had an amazing *Alice in Wonderland* themed engagement party in a restaurant called As You Like It in Jesmond, which is a beautiful venue. It was so big it was like a wedding, but of course Ricci and I managed to ruin it. It was par for the course with us. I had paid for the lion's share of it and it cost thousands of pounds, but we still got drunk and had a blazing row.

Ricci had been possessive and mean up until that point, but it was nothing compared to what was to come. I thought the engagement would make him feel more secure, but from then on I felt like I was his property. The minute bit of freedom I'd been allowed as his girlfriend completely vanished when I became his fiancée. My friends knew that if they wanted to see me they had to see both of us together because I wasn't allowed anywhere without him. I'd always found solace in my mates, but I no longer had that because girls' nights out were out of the question. I used to have to beg to leave his house and go to mine to see my family.

My relationship with Ricci's parents wasn't great either because his mam pretty much hated me. No one was ever going to be good enough for her son, and certainly not Vicky from Wallsend. I get the impression they felt that I had been dragged up, not brought up. I wasn't privately educated like him and even though I did everything to try and get her to like me, it wasn't going to happen. His mam bumped into Sophie and her mam in Durham once and said to them: 'I don't know what Ricci's doing going out with Vicky. He used to go out with much better looking girls.' Of course it got back to me straight away and you could have cut the atmosphere with a rusty knife every time we were in a room together. I knew my parents hated him as well, even though they never said it directly to me. I could just tell from the way they acted around him. They were always friendly to him but he didn't make any effort with them. Do you get the feeling this isn't going to end well?

Chapter Eleven

The Fall Girl

Just when I thought things couldn't get any worse my fall from grace was accelerated when series three aired because I'd committed the ultimate sin for a woman – I'd put on more weight. The insults were flying faster than a Twitter-branded bullet and it was like a form of torture going on there to read them. But all those horrible things gave me a massive kick up my massive arse. We finished filming series three in April 2012 and series four didn't start filming until August so I had some time to lose some lard.

I knew I had to do something extreme so I did a

shape-up feature for *Closer* magazine. I was being monitored and had to do a photo shoot at the end of the diet so there was no escape – I had to stick to it or look like an utter lazy twat. I was at the high end of ten stone when I started and I went down to about nine stone twelve doing a combination of The Cambridge Diet and working out over the next few months, so I felt pretty good.

There was a bit of a shake up with the show because the main producer was leaving to go and work on *TOWIE*, and we were getting a new one. All we were told was that none of our places were safe and they were looking for some big storylines. Unfortunately, as had been revealed in series three, that meant curtains for Jay. I was gutted because he left a real hole in the show. He was slightly older than the rest of us, he was a real homebody, and so it wasn't a complete surprise. I've always looked at Gaz and I thought 'you're a walking penis' and I can never imagine him settling down, whereas Jay really wanted a wife and kids and you could tell that. He'd really calmed down since he'd been with Chloe and he wasn't the party boy the producers needed him to be.

Sometimes being in a relationship works on the show. For instance, Sophie and her boyfriend Joel did because he was a bit of a tosser so there were always ups and downs, and I guess it was the same with me and Ricci because there were a lot of fireworks. Chloe and Jay weren't anything like us. They were *nice* together and unfortunately that's just a bit boring on reality TV. No one wants to watch two people sitting together holding hands, having a nice time and telling each other how in love they are. They want to see fights. If you want hand-holding, watch *Downton Abbey*.

Geordie Shore is carnage and if you're in a happy place with your personal life the journey kind of comes to an end for you. From what I've gleaned Jay was given an option; dump your girlfriend or leave the show, and he chose Chloe and jumped before he was pushed. I admire him for doing it because there aren't many people who would make that decision.

A couple of weeks before we were due to start filming series four Ricci and I went on holiday to Ibiza. On the first night of the holiday we were having a few drinks in the apartment when I got a call from my agent. He'd been for a meeting with the show's new producer, Amelia, and she'd told him that she wanted me but not Ricci for the upcoming series. My heart sank. I knew Ricci would be devastated. I told my agent that if they didn't want Ricci they couldn't have me either. I'm nothing if not loyal. That phone call totally ruined the next few days of holiday. Ricci moped around constantly and no matter how much money I threw at the situation it didn't work. I took him for some amazing meals and to all the best clubs – I spent thousands, but he couldn't raise a smile.

Ricci had spent all of his money from series three on my engagement ring so, once again, I was paying for everything. I think once you start to financially support a man you lose some respect for him and become resentful. I felt like I was mothering him and it irritated me. Because I'd lost some weight I was getting some of my confidence back and I started standing up for myself for the first time in ages. But, of course, Ricci didn't like that, so our arguments escalated as he tried to stay in control of our relationship. It was making me miserable at a time when I had just started to feel better about myself again.

A few days into the holiday Amelia called me directly. She was really honest and said that she'd loved me in series one but she thought I'd lost myself in series two and three. She wasn't asking me to break up with Ricci, but she didn't want him on the show because he didn't do me any favours. I was torn because he was begging me not to do it without him, and, if I'm really honest, I had become as reliant on him as he was on me. I was distant from my friends so even though I was unhappy in the relationship I was scared of splitting up with Ricci in case I found myself totally alone.

I tried to convince Amelia that we were much happier and stronger than we had been and we would be fine, but she said she needed to think about things. Eventually the day before we were flying home she called and said she would let us both go into the house. But she also said that if she saw one sign of me not being myself and being unhappy or if there were any tears and huge rows we were both out.

She also spoke to Ricci and instructed him to behave and be nice to me, but her words fell on deaf ears because as soon as were through the *Geordie Shore* doors he was back to behaving like an absolute wanker. I should have been over the moon that series because people had finally realised how boring Rebecca was and she had left the show – it was back to being us original *Geordie Shore* girls. It was also the series when Scott Timlin and Dan Thomas-Tuck joined the house – I guess they figured it would take a lot to replace Jay so had to bring in two guys just in case . . .

Scott was, and still is, the perfect addition to *Geordie Shore*. He's a lovely lad: fun, outgoing and he's got a softer side to him that a lot of people don't see. I've known him for years; in fact, when I was eighteen we had a little tash-on at his friend's party. I spent the whole time shitting myself that Ricci would find out because he would have gone mad, and to this day he still doesn't know. Well, he probably will now . . . Dan was the complete opposite to Scott. He wanted to be like Gaz but he was too naive and young. It was a shame because he was a lovely lad. One night we were all coming out of Bijoux in Newcastle and for some reason this random guy threw a six-inch ham sub at Dan's head. From that moment on Dan was nicknamed Hamiel, and it was something he didn't manage to shake off until he left the show. I wonder if he still gets called it to this day.

Either way, it should have been great but I was too obsessed by my relationship with Ricci to pay much attention to what was going on within the house. I was far too wrapped-up with what was happening with him to give much energy to my friendships. Of course, within a week of being in there he'd done everything Amelia had told him not to. He got drunk and nasty and called me names off camera whenever he got a chance. He was losing control and being sloppy and people were starting to notice just how aggressive he could be. During a particularly vicious argument Gaz had to physically take him out of the same room as me because he was being so vile, and after that he was removed from the house. Unfortunately, the stress of it was really getting to me and it all came out that night in a massive fight between me and Sophie – so in the end us girls also had to leave as well. All because of Ricci. I'd put my entire career on the line for him and that's how he repaid me.

Of course after that Ricci was full of remorse and promised MTV he would behave and begged to be let back in. He was on his last warning but when we went for a night out at Bijoux in town he showed his true colours in front of *everyone*. I'd begged him not to drink that night because I knew if he fucked up once more he'd be out, but I could tell he was in that kind of mood. I went to the toilet and when I came out one of the security guards was waiting to take me back to the table. I was chatting to him completely innocently about his girlfriend and his kids when Ricci came down the stairs and flipped. He was screaming in my face and calling me a slag in front of loads of people. The security guard stayed really calm and collected and told him he'd got the wrong end of the stick, but there was no reassuring Ricci.

I got put in a taxi so I could go back to the house and Ricci was shouting and screaming abuse at me through the window. He'd gone from being very clever and sneaky to making mistakes, and this was a gigantic one. He fucked up again by causing trouble a couple of days later – he massively kicked off about me getting a spray tan with the other girls. He said he didn't want me to strip in front of anyone that wasn't him. I'm a Geordie lass, I've told you, I need my tan! Non-negotiable. Eventually he was chucked out of the series although the producers were very fair and made it look like he left.

Amazingly, a part of me felt quite bad for him, but it was also a bloody relief. I finally had some proper freedom to be myself again in the house. Amelia was brilliant and she sat me down and talked me through everything – she was so supportive. We became friends, and even though she'll kill me for saying it because she's nowhere near old enough, she became a bit of a mother figure to me. She said she saw so much of herself in me and I can't thank her enough because she restored a bit of my confidence at that time. She didn't find mine and Ricci's arguments funny or entertaining, she wanted to protect me. Amelia was strong when I couldn't be, and without Ricci in the house I could get back to being myself. I started getting on with the other lasses again and I felt like I was a part of the old gang, finally able to engage with the series.

Little did I know that once filming for series four finished my real nightmare would begin. Despite everything Ricci and I were still together. I know you'll be reading this thinking 'you fucking idiot' but unless you've been in a similar situation you can't understand. He was my world. I hated him, but I also loved him. I cared about him so much and I was blind enough to think he loved me too.

If I'd thought things were bad up until then I was kidding myself, because from then on our relationship was constantly on a rocky footing. Ricci and I were doing two PAs in Scotland and I'd met up with a couple of male mates in a bar. It was purely platonic and we were having a really good laugh, but just like that night in Cancun I saw Ricci giving me these evil looks behind their backs. I finished my drink, grabbed him and left straight away so he didn't cause a scene, but it was too late. He'd already turned from Dr Jekyll into Mr Hyde.

We got back to our hotel room and he started smashing things up and going mad. Somehow I found my lady-balls (thank you, vodka) and I told him I was leaving. I picked up my bag and threw some things into it, but Ricci was trying desperately to stop me leaving. I think he knew if I walked out that door that I would never come back – deep down I knew our relationship was just not working. We had got ourselves into such a state that we just needed to be apart. Then his mood switched and he started crying. He was like an inconsolable child begging for my forgiveness, and I ended up comforting him. I was lying there holding him thinking 'what the hell am I doing? Why am I still here?' But despite everything I still felt really sorry for him.

It was episodes like this that meant that by this point my friends and family were sick to death of me and my dramas. Had I not been so close to all my mates for so many years I swear they would have ditched me. I don't know why anyone put up with me when I was acting like such a melt. The public were bored shitless of it too. When series four aired I was getting complete strangers coming up to me in the street and telling me I was too good for Ricci. I bumped into Ellie Goulding when she was in Newcastle doing a concert and she said to me:

'What are you doing with Ricci? He's a bully.' Everyone could see it.

People are going to ask why I stayed with him for so long and my answer is because you always hope that things will get better. Despite our destructive, unhealthy relationship I still loved Ricci and I hoped he would change and we could work things out. Ridiculous, I know.

Chapter Twelve

CAN-ned

Needless to say everything got on top of me in a massive way and I turned to food to make me feel better. I was regaining all of the weight I'd lost on the *Closer* plan at an alarming rate. Faddy diets like that are great if you've got an event and you want to lose weight quickly, but the minute you start living your life and eating normally it all goes back on. I lapsed back into my bad old habits and all the weight I'd lost came back on with a bloody vengeance.

I felt trapped and miserable, so I just ate to make myself feel better. Ricci controlled every aspect of my life and after series four had been on TV I was hardly working because we were now the two most hated people on *Geordie Shore* by a country mile.

He had become my entire world and I comfort-ate carbs like they were going out of fashion. I dug out my old size twelve leggings and lazed around in them for days on end. I convinced myself that because they still fitted I wasn't that big, but because they had loads of give in them they were growing with me. I avoided mirrors, couldn't afford to go clothes shopping and because of Ricci I didn't go out with my mates, though that made it easier for me to cut myself off. I think I was in what is commonly known as 'denial'.

It's obvious that mine and Ricci's relationship was very unhealthy. There was one time that really stands out to me. I'd been asked to do PA in Southend-On-Sea with Charlotte, Jay and James. Of course, even though he wasn't being paid, Ricci still wanted to be a part of it. Heaven forbid I tried to do anything without him. Ricci even pestered me into contacting the club promoter to see if he'd be interested in giving Ricci a bit of cash to come along – he wasn't – and as a result Ricci was in a terrible mood.

We arrived at the club and had a few drinks, but while I had my photo taken with various people Ricci got increasingly angry and ended up sitting in a corner throwing back drinks and giving me filthy looks. About an hour later, he was totally mortal and stormed over accusing me of ignoring him. I bit my tongue and tried my best to placate him but he was well and truly in one. After a few more drinks and ridiculous strops Ricci announced he was going back to the hotel. I had a contract with the club so had to stay for a few more hours and because of his attitude I was a bit like 'fuck off then'. I ended up having a really good laugh and was finally able to relax, so when I arrived back at the hotel later I was a bit tipsy and in a really good mood. Ricci soon put paid to that.

As soon as I walked into our room he flew into a rage and was accusing me of all sorts of things, calling me a slag and a bitch and then became really aggressive. He started screaming in my face – I couldn't calm him down; Ricci started taking his anger out on one of the doors and punching it repeatedly. I was so shocked I burst into tears.

Eventually he stopped and I curled up on my own and went to sleep. I woke up a few hours later, and by then Ricci had calmed down – incredibly, he acted as if nothing had happened. When I broached the subject he was full of excuses, but the holes he'd punched in the door were evidence of his appalling behaviour.

Ricci came out with his usual patter. He was 'so sorry, he was drunk', 'it would never happen again', 'it was only because he loved me so much'. The most embarrassing part was that Charlotte came to see us and it was obvious something major had gone on. I was mortified by the state of the room, but she was too sweet and polite to say anything. When Ricci and I left I had to explain the damage to the receptionist – obviously I played the whole thing down but I still had to pay for the damage.

By the time series five was due to kick off I was incredibly low. The likes of Charlotte, James and Gaz were all doing really well off the back of the show. The lads were turning down PAs left, right and centre because they were so busy and Charlotte had her own dress range. Me? I was bloody frustrated. My star was waning because people didn't want me and Ricci as a package. We were both living with our parents but I was still supporting him financially and emotionally and I was doing everything I could to try and get more money for both of us, but no one wanted personal appearances from the couple who just rowed and cried all the time.

There were several times when Ricci and I did properly break up and I thought it was for good. We'd have a massive argument, and I would leave. But he'd beg and beg me to go back to him and he would always point out that we had a holiday booked or some press to do for the show. We were so closely linked. We did come as a pair because he didn't like me doing anything solo. It was a horrible, vicious circle. We were in a bad routine that neither of us could break.

Ricci promised me wholeheartedly that he would behave if we were both asked to go back for series five, which at that point was looking unlikely. I knew that if we wanted to up our game in terms of our celebrity status we needed to get a new agent. The guy we had was lovely, but we were a bloody hard sell simply because no one really liked us. I fired off loads of emails to agents and believe it or not Claire Powell from CAN Associates, who looks after Peter Andre and Amy Childs, came back and said she wanted to meet with me. I was convinced this could be the turning point we needed. This could change everything. They were the biggest and the best agency in media and I was so excited. I thought if Ricci could start earning some money he would feel better about himself and our relationship would be so much easier.

Ricci and I travelled down to meet Claire at her house in Sussex. She was talking about branding opportunities and TV shows and all sorts, and a few days later we got a call saying she wanted to sign us. I was ecstatic. We were back on track. Claire was the answer to all of my prayers and the one who was going to turn it around for us. For the first time in so long Ricci and I were happy because the pressure was off. We didn't have to worry about going scrabbling around for scraps of work, we had clout behind us. We did a photo shoot for CAN and went up on their website – it felt properly big time.

MTV called me and Ricci in for a meeting the following week and I was shitting myself that they were going to turn around and say they didn't want Ricci again. But, amazingly, they instead told us that they wanted series five to culminate in our wedding. I was stunned. After everything they'd seen us go through in series four they wanted us to tie the knot on the show. They even said we could have a private wedding separately and just have the commitment ceremony on *Geordie Shore*, but I wasn't having any of it. I was sure by then I didn't want to marry Ricci so I refused to do it. Ricci also said no, but only because he wanted a big magazine deal. Claire Powell had already said if we were going to get married on TV she would get us our own show, so she was the bad guy who broke the news to MTV. Thankfully they still wanted us, but of course we were given a stern warning about not rowing. But, if anything, I felt things might be better in the house than out of it as I knew Ricci was always nicer to me on camera.

We went into series five all guns blazing. We had Claire behind us so despite our dodgy past suddenly we were being hailed as the next new big reality TV couple. We were going to smash it and really make a name for ourselves. Unfortunately we 'smashed it' in the wrong way. Within days we got mortal and started fighting. Ricci was really aggressive on camera so just a week into the series he was taken out of the house again.

The next day Amelia told me he was never coming back. She'd had enough. And so, finally, had I. I got to see Ricci very briefly and he asked for the engagement ring back. He may have owed me six grand at that point but he was still welcome to that ring.

The producers allowed Ricci to go into green screen where he made out he was finishing with *me*, which was laughable, but at least it was finally bloody over with. I was free. Amelia had called Claire Powell to fill her in on the situation and I knew what was coming. I found out from Claire's assistant that she couldn't be seen to condone such bad behaviour in any way, shape or form and no client of hers was going to act like that. Forget three strikes and you're out or giving us a warning, we were both dumped. I'd gone from being on top of the world and thinking I had a bright future ahead of me to having nothing.

I was so upset after Ricci left because, just like last time, I blamed myself a bit. But after a lot of tears and anger I picked myself back up and threw myself into the series headfirst. After a terrible start I ended up having one of the best series ever. It was the 'Geordie Tours' series where we travelling around and Charlotte and I went to Barcelona. We took out this stag do and I was having a laugh and talking to lads for the first time in *so* long. I wasn't being a massive flirt or tashing-on with loads of lads but I could relax and be 'me' for the first time in ages. I finally had some freedom. It was one of my favourite series ever and Charlotte and I got on brilliantly. It totally took my mind off everything that had happened back in England and it was exactly what I needed.

Once the series was over I crashed back down to earth; it was time to face Ricci and try and salvage my crumbling career. As soon as I was back home Ricci started calling me non-stop. He was turning up at my house and doing anything and everything he could to get me back. I promised my friends and family I wouldn't fall for his shit, but (and please bear with me on this because I know how frustrating it all is) before I knew it I was wearing my engagement ring again. I'd somehow fallen back in love with him. I think I'd become afraid of being on my own. I'd been in relationships non-stop for three years. I'd gone from Jay to Dan to Ricci and I didn't know how to stand on my own two feet anymore. If it helps I think I acted like an absolute twat too.

Amelia was absolutely furious with me, to the point where she stopped speaking to me for a while. I can't say I blamed her. She'd helped me to get my life back on track and I'd thrown it back in her face. I'd totally fucked things in my life by getting back with Ricci. When I look back on everything I just can't believe how I acted. I want to get into a time machine and go back and give myself a bloody good talking to. I want to stand myself in front of a mirror and say: 'Look what you're doing you fucking idiot! Look at your life! You're throwing all of your opportunities away for the sake of one man who treats you like utter shit!'

I kept coming so close to breaking up with Ricci, but I never managed to make it stick because of all the plans we'd have made together. One time Ricci and I were driving to a PA together and he was talking about us going to Ibiza again. I had hit an emotional brick wall and turned to him and said: 'It's not going to happen. I'm not here now because I love you, I'm here because we're working. Can you honestly say I make you happy?' I couldn't keep pretending to myself everything was okay.

Ricci ignored me, but when we pulled over to get a McDonalds he started a row. He got so irate he ended up throwing his food – if it hadn't been so awful it would have been laughable. The only problem was that we'd booked a holiday to New York together and he convinced me to go so he could prove to me he loved me. Has anyone seen the film *Groundhog Day*?

The news that our holiday was horrendous won't come as a massive shock. Ricci was so critical of me and made me pay for everything. All he wanted to do was drink and I wanted to sightsee. We spent five days eating, drinking and arguing non-stop. When I got back from New York I sat down with Laura and two of my best friends and I confided that I was completely miserable.

Once I started talking I couldn't stop and everything came tumbling out. One of the stones had come loose in my engagement ring so it had been sent off to be mended and I really didn't want it back. I knew that if I didn't get out of the relationship I would never be happy again – I knew I had to make that break.

At that point I was eleven stone five, the biggest I'd ever been. One thing I will say about Ricci is that he never told me I was fat, even if he did make the odd comment. One time I was desperately trying to get into a dress that wouldn't zip up and he said to me: 'Sometimes I think you think you're a lot smaller than you are and it's about time you started buying bigger clothes.' The problem was Ricci used food to bribe me. If we'd had a massive row he would order us a pizza or buy me chocolate or take me out for a meal, and seeing as we were rowing non-stop it meant that I never stopped eating. He was so jealous and possessive that I think maybe he liked me being bigger because it meant that other men wouldn't find me attractive. If any guy even looked at me or showed me any attention he would get angry, so I hid myself away. He always made me very aware of how lucky I was to be with him and was always telling me about other girls that fancied him. What he put me through was horrendous and disgusting. I went from being an extrovert, social butterfly who loved meeting new people to a dowdy wallflower.

I was so demoralised and downtrodden and I felt so unattractive, but the old Vicky was still there somewhere thinking 'fucking pull yourself together lass'. I went to my cousin Louise's wedding and seeing her and her husband looking so incredibly happy together made something inside of me snap. They were so head-over-heels in love and I thought, 'That's how a couple should be.' In his speech Louise's husband, Andrew, said he'd loved Louise since they were at school and he felt like the luckiest man in the world. He even thanked my grandma and granddad for being such an inspiration to them. Louise was pregnant so they were about to become a family which made it even more poignant. You just have to look at a couple like that to know what real love is. What the hell had I been doing? I spent an hour of the wedding hiding in the toilet crying at one point thinking 'I should be getting bloody married soon and I don't love him!'

I honestly don't think I could have got any lower than when I was with Ricci and when we eventually split up (see, I promised it was coming!) it was the biggest relief of my life. We officially broke up at the end of February 2013 and although I was so happy to be free of Ricci, I felt like utter shit about myself. There I was single, alone and fat. I felt empowered that I'd been brave enough to walk away from an incredibly destructive relationship, but every time I looked in the mirror I was horrified.

For the first time in months and months I wanted to feel good about myself again. My problem was that I was used to using food as a crutch and I had become such an emotional eater. If I was happy I'd eat chocolate, if I was miserable I would eat pizza. I'd eat with my friends and family to celebrate, and I'd eat cakes alone because I was feeling shit. I'd got into such bad habits and something had to be done. I was in one of the biggest reality TV shows in the country, yet I didn't want to go to any parties, I didn't want to meet anyone and I didn't want to be seen. I totally lost myself and my sense of fun.

I started believing all of the horrible things people were saying about me. I remember seeing Michelle Heaton talking about *Geordie Shore* on a TV show. She was saying how all of the girls had put on weight since the last series. I thought 'you horrible cow'. I'd read so many magazine articles where she'd talked how upset she was when she felt like the big one in Liberty X and had to get her catsuits specially made for her, so she should have understood how crap we were all feeling. Jesus, even Z-listers like her were talking about my weight gain!

I was by no means obese, but I was unhealthy and I had a terrible lifestyle, which didn't help how I was feeling emotionally – it was a vicious circle. My friends and family were trying to be supportive but I felt like things had gone too far. The thought of getting my clothes off in front of someone else horrified me, and I didn't want to feel like that forever. I didn't want my life to pass me by. Life is too short not to deal with something you have control over. Somehow I had to get the energy to go to the gym again. I finally had no one else to blame for not going. I wanted to be able to put on a nice dress and go out with my mates and flirt with people. I'd already lost twelve stone of utter twat when I'd dumped Ricci and now it was time to shift my own weight.

It took a lot for me to haul myself to the gym that first time, but in March 2013 I did just that. Even after the first session I felt so much better because I was aiming towards getting the slim, confident me back. I wanted to be her again so badly. I had been feeling so ugly and undesirable – feisty Vicky needed to make a reappearance. If I didn't get back into shape I would carry on feeling awful about myself. I'd slip back into going out and getting mortal with my mates, then feeling crap because I was a whale and no one was chatting me up, and then eating and drinking more. Something had to give, and it couldn't be the waistband of my leggings any longer.

I decided to do something drastic to kick off my weight-loss so I took myself away to the No 1 Boot Camp in Norfolk for ten days. It was just what I needed. Rather than sitting at home and dwelling on the break-up I threw myself into star jumps and jogging. The sense of camaraderie with the other people there really helped, plus I was so exhausted by the time I went to bed each night I fell straight to sleep without mulling over the past few months. I wasn't completely cut off from Ricci-world though. I remember some random tweeting me a picture of Ricci getting into a taxi with a girl after a night out which did hurt, but at least I was away from Newcastle and had something positive to focus on.

It was the start of my weight-loss journey, and an amazing way to help me get over Ricci. I went from eleven-and-a-half stone down to around ten-and-a-half and I felt a lot more focused. The exercise was really helping to lift my mood and the weight-loss was finally making me feel more positive about the future.

Chapter Thirteen

That's Shoe-biz

Soon, the sixth series of *Geordie Shore* was due to start filming in Australia and I could not bloody wait. MTV had confirmed they wanted me back and I knew I had to go out there and be the Vicky people liked in the early *Geordie Shore* days. The public were sick to death of seeing me crying, and now Ricci was no longer on the show I could be myself again. I needed to show people that I was strong, fun and ready to take on the world again. I had been signed by some amazing new agents called Inked Up Management after my unceremonial dumping by CAN, and they were so supportive.

They were young and dynamic and they had big plans for me – as did I.

The cast flew out to Sydney in April 2013 so Ricci and I had only been split up for a few months and I was still really hurting, but there was no way I was going to let that ruin what could be an amazing experience. And I didn't. I had the odd tear here and there because I find things a bit emotional at times, but people like Gaz and Scott were really there for me. It was liberating being over the other side of the world. I had no phone, I couldn't look at Twitter and see what Ricci was up to and there was no way he could contact me.

I fell in love with Sydney and while everyone else in the cast was having rows I was able to take a step back and not be a part of it. Sadly Charlotte and I didn't get on brilliantly that series. She had just started seeing a guy called Mitch, who she's still with now, so she was quieter than usual. Her heart wasn't in it and whereas I was having the most fun ever it felt like she would rather have been at home.

I'm pretty sure Charlotte knew at that point she'd got a place in *Celebrity Big Brother* so that was probably another reason she wasn't exactly feeling it. Holly was more subdued when she was with Charlotte too; and Sophie had Joel, so she was loved up. As a result that series was all about the lads, and I spent most of my time with them. And of course I met this bloody gorgeous man called Dan, who looked like a square-jawed Disney Prince. He made me feel so amazing and even though I knew it was unlikely to go anywhere because we lived on the other side of the world from each other, he helped me get over that massive hump in my life. It was like Ricci rehab. Dan was handsome and tall, and I discovered the best way to get over a skinny twat is to get under a gorgeous big man. Because he was six foot three and eighteen stone he made me feel really small too. It was like a form of body dysmorphia.

Leaving Australia was so hard. I was in this gorgeous place getting drunk all the time, but of course it wasn't real life. I was avoiding facing up to my world back home and the reality of being single. I knew that once I was back in the UK I would have to deal with my break-up on a more personal level, rather than a *Geordie Shore* level. You can't escape reality when it lives up the road.

I sat on the plane home feeling utterly exhausted, dizzily happy and slightly scared. I had given the series my all and I needed a proper break and some time out with my family and friends. But it was not to be. We went straight into promotion for the show, which meant travelling up and down to London doing interviews and photo shoots. I remember being in a Walkabout pub in London and getting a phone call from my agent telling me that Ricci had sold a story to *Now* magazine. He had played the part of a victim and made out that I'd been really abusive to him. Mario from *TOWIE* was with the same agent as Ricci and he'd done a similar story about how breaking up with Lucy Mecklenburgh had caused his depression a few weeks before, so it didn't take a genius to work out that their agent had orchestrated it all.

Ricci made out in the piece that he had been too ashamed to tell anyone that I'd hit him when we were together and that I started all the fights. He is an utter scumbag and that story devastated me. And for what? A few hundred pounds? I called Ricci straight away but he acted like nothing was wrong. He tried to deny that he'd even done the story, but I knew he had because *Now* had called my agent to give me a right to reply. How can you lie to someone that blatantly? He was in utter denial that he'd done anything wrong, but as horrific as it was it was what I needed to see just how low he could go.

I could have gone in hard and given the magazine my side of the story, but he just wasn't worth it. I gave them a simple statement saying: 'All I'll say on this matter is that there are two sides to every story. I don't intend to go down the same route as my ex-partner and try to embarrass him. I feel sorry for him as he's clearly become even more bitter since his dismissal from both *Geordie Shore* and my life. I hope his ridiculous notion of events has brought him solace.' Since then his career has gone from bad to worse and tragically he's still trying to ride my coattails. Meanwhile my career is going from strength to strength. One word: karma.

As amazing as Australia had been I'd obviously enjoyed the food and drink side of things a little *too* much because I came back weighing just over eleven-and-a-half stone. I was so upset that all the hard work I'd done before the trip had gone to pot. It made me realise that if I carried on doing *Geordie Shore* and drinking constantly I would be stuck in the same cycle forever and I'd get bigger and bigger.

Thankfully, my chubby salvation came in the form of a lady called Jane Irving. I'd done an interview with *Heat* magazine where I'd talked about my weight yo-yoing and how much I wanted to lose weight and tone up, but without doing faddy diets. This caught Jane's attention because she works with a company called Universal working on fitness DVDs. Jane had put together Josie Gibson's bestseller the year before which had done amazingly well, and she'd also worked on Charlie Brooks', Claire Nasir's and Jennifer Ellison's. She basically spearheaded some of the biggest celebrity shape-ups of the past few years, and she contacted my agent and said she wanted to make a DVD with me. I didn't need to be asked twice. Not only did I want to feel good about myself again, I wanted to help other people to do the same.

Jane found me a trainer called Robbie Thompson

who lived near me in Newcastle, and who I now love with all my heart. I couldn't have achieved what I have in the last year without him. Robbie's such a positive, sweet guy. The two of us started training together and at first it was incredibly hard. I would love to say that something clicked and I got addicted to exercise and looked like a Victoria's Secret model overnight, but sadly not. It was a real struggle and the weight came off gradually. I had a pretty low fitness level and barely any strength, but Robbie was really patient with me and we took things slowly.

When I lost the first ten pounds and got back to my post-Boot Camp weight I treated myself to a nice holiday to Marbella with Laura to completely relax. I needed a proper rest from everything because I was still feeling really run down. Series seven of *Geordie Shore* was just around the corner but I didn't feel up to doing it. There hadn't been enough time for me to get myself together since Australia and I still felt bogged down from the break-up with Ricci, so I asked for some proper time out. The producers effectively told me that I either took part in the show from day one or they were going to film the entire thing without me. It was May 2013 meaning I'd only had six weeks off since Australia and I was feeling really uncomfortable in myself, and the bottom line is I was depressed. The petulant, exhausted side of me was tempted to hold my hands up and admit defeat, but career-minded Vicky knew it would be stupid to throw away everything I'd worked for.

I should have stuck to my guns because I *really* wasn't ready for another full-on series, but at the end of the day ultimately the decision lay with me. The series started badly, and for me it ended horrendously. The atmosphere in the house was terrible because we hadn't had a proper rest, and the producers had bought in a new girl. Marnie Simpson is Sophie's cousin and none of us were happy about her being there because, as when other new girls had come into the house, we knew it would upset the balance.

I'd only been in the house a few days when something happened which changed my world forever. I got arrested again. Lots of you will already have read about the series of events in the press, but this is the story in a nutshell: All of the cast were all out in Florita's in Newcastle one night. We were all really drunk and having a laugh when I felt a cup of ice go down my back. I genuinely don't remember what happened in the moments that followed because I was mortal, but before I knew it security had hold of me and were dragging me through the club. Everything after that is a blur, but I think all of the shit I'd been through in those months before built up in that moment and without even thinking I threw my shoes across the club. I wasn't throwing them at anyone in particular and I certainly didn't mean to hurt anyone,

I was just lashing out and, devastatingly, people got injured.

When I got outside the club the cold air hit me and I sobered up slightly, but I still had no idea I'd injured anyone. I thought I'd just had an argument with someone and got dragged out. I got taken straight back to the *Geordie Shore* house, but when I was told that I'd hit someone with my shoes I was so drunk and upset that no one could calm me down or comfort me. I just wanted to go home and see my mam and dad. I'd been so afraid of losing my temper when I went back into the show because I knew how ridiculously stressed I was. I was worried about getting drunk and snapping and I'd gone and done it in spectacular fashion.

Reluctantly the producers let me go home but they warned me that the police may come round in the morning to see me. I told my mam everything and I remember saying 'I threw my shoe' and bursting into tears. Even then I had no idea of the magnitude of everything. I certainly didn't know the poor girl needed stitches.

At around four in the morning the doorbell rang, and when I answered it six police officers charged into my house. One of them shouted: 'Vicky Pattison, you're under arrest.' I was so shocked. One of the officers said they needed the clothes I'd been wearing that night and that they'd tear the house apart looking for them if they had to. I was drunk and terrified and they were storming into my house like I'd just murdered someone. To this day I still have nightmares about the way they treated me. I think it was all because I was on TV and it was their way of teaching me and *Geordie Shore* a lesson.

If someone in my street had been burgled that night they might have sent a couple of officers around to check it out, but I was sat at home with my parents and absolutely no danger to anyone and yet they sent *six* officers to arrest me. That must have been a great story for them to tell all their mates down the pub the following weekend. I begged them not to handcuff me in front of my mum because I didn't want her to be upset. They did it anyway and when she burst into tears this policeman growled: 'We're not upsetting her, it's *you* who's done this.' If I'd known the police were going to storm into my parents' home and arrest me I would have stayed in the *Geordie Shore* house to save my family from the upset. I'd brought all of this trouble to my parents' door and it was so unfair on them.

The police took me off to the station in my pyjamas and put me in a cell. I sat there freezing cold, crying my eyes out. I got interviewed later that morning and my solicitor Linda advised me not to give any comment. I was so scared I was shaking and all I wanted was a cuddle from my mam and dad. Eventually, after several hours, I was released and allowed to go home. But that's when the nightmare *really* began.

Chapter Fourteen

Marbella Mayhem

News of my shameful arrest was in all the papers, and I was sat in my lounge with the curtains drawn because there were paps outside. I'd been suspended from *Geordie Shore*, but to me that was as good as being sacked. I was worried that if MTV had enough pressure from the police or public they may decide I wasn't worth the hassle. Also if I ended up going to prison I couldn't exactly film the show from there could I?

My actions that night in the club were the single worst thing I've ever done in my life and as much as I don't like to have regrets, it's always something I'll look back on with a sense of shame. I'm not going to try and make excuses for what happened because I can't blame anyone but myself, though I will say that I was absolutely, completely and totally exhausted, which didn't help my mental state around that time. I am so, so sorry to the people I hurt, and I still feel physically sick every single time I think about it.

I was so down in the weeks that followed I genuinely contemplated killing myself at times. I was having nightmares every night about being arrested again, I thought I'd potentially lost my job and I was still, in my opinion, really overweight. Unbeknown to me when I was in Marbella with Laura I'd been papped on the beach looking absolutely revolting. I had been feeling a bit better about myself before I went and quite proud of my weight loss so had been lured into a false sense of security and put on a bikini. It just so happened that was the week the press printed them, when I was at my very lowest. When I saw the pictures in the paper I was horrified; they were revolting. It was like everything was happening at once and it was unequivocally the worst time of my life.

I'd lost my temper in a moment of madness and now I potentially faced five years in jail. I am dramatic about things when it comes to love or my mates, but I had never in my life before suffered from serious depression or considered suicide. I'd always thought of suicide as a selfish act and that you would be hurting other people and leaving all of your problems for them to deal with by going through with it. I was a strong person who had always dealt with my problems head on, but suddenly I got it. I felt like all I was doing was messing up and embarrassing my family. I was taking one step forward and three steps back and I couldn't do right for doing wrong. I couldn't change what happened that night in the club and I couldn't convince *Geordie Shore* not to sack me – it was all out of my hands now. I had lost everything I had going for me and didn't want to live anymore. I couldn't see any other way out.

I lay on the sofa for a couple of days just staring into space. I couldn't eat and I was barely speaking. I didn't want anyone to see me like that and I didn't want to talk to anyone because I was so ashamed, so I turned off my phone and stayed away from my laptop. I wanted to wallow in my own self-pity. My parents had a holiday booked and though they were determined not to go, I convinced them I was fine and begged them not to miss it. My friend Natalie and my sister Laura had to look after me constantly, bless them, but all I really wanted was for them to leave me alone so I could end my life.

My plan was to try and convince them I was fine so they could both to go to work. That way I knew I'd have plenty of time – there was no way they would be back in time to save me, and that's what I wanted because I didn't *want* to be saved. I didn't want to be anyone else's problem anymore.

I spoke to the show's psychiatrist, Stephen, who had been with us from the start. I'd always thought he was a condescending twat if I'm being brutally honest (he would later prove me wrong!), but I was completely truthful with him because I was petrified of the way I was feeling. I was exhausted and drained and my self-confidence was on the floor. I told him that I couldn't sleep or eat and I was having nightmares about the police coming round and throwing me in prison. I'd been spending hours going round my house constantly checking that all of the doors and windows were locked so no one could get in. Stephen asked me about my suicidal feelings and he was the only one I was completely upfront with.

I had totally fucked up my life and I couldn't go on any more. I'd been pushed to do more shows and I wasn't taking care of myself and I'd buggered up *everything*. I'd kept so much from friends and family over the years because I hadn't wanted to appear weak or for people to hate Ricci, stupidly. I'd wanted to protect him and put a brave face on things and that day on the phone to Stephen was the first time I'd ever admitted I was properly broken. I was a shell of a person.

Stephen told me that sometimes you have to reach rock bottom before you can climb back up again. Since the start of *Geordie Shore* I'd gained almost three stone, I'd had a boyfriend I thought was trying to sell stories on me, I'd had a fiancé who *did* sell stories on me, the same man who I loved and trusted, I'd completely lost myself in a damaging relationship, I'd been vilified by the public, and I'd lost any sense of self. To add to all of that I was potentially facing a jail term and I was convinced I had ruined my career. There was no way I could go any lower.

I don't know how or why, but while I was lying on the sofa the day following my talk with Stephen a switch went off in my head. It was a case of fight or flight, and I'm not someone who runs away. It was like the old me was still in there somewhere fighting to get out. I'd done the damage, now I had to deal with it. Things couldn't get any worse and I said to myself: 'Stop lying on the fucking sofa feeling sorry for yourself. Get up, go to the gym, see your friends, and if *Geordie Shore* don't want you back then it's not meant to be.'

It was that fighting instinct in me, and my amazing sister and friend who got me through that made me realise that I would achieve nothing by killing myself. I would have left the only people who cared about me heartbroken. I wouldn't have been getting revenge on Ricci or the people on Twitter who were vile to me. They wouldn't give a shit. Ricci had taken my money, my figure, my friends, my social life and almost my family, but he wasn't going to take my fucking life. I didn't want those people who had dragged me down to win, and I certainly didn't want to hurt my family and friends. Suddenly I felt a tiny bit of hope, and it was just enough to get me through.

My attitude became: 'Fuck everything, this is about me now. You've got to look after number one because not many people are genuinely looking after you. Those people you think are your friends only care about magazine sales and ratings. They do *not* care about you.' I had to do what was right for me.

It's funny because I'd always been of the opinion that counselling was a really self-indulgent process. I thought that if you had to pay a total stranger to sit and listen to you being sad you were self-obsessed and you didn't have any friends. I was wrong. I started speaking to someone and it taught me that I had been holding all my emotions in and that had been my downfall. I thought people would think. 'Oh, poor, poor Vicky, she's having to do too many TV shows' or 'Poor girl, she's split up with someone. Who hasn't?' I didn't give my problems enough weight, if you'll pardon the pun. I thought I was being a self-pitying melt. I pushed everything down and I wasn't dealing with anything properly because I didn't want to load my problems onto anyone else. I was carrying so much blame: I blamed myself for staying with Ricci, for being fat and for getting myself into the situation, so why should I make that someone else's issue?

Thankfully once I was on the right track it didn't take me long to find my feet again. I saw a therapist a handful of times and expressed how I felt lonely, isolated and lost. Once I started to get it out and allowed myself to feel sorry for myself for going through a shit time things got easier. I will always be aware that I could go back to that dark place so I have to be mindful and keep an eye on my feelings. At least now I can recognise the signs.

After I stopped seeing the counsellor training became my therapy. I went back to the gym and worked out with Robbie every day. Exercise became a constant in my life. It gave me a routine and it made me feel better about myself, and still to this day if I feel down or miserable I train. If I'm angry, I train *hard*. It's had nothing but a positive effect on me. It helps me to deal with things and it clears my head. A problem can seem completely overwhelming, yet if I go to the gym I get clarity and I can find a solution.

Working on my DVD saved me in so many ways. Robbie has no idea how much he helped me. He's become such a good friend and we used to go for long walks around that time and talk about everything. I told him all about my break-up with Ricci, and he gave me a lads' perspective on thing which really helped. Robbie became my confidant and because he was impartial and removed it was like working out with a therapist. He was one of the people who got me through.

The more I toned up and lost weight the more I felt like myself again. While my job and the court case were still hanging in the balance, my DVD, *Seven Day Slim*, gave me a purpose. My family, friends like Robbie and that DVD saved my life. I have to give credit to MTV too because they were incredibly supportive. They were the ones who put me in touch with Stephen and several of them also checked in regularly to make sure I was doing okay, including Steve Regan from MTV, who I'd known since day one and was brilliant in so many ways and Craig Orr, who was new to the team but really compassionate.

A friend of mine, Nicky, who owns a restaurant in Jesmond was really there for me too, and one day he told me that I had to get back out and start socialising again. He offered to cordon off an area for me and my mates but I didn't want any special treatment, I had to start facing the world sometime. Going there for dinner and drinks was a revelation. I had to put on make-up and get dressed up for the first time in a while and just doing that was a real boost. It was little things, and people's little kindnesses that helped. My friend Andy took me away to the Lake District for three days and we went kayaking, and those kinds of things woke me up to the fact that there are good people out there, and I would be missing out on all of that if I had done something stupid.

When you go through a hard time it really teaches you

who is and who isn't there for you. If you'd asked me to predict who would have restored my faith in mankind I would have got it all wrong. There were friends I'd had for years and years that didn't bother with me, and then people like Robbie who I'd only just met who were incredible. What matters most is that I came through the other side, and I know that if anything like that ever happens in the future I can do it again with the help and support of other people.

I continued working out like a demon and eating really healthily and when I got down to ten stone I felt amazing. Things finally felt like they were turning around and although I still didn't know what was happening with *Geordie Shore*, Steve Regan called and asked if I wanted to be involved in a new show MTV were making called *Summer of Love*. He was the one who'd commissioned the series and said he hadn't been as excited about anything since *Geordie Shore*. It involved four single guys and four single girls going off to a luxury villa in Marbella to get to know each other and look for love.

I actually asked if he wanted to me host it because I've made no secret of the fact that I want to be a TV presenter, and I was disappointed when he said he wanted me to be a contestant. To me it sounded a lot like *Geordie Shore* and I felt like it might be going backwards in terms of my career, but Steve's a very persuasive man and I was looking for a bit of a change so thought, 'why not?'.

Steve explained that he needed me in there to unite everyone and ruffle a few feathers. He piled the pressure on by telling me the show wouldn't work without me, and in the end I agreed to be a part of it. Little did I know that *Summer of Love* was *really* to become *Ex on the Beach* and the twist was that cast members' exes would be brought onto the show at various stages. If I'd known that, I might not have said yes ...

I headed out to Marbella to film for three weeks in September 2013. The cast were amazing and we bonded really quickly, probably more so than I did with the *Geordie Shore* girls. I made some friends for life while I was there.

We had this thing called the 'Tablet of Terror', which was an iPad that gave us various instructions. One morning it told Chloe Goodman, Marco Alexandre and I to head to the beach to meet a new arrival. I don't know why, but I kind of had a feeling it might be someone's ex, and when this gorgeous guy walked out of the ocean one of the girls, Chloe, went mad hugging him. It turned out he was called Ross and he was *gorgeous*.

As part of the show we got sent on dates with the other cast members. On the first night I was set up with Jack Lomax, who was like a boy version of Charlotte, but even dimmer, and then Ross and I were sent out on a date. Er, how awkward going out with someone else's ex when they're there?

Ross was from Manchester and he was dead chatty and there wasn't a dull moment, then at the end of the night we had a drunken tash-on. I fall for people really quickly and I started to really like him. I got butterflies and everything. Unfortunately, Ross wasn't feeling the same level of emotion; he turned out to be a massive player. I got really drunk a couple of nights later after a few more dates and we ended up sleeping together. He was the first person I'd slept with since Ricci and the cameras were there watching us and it was all just one giant disaster.

I was so pissed that when I woke up the next morning I had no idea we'd had sex. Someone from the crew mentioned it while we were doing interviews on the beach and I burst into tears. I'd broken my run of chastity with someone I barely even knew and I was fuming with myself. By the time I got back into the house Ross had told everyone what had happened and he went from hero to zero in an instant. What an utter helmet.

The producers knew I was fuming with Ross so they sent us on another date in a horse drawn carriage, knowing I couldn't bloody escape. I lost it and told him in no uncertain terms that he was total nob and that shagging around doesn't put inches on your dick. I got out of the carriage and stormed off so angry I started crying again.

Thankfully the following day turned out to be *much* more fun. I was told to go down to the beach by the Tablet of Terror so I suspected someone from my past would be making an appearance. I was terrified it would be Ricci, but I'd hoped so much that he wouldn't be involved that I put it out of my mind. I was stood on the beach talking to some of the crew when all of a sudden this absolute beauty walked out of the sea – it was Dan from Australia! I was stunned, but it was so lovely to see him.

I was completely overwhelmed and turned into a giggly little schoolgirl. Dan is the nicest guy in the world, and we soon rekindled our romance and I couldn't have been happier. What a turnaround in a few months.

I was having such a top time on the show I didn't want it to end. Then. They. Brought. Out. Ricci. I was *beyond* fucked off. *Beyond.* I could not believe it when I saw him. Of all the fucking people. Having done *Geordie Shore* for four years I should have expected something like that to happen, but I guess I'm still a bit too naive. He came out just before the end of filming because they wanted a big dramatic end to the series, which, because it's me, they definitely got.

I could easily have slipped back into my old ways and acted like a doormat but I was determined not to. I had the support of Dan and my best friends in the house Liam and Emily and Ricci no longer scared me. Dan hated Ricci on sight and wanted to rip his tiny little head off his shoulders, and Ricci was bloody petrified of him. At one point Dan really lost his temper with Ricci, but because he used to be a professional footballer player in Australia he's really controlled, so instead of hitting Ricci he went and kicked a bin. It was all caught on camera so unfortunately Dan had to leave the show because it was seen as a 'violent outburst' even though he didn't actually hurt anyone, which I thought was really unfair.

I told Ricci everything I felt about him. The producers said they thought it would help me get closure but, of course, it also made for great TV. It was all a bit pointless because talking to him was like trying to get sense out of a sun lounger. Ricci's painfully thick and he didn't like the fact that he couldn't play the victim in the show. He managed it for the first couple of days and put this stupid sad face on, but the cast quickly divided into two camps: Team Vicky and a bunch of losers who fell for his act. One of the boys, Liam, even turned around to him and said: 'You've been here for two days and Vicky's been here for three weeks. We know her side of the story and we don't want to know yours.'

Needless to say Ricci soon showed his true colours after a few drinks on one of the last nights out and that was that. He rowed with two of my closest friends in there, Liam and Farah, simply because they took my side. He still can't control himself, the idiot, and he was nasty and aggressive and people saw the real Ricci.

After Marbella, Dan flew back to the UK and stayed with some friends in London, and then came to stay with me for a couple of days. We had both convinced ourselves that we could make it work, but the harsh reality is that we live thousands of miles away from each other. It was horrible saying goodbye but we both knew that neither of us would be happy living away from our friends and family, so that was that.

I had to travel to London the day he left so my parents dropped him at the airport. When I called my mam later to make sure he'd got off okay she told me about the little 'gift' he'd left me in my bedroom. He'd covered the entire room in post-it notes saying things like 'Fit Vicky' and '#don'tchange'. It was really sweet, and though I'm not usually into that sort of thing, it was a really nice note for our romance to end on, especially after my long year of relationship stress. Dan now has the most beautiful girlfriend I've ever seen, they've got two dogs together and they're opening a fitness studio in Bondi Beach. I'm so happy for him. That's all I want for him because he really deserves it, and hopefully one day I'll meet a Disney Prince who lives in the same country as me!

Chapter Fifteen

Weigh To Go

I was still trying to lose weight and my goal weight was eight stone. I made sure I didn't let my new regime go to pot while I was in Marbella – I was still training at six a.m. every morning, which sometimes meant I was getting up as some of the *Ex on the Beach* cast were going to bed. Because I was drinking a lot I barely lost any weight during those three weeks, so once I was back in the UK it was time to ramp things up a gear.

I totally overhauled my diet. I had been cutting back and eating more healthily anyway, but I went and saw a nutritionist and I learned loads of new things, like the best times of the day to eat and what to eat and when. I'd always thought carbs were bad and in the old days if I wanted to lose weight I would cut out carbs completely and shift half a stone, but that's bollocks. You should never cut out whole food groups if you want to be healthy and lose weight. Gluten and wheat can be bad for you, but things like brown rice and sweet potato are great.

I learned that after I trained my body needed protein to help repair the muscles, so I used to have a protein shake or a chicken breast. I was eating oats and seeds for breakfast and loads of fresh vegetables or lean meat for lunch and dinner. I felt excited about it and how good it made me feel. I was a total health freak for the first time ever and I was seeing results.

I soon hit nine-and-a-half stone and I was back in little dresses and playsuits and sexy pencil skirts. I felt desirable and attractive and I'd left the frumpy, miserable me behind. It sounds so cheesy, but I rediscovered myself and there was nothing stopping me. I was no longer the person who sat in the corner on a night downing Jaegerbombs because I hated the way I looked. Now I was sipping gin and tonic and dancing on tables. I also got a real passion back for clothes and fake take and lashes – you name it. Glam VIP Vicky was back, and this time she was *super*-glam. I wanted everyone to see how good I felt.

Around this time I met David Souter, who was the choreographer on my DVD. Robbie, David and I started working out together to devise the routines and it was so important for me to be involved from the ground level. I didn't want to put my name to some shit DVD that people were going to buy in January, but use as a coaster by February. I wanted it to be effective and high-energy. I wanted women to train as hard as I do and see results almost straight away so they weren't demoralised. That's how we came up with the idea of basing the DVD around HIIT, which stands for High Intensity Interval Training. It's at the cutting edge of fitness right now. You train really hard for ten minutes and you're done, and that's how I was training with Robbie. You don't need any equipment and it gives you an all-over body workout literally in those ten minutes. You burn calories and that continues throughout the day.

David is incredibly well-qualified so the routines he came up with were amazing. He devised something that would train people from head to toe. Doing the training for the DVD enabled me to feel good again and I wanted it to do the same for everyone that picked it up and put it in their DVD player. By the time I finished making the DVD I was eight stone four and I felt unbelievable. I was strong rather than skinny; I was still curvy and feminine, but I was toned. If Ricci had come back into my life the day I finished shooting that DVD I would have turned my back and walked away with a massive smile on my face. I felt invincible.

I've always been very vain – I like to look nice, as I think most girls do. I've been into fake tan from a young age and I've had some hilarious disasters. When I was about sixteen and I first started going into town I thought the browner you were the better so I didn't exactly have what you'd call a 'light sun-kissed glow'. I'd start preparing for the weekend on Wednesday night by slathering on my first layer of L'Oreal tanning gel. When I woke up on Thursday I'd smell like cat's piss and look like I'd been dipped in a teabag. I'd shave and rectify any dodgy patches, and on the Friday morning I'd put another coat of gel on. Then Friday night, before I went out I'd put on some instant tan. I looked ludicrous but obviously thought I looked hot to trot. Over time I've got tanning down to a fine art and although I'm still dark it's no longer radioactive.

We're definitely into the 'more is more' look in Newcastle. We live to go out and we love our eyelashes and hair extensions and spending all week planning your outfit. Nowadays I've got my own range of fake tan that I use and I still love being brown. It makes you look so much healthier and I can't live without it, I'll will never stop using it. I would never use a sunbed nowadays, not in a million years, but you'll still rarely catch me looking pale.

I started wearing eyelashes when I was seventeen and the only time I don't wear them is when I'm in the gym. I even wear natural ones during the day, and again, I've got my own range now so I've always got loads at home – no need to reuse them anymore! The same goes for hair extensions. I've worn them since my teens but the quality didn't used to be as good so I was often left with bald patches on my head. I had to artfully style my hair so you couldn't see my scalp and every time the wind blew I had to hold my extensions down so you couldn't see the damage they'd done. I practically had a combover. The things we do for beauty, eh? The one thing I've never done is get a tattoo. I change my mind about everything constantly, from food to clothes to boys, so if I was to make a big statement like that I would be petrified I'd hate it within weeks. My sister's got a pattern on her wrist that she hates and she's only twenty-two so I've learned from her. I haven't got any piercings anywhere apart from my ears, either. I'm too prudish. I've made a lot of beauty mistakes but there's been nothing I can't change back.

Before I discovered good products I used to go out looking what I would class as glamorous, but by the end of the night everything would have been falling off and my fake tan would have mottled. If I was going out with someone I would have to get out of bed early so I could sort my hair and eyelashes out before they saw me, unless I was really comfortable with them. I've learned to look after my skin more as I've got older. Because I use fake tan on my face I do suffer with blackheads so I've always got a good face scrub to hand, and if I've had a breakout I'll make sure I cleanse, tone and moisturise. Then again, if I've been out for a big night and I'm drunk I generally pass out so my face will be lucky if it sees a wipe.

Some people may have read in the press that I plan to have a boob job one day and that is true. One of the first things that go when you lose weight are your boobs. I've never had a particularly enviable chest and it's never been as perky as I'd like. Now I've lost weight they feel like even more of a non-event. They're a bit empty and saggy and even though I love being able to show off a bit of side-boob because they're a good size, they're not the size and shape I'd like them to be. I'm not going to go massive, though. I'm a 32C now so I'll maybe go to a 32DD and I want to have a nice teardrop shape. I don't think I'll ever do anything to my face though. I haven't had Botox or any other fillers or injections yet but never say never. In my work I need to have expression and I worry I would look ridiculous if you couldn't tell what I was thinking. I like having a full range of facial movements, but that's not to say one day I won't succumb to the needle ...

I went to Ibiza with my mates just after I lost all of the

weight and I really wanted to flirt and have fun. It was there that I met Charlie Sims from *TOWIE* for the first time. I was in Ocean Beach Ibiza and I ended up sitting on a giant bed next to Charlie, Joey Essex, Mario Falcone and Tom Pearce. Joey is such a sweetheart, Charlie is dead friendly and Tom is such a lovely guy. The only one who didn't say hello was Mario, but funnily enough he couldn't wait to private message me on Twitter when I later lost even more weight! He obviously wasn't keen on me when I was carrying a bit more timber. I guess he doesn't like more cushion for the pushing.

When the others headed back to their hotel Charlie stayed on and chatted to me. We were chatting about our respective shows; his girlfriend Ferne and my arrest drama. He confided in me that he was on the cusp of breaking up with Ferne because things weren't working. He seemed like a really nice lad and I told him that life is too short to be with the wrong person so he's got to do what's best for him.

Charlie asked for my number and we talked about meeting up later, but I totally thought he meant as friends and in the end it didn't happen. Unbeknown to me it turned out to be the same day that he cheated on Ferne with a random girl and got papped, so I'm glad I hadn't been around. We stayed in touch when were back in England and after he and Ferne broke up we texted each other a few times and I let him know when I had a PA in Kent coming up. He asked me if I fancied dinner and I had a bit of a 'why not?' attitude. We met up in Kent and he whisked me off to London. I was a bit taken aback as I thought we'd go somewhere quiet and local. Instead we arrived at a lovely restaurant called Sushi Samba and as soon as we got out of the car there a pap was there waiting. I was so angry I put my head straight down, put my hand in front of my face and walked into the restaurant.

A couple of weeks earlier I'd been papped out with Natasha Hamilton's ex-husband, Riad Erraji, just after they'd split up. Absolutely nothing had happened between us but the shot they got of us was him helping me to walk across some cobbles in my high heels so it looked like we were holding hands. There were stories in the press that I was helping him get over his heartbreak from Natasha Hamilton. Even though the shots of Riad and I were all totally innocent I didn't want to be photographed with two different guys who had recently split up with people.

I felt really embarrassed and when I got inside the restaurant I was shaking because I had a suspicion Charlie had set it up so the photographer was there. He swore blind he hadn't, but how else would they have known we were at that place at that time? I decided to go ahead with dinner – mainly because I was bloody hungry! – but I had a bad feeling about everything. We ended up having a good laugh and a little kiss later that night, and I thought he was a nice lad, but I couldn't shake the feeling that he was after publicity. Of course the pictures did make it into the tabloids, alongside a story that I was helping him get over his heartbreak with Ferne. I was clearly the go-to girl for heartbreak at that time!

I got linked with Tom Pearce shortly afterwards and at that point I started to panic that people would think I was some kind of slag. Don't get me wrong, I would love to be linked with Tom Pearce because he's a gorgeous guy, but absolutely nothing ever happened. I'd met him in Ibiza and we'd chatted and it had been lovely, and when I went to Sugar Hut for my birthday he came over for a drink, but it was purely platonic. He was seeing Lucy Mecklenburgh at the time and because I like to think of myself as a bit of an agony aunt I was giving him advice about their relationship. I swear, I thought I was in an episode of *TOWIE*. Someone took photos of us which got into the papers and the next thing I knew Lucy was commenting on the situation. To be fair she was very dignified and lovely about it, but it was just an innocent birthday kiss between friends which got misconstrued by the press.

That period of time made me feel a bit distrustful of everyone. Although, apart from Ricci, I've never been burned by anyone close to me selling stories it did make me realise that now I was in the press more it was a possibility. There have been 'close sources' quoted a lot in magazines over the years but I have no idea where the quotes have come from though of course I do wonder ... I know that sadly, these days, I have to be a lot more careful about who I say things to because I don't always know who I can totally trust.

I'm a firm believer that everything happens for a reason, and even though I can't explain some of the horrible things that happened to me in 2013, the DVD was my saviour. It made feel like life was worth living again. I used wake up in the morning and think, 'Come at me day. Give me whatever you're got, I can take it.' When I was depressed something as small as there not being any milk in the fridge could reduce me to tears, but things had completely turned around for me. I remember thinking 'I look good in clothes, I am mentally and physically strong and there's nothing I can't do'. That strength was exactly what I needed to deal with the court case coming up. It was not going to be pleasant.

Chapter Sixteen

Court, Kirk and a Comeback

The court case had been hanging over me like a million giant, black clouds for six months. I was desperate for it all to be over so I could get on with my life but I kept getting bailed, which meant it got dragged out. My solicitor told me the fact I was getting bailed was a good thing because if the charges were really serious I would be straight up in court. In fact, until I got the official letter with my court date I was being told there was a chance I could get off with a caution. I was praying that would happen.

It was such a stressful situation and it was eating me up inside every single day. Some people were really making light of it. I know it was a very serious business and I don't want it to seem like I wasn't taking it one hundred per cent seriously, but the small moments of lightness kept me going in a dark place.

I got so much abuse on Twitter, but I think that the people who are vile to me generally must have been really unhappy. It's the tall poppy effect. When you get famous people support you, but then as soon as you're in a position when your star could be waning they wade in and try to knock you down. I read all kinds of posts saying I should go to prison and they hoped I'd get beaten up. These people were saying this to a terrified twenty-six-year-old girl so at the end of the day they're the scumbags, not me.

Weirdly it also wasn't the national press who really went hell for leather and slagged me off, it was the local papers. To this day I won't give them interviews. My grandma used to be on the phone crying to my mam because she'd read all of these horrible things about me and I will never forgive them for that. One newspaper even printed my home address, which is disgusting. How can they be allowed to do that? How is that in the public interest? It made me so fearful that people would turn up at my house wanting to harm me.

My first court appearance was in the local Magistrates Court in December 2013 and I was shitting myself. All I remember as I left the house is my mam saying: 'It'll all be over by Christmas.' That morning my amazing solicitor Linda held my hand, looked me in the eyes and said: 'Don't worry. You threw a shoe, you were drunk and you're not going to prison, dolly.' I really wanted to believe her, but when I got the news the same day they were bouncing my case up to the Crown Court I was skeptical. That's where murderers, rapists and paedophiles are tried and I couldn't believe my case was considered serious enough to sit alongside those kind of trials.

I ended up having three hearings in Crown Court, which made it very hard for me to believe I wasn't being judged (quite literally) because of who I am. Every day there were twenty reporters outside the court with video cameras. This was a serious trial and yet all the journalists wanted to know was what shoes I was wearing and how I'd done my hair. I wanted to be left alone but at the end of the day it was news, and they wanted as much of it as they could get. I didn't want anyone to think I was turning it into some kind of fashion show so though I dressed smartly I also dressed down each day, and I kept my head down and I got on with things with the least amount of drama possible.

Being in court was harrowing. I would have to put my hair over my face and lean forward so I could hide the fact I had my fingers in my ears. I just couldn't bear to hear people repeating the details of what I'd done. Of course it was the prosecutors job to make me sound as bad as possible but there are only so many times you can hear you're aggressive and vile until you start to believe it. They made out I'd gone out to attack an innocent person, which was so far from the truth.

I didn't let my parents come to any of my court dates because I didn't want them to see me in that situation, but my sister Laura was there with me every step of the way and one of my best friends, Gav even flew up from Southampton to accampany me to court. I'd spent the previous seven months unsure if I was going to prison or not. Even in the courtroom on the final day – despite having been assured by the judge I wasn't being given a prison sentence – I still thought there was a chance I could. I don't have a great understanding of the law so I was convinced he was going to change his mind.

With just hours to go before I was due to be sentenced the prosecutor got up and said something that sounded like she had new evidence, and I thought that was it. I nearly collapsed with the stress. In the end there was no new evidence so that came to nothing, and I was given a suspended sentence but it wasn't until I walked out of that court I relaxed for the first time in seven months.

I was so drained that I just went home to my family. There was no celebration, because I had nothing to be happy about. Of course I took solace in the fact I wasn't in prison, but nothing good came out of a hideous situation. I feel like I've got a target on my back now. If I ever put even the slightest step wrong again the reality is that I would probably go to prison. I have to be so careful in case anyone starts trouble just for a laugh. I've got a bit OCD about where I'll go out and there are certain places I avoid now. I'm not the same Vicky I once was. I know life changes you and everything happens for a reason and all that, but I am struggling to find a reason for what happened. I'll get over it but I still feel a huge sense of injustice and that's hard to move on from. I've got to complete one hundred and eighty hours of community service, and I had to pay almost ten thousand pounds in fines. But I have to suck it up because what I did was wrong, and of course I deserved to be punished – if you make that kind of mistake you have to pay for it.

My community service involved me working in a local charity shop. It's not like I was in some fancy charity shop in Notting Hill picking through Kate Moss's old hot pants. I'd sort out Bon Marché cardigans and old underpants, talking to old ladies, but doing something like that was very grounding and all of the people I met there were lovely to me. It was ridiculous because in a week I'd spend a Monday in London doing a photo shoot, on a Tuesday I'd go and do a PA in a club, then on a Wednesday I'd go to Wallsend High Street and tag clothes in the charity shop. My life was bizarre.

I will always feel terrible towards the two people I hurt and I would never choose to hurt anyone, either physically or emotionally. But I can't take it back now so I have to live with it and try and salvage what I can from a really horrendous situation. It certainly taught me a lot and I'm grateful for that. I'm not a monster, I'm just a girl who made a mistake. If I could go back in time and live that night again of course I would do things differently. I don't even recognise the person who did those things. I really hope that people can see past it and understand that I'm a human being and I don't always make the best choices. In retrospect I should have *demanded* some proper time out before series seven of *Geordie Shore* so I could get my head together and have a proper rest. I wasn't thinking straight and it scares me to think I could have lost everything that night.

It also breaks my heart to think that had I not made that mistake that night Sophie would never have been involved. But you can't dwell on the past. I've seen the footage of what Sophie said that night when she was very drunk and she said something stupid in the heat of the moment that she didn't mean. She is by no stretch of the imagination a racist or a bad person. She made a mistake, just like I did. I'm not a violent criminal, but I acted like one that night. You can do things that are totally out of character when you're pissed or in a stressful situation and that happened to both of us.

Sophie misjudged the situation and it was a stupid, stupid mistake that's cost her so much. We all missed her loads because she's a truly original girl, but I think she was getting a bit sick of the process of *Geordie Shore*. She was growing up, she was in love with Joel and I don't think she enjoyed it like she did in the beginning. She's been doing different things work-wise and has brought out a clothing range, and I think she's happy.

Having said all of that of course I missed her a lot and I am totally gutted for her but she's a positive person and she'll be fine. Sophie and I will always stay in touch and be friends. Arguments aside, no matter what us girls have done and said behind each other's backs we've all come through it together. They may have bought in other girls but until now they'd never got rid of any of us original female members of the house, and I think that says a lot about our bond.

I can't even begin to describe the relief I felt now the court case was over. I'd been through months of agony and it was time to start living my life again, away from the shadow of what had been happening. I had this new-found self-esteem thanks to getting in shape and I was ready to throw myself back into the world of men. I'd been single for about six months and I wanted to have some fun. I had definitely lost my confidence when the weight went on and I needed to see if I still had 'it'. I'd always done well with lads and got attention and been a big flirt, and I'd had my lovely fling with Dan in Australia, but I hadn't tested the water back home yet.

My first foray back into the dating game was with none other than Kirk Norcross from *TOWIE*. Early in December 2013 I was at *The Clothes Show* in Birmingham promoting my clothing and beauty ranges – it was my first big event for ages so I was raring to go. It was the first proper celeby thing I'd done and I was like 'bring it on'. I'd been to premieres and parties before but this was different. Literally everyone from every reality TV show was at *The Clothes Show* and it was so much fun.

Me and the girls who were working on my stand went out to a club called Bamboo on the first night. Kirk Norcross was sat on the table across from me and he walked straight over and gave me a bottle of vodka because his group had two. It was so kind of him and I thought he was absolutely gorgeous on sight.

I've got this terrible habit of walking off by myself in nightclubs and often people want to come up and chat to you, so you can get trapped for hours. When I went to the toilet that night I saw Kirk outside and he was getting totally bombarded by fans. I walked over, grabbed his hand and led him away like I was his knight in shining armour. He was so grateful, and I joked that it was payment for the vodka. We went back to his table and we chatted for ages, but both our groups had different plans for the night so we went our separate ways and didn't exchange numbers or anything. I was disappointed, but if it was meant to be ...

The next day I was in the VIP area, hungover to fuck with a glass of wine in my hand at one o'clock in the afternoon. It was the only way I was going to get through the day! Kirk came over to say hello with his manager and again I found myself getting butterflies. I definitely fancied him a lot but I *tried* to play it a bit cool. That night Kirk messaged me on Twitter and ended up coming to meet me and the girls and we had great banter.

There was also a stupid little girl in the bar that night. This girl was once on *Big Brother* for five minutes and for no apparent reason she hates me. She took a photo of Kirk and I and posted it on Twitter along with a message saying 'you heard it here first'. So within hours of meeting him, and before we'd even kissed or anything, people were talking about us being a couple which was loads of pressure.

Kirk was furious and told me he'd only split up with his fiancée a couple of months before so he didn't want things being written about us in case she saw it, and I certainly didn't want to be gossiped about for something I hadn't done. Again. We ended up going to another bar and we didn't leave each other's sides all night. I really liked him but my one bugbear was that he'd slept with Sophie a couple of years before, but I knew I had to get past that if I wanted anything to happen. And I did – we had our first cheeky kiss at the end of the night. For the next few days we were pretty much inseparable and I was smitten. He used to call me a 'sort' and my heart just melted.

I felt so sad when *The Clothes Show* came to an end and Kirk and I had to leave each other. We texted non-stop and we would Facetime every night before bed. I thought about him as soon as I woke up in the morning. It was so nice to be excited about someone because I hadn't properly felt like that since the beginning of my relationship with Ricci. We 'got' each other really well. Kirk had been in high-profile relationships and through public break-ups like me and, of course, he knew what it was like being on a reality show.

We had our first official date at Winter Wonderland in Hyde Park which is when our business officially became everyone else's business and the floodgates opened. His ex got involved saying things on Twitter, and magazines wanted joint interviews. We'd barely had a chance to get the relationship off the ground let alone do a photo shoot and talk about our future. I wanted to decide for myself what was going on between us before everyone else made their minds up.

That put a real spanner in the works because everyone was speculating about whether or not we'd last. One magazine gave us a four out of five love rating. They were talking about us getting *engaged* and we'd only been on one date. We also lived miles away from each other and barely got to see each other so other cracks started to appear very quickly. It was a total whirlwind romance and I was getting busier and busier with work and I was just stressed trying to juggle everything. Kirk and I had a brilliant couple of months together but then we started bickering over silly things.

Hand on my heart I could definitely have fallen in love with Kirk, but it wasn't to be. We knew that it if was going to work we could need to move closer to each other and it wasn't an option, so we decided to go our separate ways. I do wonder if people hadn't got involved and we'd kept it private it may have worked, but I guess we'll never know. I really don't have a bad word to say about him because he was a complete gentleman and treated me like a princess, but we were doomed to fail.

It's a shame because Kirk was the first person I let myself get close to after Ricci and now I'm kind of scared to let anyone get close again because I don't want to get hurt. I'm also scared of losing my independence again. I don't want anyone else I meet in the future to suffer because of what happened between me and Ricci, and I think if I were to meet someone now I would try my best to keep the relationship out of the limelight. I need to be selfish about it and keep it for *me*. It's going to take a special man to restore my faith in relationships but I hope he's out there somewhere.

When I look back at how my life has changed since I started on *Geordie Shore* it's hard to fathom the differences. There have been times when I've struggled and I've wanted to give up, but it's everything – both good and bad – that's led to who I am now and I wouldn't change a thing.

These days I feel better than ever, both inside and out. Don't get me wrong, there are still some nights where I want to sit down and drink a bottle of wine and eat a family-sized bag of Oreos and feel a bit sorry for myself. There's a famous Kate Moss quote that goes 'nothing tastes as good as skinny feels', well, Ms Moss clearly never had an M&S Profiterole Tower.

I'm never going to be the kind of person who wakes up at six *every* morning and can't wait to go to the gym and then eat green vegetables and a bit of lean protein. Most mornings I'll wake up and think, 'I'd love a bowl of Crunchy Nut Cornflakes, and then a couple of croissants and jam, and then a fry up', but I've learned what makes me feel good and what doesn't. For me personally, eating too much crap and being overweight is a fast track to misery.

I'm naturally a quite curvy girl who loves her food and so there will be always be a fat girl inside of me trying to get out and eat three McDonalds in a day. But I didn't lose all this weight to spend the rest of my life worrying, and I do treat myself. It would be awful if I was scared to go and eat in a restaurant because I was worried I couldn't control what was being put in my food. If I had to worry whether something was being prepared with extra virgin olive oil or butter where would be the fun in eating? I didn't lose weight to put more restrictions on myself, I did it to lose my inhibitions and get my confidence back but still be able to enjoy myself. I don't beat myself up because I still work out and it's not about being skinny for me. It's about having a way of life that helps me to deal with my emotional issues in a more healthy way.

I'm so aware of how easy it is to put weight back on after you've lost it, and sometimes losing the weight can feel easy compared to the effort of keeping it off, but I have put things in place that help me. I'm not super-woman and if I fall off the wagon and eat carbs all day, then so be it. If I've had a big night on the booze there isn't enough bread and mayonnaise in the world to satisfy my hangover the following day, but I'll give it a good go.

We have to accept that we're human and we make mistakes. The best thing I can say to everyone is don't give yourself a hard time if you slip up. If you go out on a Friday, get drunk and eat crap all day on Saturday don't think 'I'll start again on Monday' because every day is a new day. Start again on the Sunday otherwise it will drag on and you'll end up feeling more and more guilty. Do things that make *you* feel happy. Buy yourself something in a size that you couldn't wear before you were slim or give yourself the afternoon off to watch really crap films. Think of how many positives there are. The first time I wore a size six skirt I felt incredible, and the fact that I can walk into River Island and pick up a dress knowing it will fit is the best feeling *ever*.

My style has really changed. I've always been very daring – backless, frontless, short hemlines, you name it – and even though I'm older now, I'm starting to take more risks. I enjoy things that are nipped in at the waist, and I love getting my arms out. I never knew they could be sexy. I know it sounds vain but that is one of the amazing payoffs. And I will also say that looking good is the best revenge. Revenge is a dish best served slim, and as much as I didn't lose weight for anyone else, it was lovely to be able to say 'fuck you' to all the people who had made nasty comments about me over the years.

Another tip about staying on track is to put things in place that will help you to stay on the straight and narrow. Personally I always want to be putting something in my mouth (no jokes please) and back in the day it used to be Haribo and crisps, but now it's carrot sticks and hummus, or almonds or blueberries, all of which taste great and make you feel like you're having something nice. You don't have to miss out on anything. I still go to Nando's with my mates and I'll have an avocado and green bean salad instead of a chicken burger and it's amazing.

I treat my body like a machine now, and I know it runs better when I'm giving it eight hours sleep, looking after it properly, feeding it good fuel, going to the gym, cleaning it with a detox three times a month, and drinking loads of water. I know it's a cliché but a healthy body really does equal a healthy mind. I used to worry when I was big that no one would ever love me again, but now I feel like I could be loved by all manner of men if I want to be!

Chapter 17

Nice to Meat You

All my health efforts were about me getting ready to go into series eight of *Geordie Shore*, and it was my big comeback after a year away. I'd heard we were getting some new cast members and I was raring to go. I went into the show a bit later than everyone else because the producers wanted to tease the audience with a bit of a 'will she, won't she?' scenario. I made my entrance in episode two, about five days after everyone else started filming.

It felt great to be back and as soon as I met the new boy, Aaron, I thought he was really handsome but an utter melt. He was mortal drunk and within about five minutes of meeting me he was telling me he loved me. I later discovered that he's a terrible drunk generally. He either gets soppy or he gets quite angry – but who the hell am I to judge? People in glass houses shouldn't throw stones and all that! So, regardless of his behaviour after a few too many, I love Aaron to bits! He's actually been on *Geordie Shore* before because he shagged Holly in series two. You may not remember him but you may remember the noises he made Holly make. (It was the night when Holly and James awkwardly had sex in the same room and tried to compete for the 'Loudest Buck Award' . . . needless to say, Holly won! Go on lass!)

Aaron has always wanted to be on the show and I think he's a great addition. He's not afraid to say what he thinks and stand up to people. A lot of the boys are up each other's arses and they want to come across as ultimate lads, but if Aaron likes a girl he'll say it and if he thinks someone is in the wrong he speaks his mind. He's very genuine.

I hadn't experienced the house with Marnie in it at all so that was new to me as well. I saw the reaction she got during her first series, series seven, and I felt bad for her. To the public it looked like Sophie and I had been kicked out and Marnie was there to replace us, so she got the blame. But that wasn't the case at all! No one likes to see original cast members leave, so unfortunately Marnie received a lot of unwarranted backlash. Mind you, she didn't make things easy for herself either – she exploded on to the scene like a hurricane: getting with Scott, flirting with Gaz, then rowing and eventually fighting with Holly – not bad going for your first series pet! I suppose it's because of all this that she didn't go down well at all with the public and when the show came out and I saw the reaction she got on Twitter, I really felt for her! We've all been there ... we've all had those series where you come across like an utter bag of piss and everyone hates you.

When I saw what everyone was saying about her on Twitter I extended a bit of an olive branch to her over private message and said:

Seen a bit of the rubbish on Twitter mate, don't let it get to you – we all have shockers! Just surround yourself with family and friends and you'll be fine!

Marnie seemed genuinely grateful for my support and because of this I thought we'd really get on and I'd have a bit of an ally in the house. Holly and Charlotte are a double act and so incredibly close and, even though I love them, I thought it would be great to have a BFF in Marnie. It turns out that was *never* going to happen.

I went into series eight single and skinny so I was thinking 'I'm going to have some fucking fun here'. The only thing I was apprehensive about was the drinking side of things, and potentially putting myself in a situation like the one I'd been in the previous year with the nightclub incident. I knew I was in a happier place in myself and I was ready for fun, but that was still in the back of my mind.

Charlotte was in a relationship with her boyfriend Mitch so the lads only had Marnie and Holly to crack on with for the first few days. When I walked in they had someone else to flirt with, which always makes them happy. As soon as I walked into Riverside Holly gave me the lowdown on what I'd missed – which was a bloody lot considering I was only five days late, Marnie had moved on from Scott to her next victim – Gaz, and she'd shagged him on the first night back! Now I didn't know an awful lot about Marnie but this seemed pretty quick . . . almost too quick? But it was nothing to do with me and I only really had one thing on my mind – getting pissed with this bunch of bellends! Obviously it was later revealed that she'd shagged Gaz straight after filming series seven and kept it a secret from everyone. This sparked one of the biggest rows *Geordie Shore* has ever seen and of course Marnie was at the middle of it!

Aaron was trying to crack on with Holly and James was with his girlfriend, so that just left Scott. He started flirting with me straight away but I think he just wanted a good storyline, bless him. I've always loved Scott but we didn't properly neck on or anything. We had a bit of a kiss but every time we got close to anything else I'd get giggly because he's like my big brother.

With the exception of Ricci, Aaron is the only lad in the *Geordie Shore* house that I've ever really 'dated'. We went on double dates with Gaz and Marnie, got drunk and tashed on, enjoyed each other's company and even shared a bed together – and a Yurt! (Practically married in *Geordie Shore* terms!) But as our third date approached Aaron pulled me to one side and told me that the producers were egging him on to push our relationship further – they wanted him to try and have sex with me after our next night out. Being new to the show, and the closest thing we have ever had to a gentleman, Aaron was genuinely confused and came to me for advice. I was never going to sleep with Aaron, that much was painfully clear to everyone, we were friends and in that house we'd been drawn to each other because we were a similar age and had a similar sense of humour. We'd mistaken that friendship and general affinity as romance – and that was fine when you were just tashing-on in bijoux, but I couldn't allow it to head to the shag pad! Me and Aaron decided that we'd fizzle what we had out on camera and that way the producers wouldn't complain as the audience would see us reach the mutual agreement that we were just friends. Sounds simple doesn't it? Well that was until my great big mouth got in the way . . . I was having a chat with the lasses in the kitchen and they were asking me about Aaron and our big date that night. I started off going with the plan – saying I wasn't sure about him anymore and thought we were better as friends, but then I got carried away with myself didn't I? We had been told Aaron was in green screen so me and the lasses started doing what lasses do best – bitching! It was all good natured, bit of banter, bit of bravado – we were just messing around and trying to make each other laugh and weren't thinking about Aaron or his feelings. But it turned out Aaron wasn't in green screen – he was upstairs in his room and he'd heard every last word! I had just been trying to lay the groundwork for us calling it off and instead I'd got carried away and hurt his feelings.

I went about it totally the wrong way and that will go down in history as one of the worst things I've done because Aaron is such a nice lad. It was his first series so he wasn't used to how cutthroat the house can be and he took it all to heart. He kicked off with me and then I kicked off with the producers and it was a big fucking nightmare. It took Aaron days to forgive me and over those days the atmosphere in the house was terrible. When he eventually did things were strained for a while – I suppose he felt like he couldn't trust me anymore, which broke my heart as I really was growing fond of him. But I've worn him down and we're firm friends again now. (I'm a persistent little fucker and hard to stay mad at!) But I definitely learnt my lesson that day – there is always someone listening in the *Geordie Shore* house!

Once I'd kissed Aaron and Scott they were both out of the picture and I thought that was my lot for that series. Then our other new boy, Kyle, entered. He used to man the VIP area at House of Smith and I already knew of him – in fact, I'd snogged him outside a club once. He'd also dated Charlotte several years before so they had a bit of history too. So he wasn't really our 'new lad' at all – he was everyone's fucking 'old lad'! He was a great addition because he was young and he loves going out and he's not afraid to stand up for himself.

Needless to say we ended up having a very awkward kiss one night, which meant I'd snogged three of the four single guys in the house. So what did I do? I decided to go for the full set.

I'm not going to lie to you; I got with Gaz predominantly because I felt like Marnie was getting too much screen time ... the rest of me just wanted to see what all the fuss was about! (I still have no clue to be honest!) I've never really cared about screen time or getting a big storyline, but there was something about Marnie's attitude which was really starting to grate on me. Outside of the show Marnie is a really nice girl and I enjoy her company in small doses, but she was very draining in the house. I think because of mine and Sophie's abrupt exits in the series before and with Marnie being the new girl, she'd found herself the centre of attention and she wanted to keep it that way!

It was like being in 'The Marnie Show' and the rest of us merely supporting actors. I wouldn't have minded if she was a brilliant character: strong, opinionated, witty, adorable or ditzy – but she was none of those things! She's not a girls' girl and I quickly realised that she wouldn't be anyone's ally in that house – Marnie looked out for number 1. In the end I said to myself 'what can I do that's going to take the attention away from Marnie?' I had to do something dramatic. And that something was Gaz. It was a personal low point and even as I was kissing him I was thinking 'you're going to fucking regret this in the morning Vicky'. But my God, it worked. Instantly everyone was talking about us and Marnie was on the backburner. Mission accomplished. I was still Queen.

Series eight was my slaggy series but I did have some really good times. Our visit to Iceland was brilliant and we had some great nights out in Newcastle as we always do. Of course, there were some low points during the series too. The 'shite night' where I got drunk and called everything shite was pretty awful, and I did pack my case to leave the house a couple of times when I got pissed off. I was also furious when I realised that I'd put on almost a stone in five weeks from drinking loads of booze and eating shit. We would come home after a night out and attack the sweetie cupboard like a pack of raccoons. I'd be walking around with both hands in a packet of Doritos so, to be fair, what did I expect? But it still really annoyed me. I felt like all of my hard work had gone to waste.

I think that signalled the beginning of the end for me – my heart just wasn't in it. My relationship with Marnie hadn't turned out how I'd wanted it to, Charlotte and Holly were closer than ever and I'd kissed each of the single lads in the house. What was left for me to do? I love all the other cast members but I'm so different to the other girls, and quite a bit older – every series that age gap was becoming more obvious. All the lads were more like my brothers now than anything else so from then on tashing on was off the cards!

For the first time while I was in the house I was constantly thinking about my life outside and really missing it. My autobiography was about to come out, my DVD was still doing really well and I had my fingers in so many business pies. It felt like I was living two contradictory lives. I'd also met a lovely new guy called James and he was on my mind a lot. We weren't in a relationship or anything at that point, but I knew I really liked him. We randomly met on Twitter during Valentine's weekend. I was sat at home on the sofa, dateless, eating pizza and feeling sorry for myself. I was looking at all these posts on Twitter and Instagram where lasses were showing off their bouquets of roses, Michael Kors watches and boxes of chocolates all captioned: 'Didn't he do well?' Eurgh! Every time I read another one that annoyed me I'd stuff another slice of Pepperoni Passion into my mouth.

James had been looking for a celebrity to front a new protein range he was working on and he tweeted asking his followers for suggestions. Loads of people suggested me and started tweeting him adding me in. I was pissed off and miserable and had no idea who this guy was so I ignored all of the messages. Getting hassled by a total stranger was the last thing I needed.

Later that night I got a drunken message from Charlotte all the way from Australia saying: 'Follow the meat man,' and I was like: 'What? Who?' She replied: 'The man from Stilton Butchers. He's got the wicked meat.' I followed her advice and as soon as I followed him he private messaged me saying: 'You took your fucking time.' We started having a conversation and then he said: 'By the way, you're really pretty.' I replied: 'Is this a business proposition or are you putting a fucking shift in? You can only do one or the other.' He said he wanted to take me for lunch the following Saturday so we could decide – to this day I still don't know if it was an elaborate ruse to meet me or not!

James and I hit it off straight away and I found myself thinking about him all the time. Suddenly things that had seemed really important – the show, getting drunk, kissing loads of lads – became less important. I wasn't twenty-one anymore. All I'd had to worry about during previous series was being caught not wearing my work top by Anna, but now I had *real* things to think about. At some point I stopped being able to switch off and just enjoy it.

I was almost playing a role in season eight. I still wanted to be the big character so I ran around and kissed people and tried to convince myself I could still love it, but it felt forced. And on top of everything else I was fat again. It took me six weeks of working out with my trainer, no booze and eating really healthily to get the weight back off after the show, and I was bloody miserable during that time.

Thankfully work was really busy so that gave me a focus away from my gruelling weight-loss regime. I did photo shoots, interviews, book signings or community service during the day, and PAs most nights. Things also things started really picking up with James. We'd been out together quite a few times before series eight but we'd always known I was going back into the show so we'd kept each other at arm's length. When I left the house something inside me clicked. It was a bit like 'well you've snogged the rest of the world. Maybe it's about time you look for something more and something real?'

James and I started properly dating and life settled into this really nice place, which consisted of nights on the sofa and long Sunday dinners with his family. Call me boring but I felt so content. I fell in love with him and I felt happier than I had done in years.

James didn't come on his own, either. He came as a package with his six-year-old daughter, Talia. She was the most rumbustious, amazing little girl I've ever met. I think she's probably similar to how I was at that age. I'd never imagined myself taking on a stepmother role before because, if I'm being honest, I've never been that fussed about kids. I don't know if it's because when I looked at her I saw someone James loves and I saw him in her, but she's ridiculously adorable. An adorable handful.

My life totally changed over those six months and I guess I matured. James was thirty-two and he runs a really successful business called Stilton Butchers with his family so he's got a lot of responsibilities. Because of that I couldn't play at being a grown-up anymore; I had to be one.

But I hadn't gone 'public' with a boyfriend since Ricci. I wanted the world to know I was dating James because I was proud, but I was also worried about what the press would say. James used to go out with someone else who was in the public eye and I knew that would be picked up on straight away. And once you put something out there you can take it back, so I was petrified that it would damage our relationship. The press interest in me was pretty intense and it was never going to be a cheery situation where people were like 'Ah look, Vicky's in a nice relationship. How sweet!' I knew they would want a story.

I think James thought something shady was going on or I wasn't sure about him because I kept our relationship quiet for quite a while. From his point of view we were in love and he wanted people to know. He didn't want people to think his girlfriend was single. So after we'd been seeing each other for a while I started putting a few things on Instagram. To start with it was just a bunch of flowers he sent me, but straight away I started getting weird messages from his ex and people started comparing me to her. No one compared James to bloody Ricci, but I suppose I should have expected it really.

I'm pleased I had the sense to wait until I was totally sure James and I were going to make a proper go of things before putting it out there because it meant we were prepared for the onslaught to a certain extent. Forewarned is forearmed and all that. We got through it by sticking together and not letting any of the negative stuff in.

Life was good and I was buzzing. Every day was different and exciting and I was constantly being challenged. I was on such a high and I woke up every day with a smile on my face. Then MTV called and said they wanted to film another series of *Geordie Shore*. My heart fell.

Chapter 18

So Long, Farewell ...

It was less than two months since I'd finished the last series of *Geordie Shore* and my whole world came crashing down when I got the phone call about the next series. The thought of having to go back into the house and get pissed for weeks on end filled me with dread.

I arranged to meet up with the producers to talk things through and my agent gave me a pep talk beforehand, saying: 'They know you don't really want to do it and they're looking to cut some people, so if you're not really positive and excited and don't tell them you want to be in *Geordie Shore* for the rest of your life you're going to be in trouble.'

I walked into that meeting determined to give them the dog and pony show but I just couldn't. I wear my heart on my sleeve and you can always tell what I'm thinking – and they knew. I really respect the producers they've got at the moment, Jake and Kate; they understand that there's got to be some semblance of your real emotions in the show and they're respectful of that, so I couldn't lie to them. They asked me what they could do to make the show more enjoyable for me. I knew we would never film abroad again because of *Ex On The Beach*. So we were going to be stuck in that fucking warehouse on the River Tyne again, going to Bijoux and House of Smith and Tup Tup and looking like we're having the time of our lives. But I wasn't anymore.

I was totally honest with Jake and Kate and said: 'I'm sorry, I know you want more from me but I've made it clear for a while now that I'm only here until I get something better.'

The show is amazing. I may be biased, but I don't think there's a better reality show around. But the last series had scared me a bit. I had felt like I was outgrowing it and as a result I had tried harder than ever to be 'crazy Vicky'. I was a caricature. I was trying to be what I thought the producers and the *Geordie Shore* fans wanted, which is ridiculous. It didn't sit well with me and it didn't sit well with the producers. They even said to me that the role of being 'the one who tashes on with everyone' didn't suit me. They thought I was better when I took a step back and could watch everyone else doing it and be a bit self-righteous. I guess it's hard to be self-righteous when you're the one being a bellend.

Jake and Kate told me that what had stood out to them from series eight was how good I'd been at the *Tash-On Tours* side of things. I think I must have been an 18–30 club rep in a previous life because I'd loved it. Their idea was to expand that role and make me the boss of everyone, which, funnily enough, I really liked the idea of, so that's how Queen V was born.

I was still really apprehensive about series nine because mentally I had moved on. But I still thought I could make it work. Being the boss was a way of giving me a purpose in the show. However, it turns out that when you segregate yourself like that you feel even more isolated – I instantly felt ostracised. I felt like I was fighting a losing battle from day one. The other cast members thought I was taking it really seriously but actually I couldn't have cared less. I wanted to be sitting at home with my boyfriend watching a film and having a Domino's.

Another thing that made me feel like a bit of an outcast was that I didn't want join in all of the drinking sessions. Having put on so much weight in the previous series I was paranoid it was going to happen again. I was almost obsessed with not piling on the pounds so I was getting up first thing and training hard, as well as eating as well as I could. Don't get me wrong, I still love a night out where I get *Geordie Shore* pissed and eat a questionable kebab, but I couldn't handle it every night. My body can't take it. If I have a big night out now I feel poorly for days. I used to scorn at people who said things like that and drink through the hangovers but those days are over.

On top of all that I'd dyed my hair blonde just before the series and I *hated* it. I'd done a piece for *Now* magazine about my weight loss transformation and they said they wanted to take things a step further and cut off my hair and dye it. Summer was coming and I was up for an image update so I agreed. When it was first coloured it was a rusty auburn colour and I liked it. But I felt like it was something and nothing so a couple of weeks later I went back and asked to go blonder. I clearly got a bug for being blonde because I went to my hairdresser and got it lightened even more. Because my hair had been black before the blonde dye washed out really quickly so by the time I got onto green screen my bloody hair also looked green.

I started to really loathe it and missed it being really long, so I had some blonde hair pieces sent in. As soon as I saw them I knew that none of which really matched, but I went ahead and wore them anyway. My God, have

I been ripped apart on Twitter since. Sorry about the dodgy hair, guys!

The crew realised how down I was and they rallied around me, but I noticed that I was needed less and less. One thing I can't be is surplus to requirements. I don't want to be a supporting cast member. What makes *Geordie Shore* so brilliant is the fact it doesn't have a stand-out star. It has eight or nine people who all contribute something to make it great, but some characters *are* bigger than others and are at the forefront of the show. I'd always considered myself to be one of those but all of a sudden I was superfluous.

The production team asked me to speak to Kate, the main producer, before I made any big decisions. I really didn't want to because Kate is like a Jedi. She's got some kind of hold over me. I can be irate and then I'll hear her voice and instantly calm down.

I really respect Kate so I agreed to talk to her. She basically said that if I walked that night it would make her life very hard because she wouldn't be able to explain it on the show. I totally got where she was coming from but at the end of the day I was hurting. I'd been there for every single one of the girls and boys in the house at one time or another and they hadn't been there for me. Not one of them had asked how I was and it just cemented what I already knew – that I didn't have a place in the *Geordie Shore* house any more.

At the end of the conversation with Kate I agreed to stay that night and I'm really pleased I did because it was the start of me leaving in a proper way. It meant that I got to do it right. James came and visited me the next day and I talked it over with him, and then I took a couple of days off. I think some of the other cast members suspected I was planning to leave because they said: 'You are coming back aren't you?' I said I was, but really I was only coming back to say goodbye.

When the rest of the guys were filming series seven I remember feeling so angry that I was missing out, but during those two days away I didn't give it a second thought. I didn't care if they were in Bijoux or having a big house party, I was on my sofa cuddling up with James. I went back to the gym the next day and because I had that freedom it felt like a weight had lifted. I knew then I'd made the right decision.

I went back into the house and on the last day of filming we had a big Christmas dinner and gave each other stupid Christmas presents. Everyone was in such a good mood so it was heart-wrenching saying goodbye. It had been my life for four years and it was the longest relationship I'd ever had! I honestly felt like I was divorcing all of the other cast members at once.

I think everyone else in the house was really shocked. They still love the show and it's totally beyond them why anyone would want to leave. I explained to them all I loved them and that having that experience with them had been amazing but I had to go. I still cry when I think about that moment now. I didn't just walk away from the cast members, I walked away from the crew and the house and the bubble. Charlotte and Holly were in floods of tears, and Marnie tried her best to squeeze some out but she was clearly thinking 'Yes, I'm the Queen now!' Marnie love, you will never be Queen.

After dinner I walked out of the *Geordie Shore* house, got into a car and left the others to discuss my departure. That was my time in the show over. It felt surreal but right.

I went straight home and I woke up the following day next to my lovely boyfriend with my amazing sister in the next room and my brilliant dad downstairs making breakfast. There were no random slags tip-toeing out of the house and there was no hangover self-loathing. Sun was streaming through the windows and it may sound cheesy but it felt like the first day of the rest of my life.

We had a big family meal that day and then I caught up with my friends. I've seen them so much more since I've left the show. All of us lasses started planning to go to Ibiza the next summer and I felt like I'd got my freedom back. My mum was so thrilled I'd left too. She hated it! Whenever I was filming she was always waiting for that sobbing phone call from me. Now she doesn't have to worry anymore which makes me so happy.

I felt good within myself and about myself. For the first time ever I came out of a series slimmer than when I went in because I had been so careful. I still work out regularly and I love the gym as a mood regulator as much as anything else. I'm a bit gentler with myself these days and I have everything in moderation so I do have treats, and I've found that my body is more in harmony as a result.

While we're on the subject of my body, it's no secret that not long after I left *Geordie Shore* I finally went and got my boobs done. New start, new boobs! I'd been talking about it for so long and it felt like the right time. I was so unhappy with my chest I didn't even like taking my bra off when I had sex because my boobs were so lifeless.

Once I knew I was having it done that was it – I became tit obsessed. I was checking out everyone's boobs, and I would get caught out staring at random women's breasts wondering if they'd had theirs done. I knew what kind of look I did and didn't want. I've worked so hard to get this smaller frame and the last thing I wanted to do was ruin it with great big tits. I decided on a C/D because I've got quite a small back at 32". I've got a bit of a bum and hips on me so I wanted to balance myself out and have more of an hourglass figure.

One of my main issues is that my boobs not only

looked shit, they were two different sizes. They were like little and large. My right one was much bigger and hung down like an empty condom, whereas my left one looked like a bloody moob. If you looked at them both together it looked like the right one had eaten the left one.

I explained all of this to my surgeon, Dr Frati at Mya, who is known as 'the tit doctor'. He was so funny. He didn't even try and hide the fact he thought my boobs looked weird. He was staring at them with this really confused look on his face and eventually he said that my right one needed an uplift and implant and left one just needed . . . something!

I was nervous and excited on the day of the operation. I got dressed in my hospital gown and compression socks and then it was time to have my anaesthetic and go down to theatre. When I came round I looked at the doctor and slurred: 'Are we going to get this show on the road?' and he replied: 'Actually the show's over, we're all done here.' And there they were. My lovely, shiny new boobs. Except they weren't shiny. They were bloody painful and wrapped in tons of bandages.

Because my right one was bigger I needed a slightly smaller implant in there so I had 250mls in my left boob, and 300mls in my right boob. Who's the winner now, eh lefty? The underdog – or underboob – triumphed in the end. The left one healed really quickly because it didn't have an uplift, but the right one took ages because of all the internal stiches.

I'm so pleased I did it and it's made me feel so much more confident. I'm happy to go braless and I can wear a bikini without shitting myself for the first time in years.

I'm not going to lie, it was bloody painful. When people say they were shopping for bras four hours after their operation I think 'you must have a very high pain threshold' because I was wiped out. I was bed/sofa-ridden for about nine days and my mum, Laura and James all look after me. They all had some kind of competition as to who could be the best Florence Nightingale, which was brilliant because it meant they made a lot of fuss of me.

I lay around for days eating Ben and Jerry's and watching box sets and, unfortunately, some of *Celebrity Big Brother*. I was on medication so I was drowsy through the day and awake at night and sometimes *CBB* was the only thing that was on. Needless to say the last thing I wanted to see when I was recovering from surgery was Ricci's face.

I'd been given the heads-up that Ricci was going into the house so I knew it was coming. I didn't begrudge him the opportunity to go on the show at all and I was pleased he'd got that chance, but I was nervous that he was going to talk about me on camera. Thankfully he didn't, but I do think he showed himself to be everything I have said about him in this book.

As much as it was lovely being taken care of I struggled with the lack of independence because I had to have help with everything. Certain movements can rip your stitches and you're so aware of your boobs because they don't feel like yours at first. It was only after about six weeks that I properly got used them. I was very precious about them and I lived in a sports bra for about eight weeks and I think because of that they healed really well. When they were finally ready to roll I treated myself – and I guess James too! – to some lovely new underwear and it felt amazing.

I finished my community service in November 2014. It ended up being a real blessing. I did it at a time when my career was massively on the up and I could easily have got quite arrogant and believed my own hype. But there are certain experiences in my life that have stopped me being an utter nob, and I believe that one of those is community service. I remember being on a PA in Bangor and having to drive six hours back home and then go straight to the charity shop on no sleep whatsoever. But I still put in the hours and I did the work and I felt good afterwards.

I've met genuinely nice people through it, and it also opened my eyes a lot. Years ago I would have been ignorant enough to think that anyone who did community service was a nasty criminal, but the people I've met just aren't like that. It makes you realise that you're not alone and many people make mistakes. It's life. Even though I've finished now I'm still going to go in and volunteer one day a month in the shop to keep myself grounded. It's an amazing leveller.

So once again it was time to look to the future. Sadly, that meant that James and I decided to break up. There's no great story – though the press like to think there is. I just needed to be single and free to make the most of the once-in-a-lifetime career opportunities I've been given so we agreed it would be best for both of us to take a break from each other and concentrate on our work! We still speak regularly and I think so highly of James and his entire family – he was such an amazing support through my leaving *Geordie Shore* and surgery, it really was a life-changing time and he showed me how amazing a (slightly!) quieter life can be, it's just the relationship wasn't right for either of us at that time. I still wish James the very best of luck, and who knows what will happen in the future . . .

Geordie Shore was an incredible experience and even now I know how lucky I am to have been a part of it. I travelled the world, met amazing people, been on the front cover of magazines and been pissed in more countries than most people will drink in in a lifetime, but most of all I have made some real friends. Not just the eight cast members but those who have been and gone over the years and also the amazing (and long suffering) crew! We ended up being like one big family and I genuinely miss them all.

But *Geordie Shore* is about being young, wild and care-free and I suppose I just wasn't in that place anymore! I was too old for it! I know what loads of you must be thinking – 'you were twenty-six, that's not old?' But I didn't feel twenty-six – every year that passes in *Geordie Shore* ages you by about seven years. It's like dog years! So in *Geordie Shore* years I was about fifty-four. And fifty-four is too old to be sleeping in the same room as three of your mates and listen to them talk about getting fingered, man! I wanted to try something new, to really carve a career out for myself and it felt like the right time to make that leap. That great big, scary leap into the unknown!

Life was good. I was happy, I was in a great place and I was looking to the future. Okay, so I was effectively unemployed, but I was both petrified and excited at the same time.

And with good reason . . .

Chapter 19

I'm a Celebrity . . .
But I'm Not In There

The end of 2014 proved to be a very strange time for me. So many things were changing in my life and I felt like I had no real direction. In November I flew out to Australia to do a tour of PAs just as *I'm a Celebrity . . . Get Me Out of Here* was about to kick off, and that was a proper punch in the dick. I was desperate to go into the jungle but at that point ITV wouldn't entertain the idea of even seeing someone from *Geordie Shore* let alone putting them on the show.

The nation was convinced I was going in and the odds

were something like 8–1 on me to win – not bad considering the closest I'd get to any sort of jungle would be the fake plant pots in my various hotel rooms. So while everyone was speculating, I was doing a load of 'schoolies' with Scotty T. Schoolies are Australia's version of Fresher's Week, except they do them when everyone is sixteen and about to enter their final year of school. They can't legally drink but they all go absolutely nuts. Scott bloody loved it – you can imagine what he was like – I mean, he's essentially a big kid himself really! But it all made me feel a bit old and uncomfortable. I felt like their mam or something. I ended up leaving Scott up there and going to Sydney to spend five days with Dan, and it was definitely the best decision I could have made. We had a lovely time going for dinner, walking his giant dog, King, sightseeing, going to the gym and just chilling out.

When I eventually got back to England I had a real crisis of confidence. MTV were already filming another series of *Geordie Shore* so even if I'd wanted to go back – which I didn't – I couldn't, that ship had sailed. The wheels were already in motion and they had my replacement. I never once mourned the show – I respected it and I loved it for everything it gave me, but I was over it. But I also had no idea what I was going to do next. I was effectively unemployed. And single. Balls.

After splitting up with James I was genuinely much happier on my own. James was a nice lad who thought the world of me and had a lovely family, but in the end I think I loved his family more than I loved him. James has since met someone else and got engaged, and I'm happy that he's happy. I've come to realise that I'm basically a female Good Luck Chuck for all these lads who want to find 'the one'. I always seem to be the last girl lads go out with before they meet the girl who becomes their wife!

I was kind of free-floating, so threw myself into promoting my Mini V range of nutritional supplements. It was nerve-wracking starting something so different to what I had done in the past, but I'd had such a good reaction to my weight-loss transformation that it made sense for me to try and help other girls. The Mini V range has been phenomenal and I am incredibly proud of the business and my customers. Seeing their transformations is unbelievable and knowing I have been part of that somehow makes me very emotional.

It was a scary time because I didn't know where my next TV job was coming from and I felt a bit paralysed by fear. I was trying to be positive but I'd just walked away from one of the biggest reality TV franchises going – and straight into nothing. Then out of nowhere, two weeks before Christmas, ITV2 asked me to appear on *Dinner Date*. It went really well, and I think that was a big turning point in my career – it was the first time I'd been on ITV's radar. It was absolutely hilarious to film, and the confidence boost I'd needed, but in true Vicky style it wasn't exactly straightforward ...

There were five days of filming in total and it all started off really well. On the first day I chose my menus, and over the following three days I had three dates before deciding on my winner. All the lads were from Newcastle and I was convinced I was going to end up on a date with an ex-boyfriend or something – that would be just my luck. Sort of an *Ex on the Beach* situation only this time with beef casserole and chocolate soufflé.

When the car arrived to take me to my first date's house we drove for – I'm not kidding – less than two minutes and then stopped. I knocked on the door, convinced I was going to know whoever was behind it, and this lad called Nathan answered. I've partied with him a lot in the past and his brother, Keiron, is a good friend of mine so I'd known him for years. He *also* happened to be my mate's 'friend with benefits' – if you know what I mean!

When he opened the door there was no: 'Hi! How are you?' Instead, he first thing that came out of my mouth was 'Oh my God, I can't date *you*!' The producer was horrified, but Nathan and I actually ended up having a lovely, funny date and he was a great cook – although obviously there was no romance there.

I was having fun doing the show and looking forward to the next two dates, but things didn't quite go according to plan. The week before I filmed the show, against all my better judgement, I'd started seeing an ex of mine called Josh, who lives in Canterbury and runs club nights there. He was hosting one on the Wednesday night, the same night as my second date, and was desperate for me to go. There was no way I'd have had time to get there by car, so he hired a private jet for me. It was *so* swanky and howay man, you can't say no to a private jet, can you? So after my second date with a lovely wrestler chap called Jason, I went to a private airport in Newcastle and flew off. It wasn't as glam as I was expecting because I was cold and tired, but when I got to the club I had such an amazing night. And at least I can say I've been on a private jet! I felt like William large penis. Scotty T, our friend Brad and my mate Farah from *Ex on the Beach* were also there, and we had a wicked night just drinking and letting our hair down.

I had a really early flight back from Gatwick the following morning so Josh offered to drive me, but as we were halfway there Scott called to say he and Brad desperately needed a lift. Josh promised me we'd still be on time even if we went back and got them, but he wasn't accounting for the morning traffic into London and of course we all totally missed our flight – by a country fucking mile! There wasn't another one I could get that day and I could have cried. I was set to go on my third and final date later that day and there I was stuck at Gatwick having had no sleep whatsoever. In the end we decided we'd have to get a train to Newcastle – and I thought to myself, 'ah well, I'll sleep all the way so I'll be fine by the time I get there'. But I hadn't factored in party animals Scott and Brad. It was the week before Christmas and the train was packed, so I told myself I'd just have *one* small wine to send myself to sleep. Three hours later I was three mini bottles of white and four cans of gin and tonic down, and we had the whole train carriage up singing and dancing. I don't think the drinks trolley moved the entire journey – we were holding it hostage.

By the time we got to Newcastle I was absolutely mortal and I had to head straight home to get my make-up done for *Dinner Date*. I fell asleep on the sofa and my make-up artist Lo cracked on and did my face while I lay there passed out. When I eventually woke up Laura came down the stairs, took one look at me and told me there was no way I could go, I looked like a bloody wreck, and the hangover was starting to kick in! But I had no choice. So in the end I went to my final dinner date absolutely mortal having not slept for twenty-four hours.

I'd gone past the point finding it all funny and all I felt was *utter* regret. I smashed some Red Bulls before I knocked on the door, and luckily the lad who opened it, Mike, was a real laugh. We shared a couple of bottles of white wine and then he bought a duvet downstairs so I could have a little sleep on his sofa in between courses. He was so canny that, even though I didn't fancy him, I chose him as my winner. Any lad who lets me sleep off a hangover on his sofa evidently does it for me – apparently I'm not that fussy!

So that was my first 'in' at ITV, and it could have easily been my last. What a way to announce my presence, eh?! But you've got to be yourself in these things haven't you? I was pleased it had been such a laugh, but I was feeling pigeonholed. I really loved my managers Kay and Shaq at IMA, but I'd been approached by two girls I knew called Gemma and Nadia, from a new management company called Mokkingbird. They had a background with CAN Associates but they had left recently to set up their own company and I agreed to meet them. It was all very cloak and dagger, but I instantly got a good vibe from them – I'm drawn to strong women like a moth to a flame.

Gemma and Nadia represented Millie Mackintosh, and they were talking about signing Binky Felstead, who are two people I love in the industry. I just knew they'd be the girls for me. I talked to them and they seemed to understand and be on my page. They wanted to take my image down a more clean-cut route and get me mainstream work – everything they said really resonated with me.

I fell in love with Gemma and Nadia but it was important to me to get my mam's opinion. I wanted to get her view because it was a big decision for me to make. I'd been with IMA for a long time and they'd be there with me throughout really tough times, like the court case. I felt like I owed it to myself and them to be sure I was making the right decision.

Mam loved the girls but still I really didn't know what to do. I'm loyal to a fault so the thought of leaving IMA made me feel awful ... but something was strongly drawing me to Mokkingbird. Then just before the end of the year I heard that IMA were signing Marnie. I was so angry with her as she had been mouthing off about me no end in the press. The next day I gave IMA my resignation and told Gemma and Nadia I was going to sign with them. It was the best thing I've ever done because I love the bones of them.

Not long afterwards a guy called Jake Attwell, who is an executive producer at MTV and worked on *Geordie Shore*, called me to say he had an idea for a new TV show. He'd always been a big champion of mine and told me he wanted to make a show that was like *Catfish* crossed with Jeremy Kyle – and he wanted me to front it. I was totally baffled but none the less buzzing like an old fridge!

He went on to explain that I would travel around the country solving people's relationship problems. He'd pitched it to MTV and they liked the idea, but he needed to show them a pilot in early January. It was now or never, and I've never been one to shy away from a challenge, so the following day I flew back from a PA in Ireland and went to a studio in Staines to start filming so we could squeeze it in before the end of the year.

The show hinged on me telling people what for and I knew as soon as we started filming that it was going to be good. The first situation we had to deal with was a girl who said her sister had stolen her man. I went to see the sister and told her in no uncertain terms that it should be sisters before misters. She was dead cold with me, and I thought 'awww no, I've got my work cut out with this one', and it later transpired that the woman who'd got in touch was actually the other girl's *mother,* and she was jealous that her daughter was young and loving life. I was on my soapbox giving the mother what for and I suddenly thought 'hang on, I'm getting paid to meet all these wild and exciting people and dish out my opinions and home truths? This is home.' All I

The original *Geordie Shore* cast in 2011 – if only we'd known what we were in for! (Top row, L–R: Jay Gardner, Greg Lake, James Tindale, Gaz Beadle; bottom row, L–R: Charlotte Crosby, Holly Hagan, me, Sophie Kasaei.

Me and Greg, hanging out in our classy dressing-gowns.

Things are starting to get a little more glam after season two. With new castmate Rebecca Walker, Charlotte and Sophie at the premiere of *The Dictator* in 2012.

With Ricci Guarnaccio at the MTV EMA awards in Frankfurt, November 2012. We were engaged by this point, but I wasn't happy.

Presenting the award for best male at the MTV awards with the rest of the gang.

Me and my *Geordie Shore* girls at the aftershow party.

My relationship with Ricci was tumultuous from day one, but there were moments when I thought we really could have a future together.

Ricci and I never made it this far – would have been much more fun going down the aisle with Charlotte!

Single, at last, and ready for a fantastic time tashing-on in Australia for series 6!

Me and Charlotte on the beach in Australia.

My lowest point – on my way to court in February 2014.

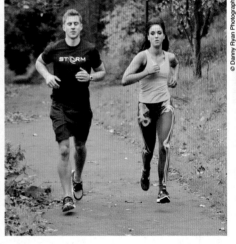

Thankfully I had *7 Day Slim* and my exercise regime to take my mind off the other things going on.

The snaps that caused all that trouble . . . with Charlie Sims (left) and Riad Erraji (below).

Me and Kirk in our little love bubble!

Her Royal Highness Queen Victoria of the jungle! Long may she reign.

Celebrating Geordie style with Ant and Dec.

could do was hope MTV had the same amount of faith in it that I did.

From the moment I walked out of the *Geordie Shore* house people were waiting for me to fail. Sadly that included other people from the show, which still makes me feel incredibly sad. I stayed in touch with all of them when I left and it all seemed pretty friendly, but it didn't take long for things to sour.

A lot of the problems started because Charlotte bought out a fitness DVD and people started comparing us. Journalists would say to me, 'How do you feel about Charlotte copying you?' and it's very hard to redirect a question like that. You can be the most articulate person in the world, but when someone asks you a loaded question they clearly only want one answer to it's very hard to swerve the subject – especially if there's even a single grain of truth in what they're saying. I used to smile and say, 'Yes, of course there are similarities between mine and Charlotte's career, but it's not as if I'm the only person in the world who can make a fitness DVD!' I did my best to keep things positive.

I tried so, so hard not to say anything out of order because I had no bad feelings towards Charlotte at all. I truly believe that you should want everyone in your team to be winning. That's *real* success. If everyone around you is doing well it means everyone is happy.

Lifting people up is the best thing you can do. Dragging people down and being bitter gets you nowhere. I told Charlotte when I saw her that I wished her well, and even gave her advice while she was making her DVD. There was no chance I was going to stab her in the back. Sure there was healthy competition between us but if anything we spurred each other on, there was no malice.

But of course nobody wanted to hear that we got on and I was happy for her, so when interviews came out it was made to look like I was pissed off with Charlotte. I'm not mad at the press because that's how they sell magazines, but I am mad with people for believing I would say those things. Charlotte read some comments that sounded like I'd been slagging her off and she reacted, in my opinion, childishly.

Initially she came to me and asked me about it, and I told her straight there was no truth in it and thought that was the end of it. I told her I thought very highly of her – and I still do – but it turns out Marnie was shit-stirring no end. Even though I've never truly got on board with Marnie, I always kept my opinions about her to myself – until it transpired that she didn't have the good grace to do the same.

Thankfully Charlotte and I managed to solve things. Last summer she had a big night out with some of my mates and they all told her the truth about what had happened. She texted me while she was drunk saying, 'We need to stop all of this,' and I messaged her straight back saying I'd never, ever had a problem with her.

I still get people coming up to me and saying they cried when I left *Geordie Shore*, and I always tell them that the show is still amazing. I would never slag it off. I think it scared other cast members when I left the show because it held a mirror up to them and made them wonder if they should have been doing the same.

As much as it hurt when people stabbed me in the back or said unkind things, they actually did me a massive favour. They're idiots for thinking their attitude would ever make me anything other than more determined. They made me up my game and be better at everything I did. The more I knew people didn't want me to do well, the more I wanted to prove them wrong. What's sad is that if those people had channelled even half the energy they put into hoping I'd fail into their own careers they'd be able to do really incredible things.

I knew *Judge Geordie* had real potential and could only hope that MTV felt the same way. It was outside of their usual format and I needed the whole network to get behind me, so it was a waiting game. And it's never nice waiting over Christmas.

I hung out with Josh a lot, which helped to take my mind off things. We spent Boxing Day in Manchester, and then flew to Madrid for New Year. I was feeling really happy: Mini V was going well, Josh and I were getting on brilliantly, and my clothing range was flying. When I found out in early January that MTV were going ahead with *Judge Geordie* it was the icing on the cake. I felt like I was really finding my feet and things were changing in my life in every way.

The first couple of months of 2015 were very much about me realising who I did and didn't want around me because there had been people in my friendship circle that didn't have my best interests at heart. I found a lot of new friends who were more on my wavelength – I met Casey Bachelor through a mutual friend, and she is one of the loveliest people in the world. I also hung out with Jess Wright a lot, as well as Talitha and Farah from season 1 of *Ex on the Beach*. It was then I started to develop a bit of an obsessive work ethic – and worked out that your vibe attracts your tribe. I needed to be around strong, like-minded people who want success. Yes, my friends can party for three days at the weekend, but when Monday morning comes their heads are in the game. I need that – I was meeting so many brilliant new people around that time. And then I met Alex.

When *Judge Geordie* got the go ahead I knew I didn't

want it be a one series thing. I couldn't be given this amazing opportunity and then have it taken away. MTV know what they're doing and I had the best people behind me, but we all agreed on one thing; I was great at reality TV but one person cannot carry a show. I needed someone to bounce off, I needed a sidekick.

I can't drive and the plan was for me to travel around the country, so it made sense I my sidekick was someone who could drive me around. I also needed a bloke so we could get some banter going. We started holding auditions and rigged up a car exactly as it would be on the show.

The first day of auditions was dire. Some of the blokes were trying way too hard. One of them turned out to be the ultimate Vicky stalker and I was worried was going to skin me and wear me like a coat! This stripper came in who had obviously lied about his height on the application form and I was like, 'What are you going to protect me from? Borrowers?' It was a disaster.

Then the next day Alex walked in and things started to look up.

Alex is the most beautiful person I've ever seen in my life. He is completely carved by angels. I was more worried I wouldn't actually be able to speak in front of him than anything else. Then he opened his mouth and he had this thick Scouse accent and I was completely sold. I warmed to him immediately because he had a real presence and he's so charismatic and warm. I just hoped he had the banter to back it up.

Alex and I were given a potential scenario to deal about a guy who thought his girlfriend was cheating and I said to Alex, 'Everyone cheats don't they?' He turned around and said, '*I* don't. I think it's disgusting.' I'd said that as a test and he had passed with flying colours. A lot of men would have just said yes trying to act like ultimate lad but not Alex – he was opinionated but moral and marched to the beat of his own drum and that was something I wanted in my sidekick. We laughed so much together that when he left one of the producers said to me, 'We've found him.'

Alex and I were invited for lunch in London with all the bigwigs from MTV the following week so I had a pretty good idea he'd got the job. Everyone sat there and said, 'The chemistry between you two is amazing. We love it. But you must never, ever shag each other.' It was the 'will they, won't they' quality they loved about us. It was bizarre. I'd come from *Geordie Shore* where you were encouraged to shag your co-stars, and now it was forbidden! Which made it even more tempting, of course.

Alex turned around said, 'Hang on, you haven't told me if I've got the job yet, but you're still saying I can't get with Vicky? Tell me whether or not I've got it now, because if I haven't I'm taking her round the back of this restaurant and I'm going to blam her head off.' We were all in hysterics.

Needless to say Alex did get the job and without a doubt he has been the best thing that's ever happened to me. I wouldn't have been able to cope with the *Judge Geordie* schedule or won the jungle without him. He's like a breath of fresh air. He's taught me so much and instilled so many brilliant things in me. Everyone needs an Alex in their life.

I was still seeing Josh at this point and I adored him so much. He kept me on my toes and he had his own life and career going on, which I really liked – or at least I thought I did. He was so switched on and together, whereas every other boyfriend I've had has smothered me. I always thought I wanted someone who was really laid back, but the grass isn't always greener, is it? I started to feel like I wasn't a priority for him, and it wasn't very nice. I was running around after him, meeting his friends, getting to know his family – you name it – but I wasn't getting anything back. I'd try and act really cool and nonchalant like he did, but as soon as I got drunk I'd start asking where things were going. Now I can see he just wasn't looking for a proper relationship. He used to bat me off by saying 'don't put a label on us' or 'what's the rush?'. I never knew if he was seeing other people or if it was OK for me to see other people. I was never *his* as such, but I wasn't anyone else's either. It all started to play on my mind and drive me a bit mad.

When I was sober I was quite desensitised to it all and I'd only text if he texted me first. It became a bit of a power struggle, and that's not what a relationship should be. I think he liked me and he cared about me but I felt unappreciated and more like his mate than anything. That's fine and I can cope with being his mate if that's all we were because at least then I could go off and start seeing someone else, but I was so confused.

Casey and I went to one of Josh's nights in Canterbury and I got absolutely mortal and he was working, so it wasn't ideal. I got drunk and I became that person I didn't like again. I got dead paranoid that he didn't want to be with me, and I didn't know how to be in a relationship where someone wasn't obsessed with me and trying to control me. I tried to hold his hand that night and he shrugged me off so I flipped. I started shouting at him demanding answers about our relationship, and I will forever thank Casey for being the voice of reason and taking me back to our hotel. She sat me down and said I was driving mad myself over a lad who didn't seem like he was ready to commit, and she was right. I needed to be with someone who wanted the same things as me.

I got up the next morning and had a good think about

things. I couldn't be with someone who was detached and I had too much else to focus on to worry about a relationship not being right. Knowing my luck Josh'll probably marry the next girl he finds – good luck Vick strikes again!

It turned out to be a bloody good that Josh and I broke up because *Judge Geordie* took over my entire life for the next four months. With the exception of a two-week break to film *Ex on the Beach* and have a holiday with my family, I worked on it non-stop. We were travelling constantly and my life became all about the show and making sure it was a success, and during that time Alex became everything to me. I believe people are brought into your life for a reason, and he could not have walked in at a better time.

The show was amazing but exhausting. We were dealing with some really emotional situations and sometimes it could be really draining. I didn't have any kind of social life while I was filming. There were no pap shots of me and Casey having a night out for months – people must have thought I'd died! I literally couldn't do anything while I was filming the show because I was so tired. MTV had invested so much in me and I wanted the show to work for them as much as I did for me and Alex. We worked eighteen hours days and the crew became my family. I bloody loved it.

I spent all my time with Alex and he was there when I needed a good friend. I was getting asked a lot of questions by the press about people slagging me off, and the old me would have replied really angrily. But something about being around Alex made me feel calm and I didn't feel the need to be that anymore. He'd taught me new ways of thinking, and it's all about being positive. He taught me that winners focus on winning, but losers focus on winners – he's always coming out with amazing quotes. One of my favourites is: 'If anyone is trying to drag you down it's because they're below you already.' As a result I grew and I changed and I became a better person. I would do *Judge* for the rest of my life if I got the opportunity because it means I'd get to drive around with Alex every day. I am aware that I'm fangirling but I don't care – I can't help it! He's the dream!

Everyone thinks there more to us than just friend-ship, but there's not. We've been linked many times, but honestly nothing's ever happened between us. I will admit that when I came out of the jungle we were caught having a drunken kiss, and as if it couldn't get any worse we were in Sugar Hut – but I had been locked in a jungle for three weeks and we were both mortal.

Alex and I love each other as friends but that's it. There are a lot of blokes in the world I can fuck things up with – I've proved that time and time again and I'm sure I'll continue to – but Alex is the one guy I never want to lose. I can kiss anyone, sleep with anyone and have a relationship with any reality TV helmet going, but he's the one man I can't have ill feeling with. He's too important to me, and it would be a totally different show if anything happened between us. I don't want *Judge Geordie* to become *Geordie Shore* on wheels. We're just there for each other. He asks my advice about birds and I ask his advice about lads. He's taught me that I'm the prize and lads are lucky to be with me, not the other way round.

*

Judge Geordie ended up completely running away with itself. It was MTV's most successful launch in years and their most successful show in that time slot *ever*. But of course with success like that comes more pressure and the producers wanted more and more.

We were constantly driving around and staying in really crap hotels. Forget five star luxury, we were in Holiday Inns because the whole crew had to be put up. We'd finish a really long day and everyone would go for a drink, and of course I wanted to hang out with them. I had to be up two hours before everyone else because I had to be in make-up and because of how tired and usually hungover I was it was no mean feat making me look presentable! I'd wake up knackered and hanging like me old tits at times. The show hinged on Alex and I having quick wit and being really emotionally invested, so it took a lot out of both of us. It got to the point where I was so drained I'd sit in the car in between takes not being able to speak. Throw the *Ex on the Beach* debacle into the mix and you've got a recipe for disaster.

Doing series 3 of *Ex on the Beach* was a huge mistake. Full stop. When I got given *Judge Geordie*, MTV said they'd heard I'd booked a family holiday to Mexico in March, and dropped the bombshell that they were filming *Ex* out there at the same time. How very convenient. They asked me if I'd film a cameo and it was all very jokey – I didn't agree to anything, but I soon found out they thought I had.

I hated the idea of doing another season but the wheels were already in motion. They had Kirk Norcross, Cami Lee and Jordan Davies, and I was the link. They had it in their head that because I was MTV talent I would do it. *Ex* was dangerous territory – I was the face of my own show and I felt like it was a step back as well as Mokkingbird trying to clean up my image. But at the end of the day, it wasn't worth chucking away my great relationship with MTV over three days of filming so I reluctantly agreed.

It couldn't have come at a worse time. I needed a

holiday, not more work. Everyone who was working on *Judge* was worried I was heading for a breakdown because I was working too hard; simple as that. We were filming the show five days a week, and on the other two days I was doing PAs, working on my first novel, *All that Glitters*, doing press days and photo shoots, and anything else that came my way. Now I had new agents I had more freedom to say no to things, but I was so used to working my arse off that I still never turned anything down. I remember sitting up one night until 5 a.m. working on my novel and then I had to get up at 7 a.m. to film *Judge*. I was crying all the time, I wasn't sleeping properly – if at all – and I was exhausted. I was so overwhelmed. I wanted success but I hadn't seen my family in weeks and I had no balance in my life. I was careering towards a meltdown, and disastrously it happened the minute I arrived at *Ex*.

The day before flying out I'd worked for twenty-two hours straight filming the advert for *Judge Geordie*. I'd been woken up at 6 a.m., taken straight to Gatwick airport (where I got a spray tan. Priorities) and then got on a flight to Mexico. I only had eight hours to acclimatise and I was ruined. When I first arrived I think I was surviving on pure adrenalin and caffeine, and I was like 'yeah, let's smash this!' Then the jetlag hit and I decided to have a couple of drinks to perk myself up. And then a couple more – you can see where this is going I'm sure.

I was drunk when I first walked out of the sea. I say walked but I literally fell out, and my opening line to Kirk Norcross was, 'Kirk, I've had my carpets done!' Not exactly the sexy, glamorous opening the producers were hoping for.

I walked into the apartment and gave Jordan a hug, told all the girls how pretty they looked, then I saw Cami Li giving me proper daggers across the table. I felt very wobbly and alone and I didn't know how I was going to deal with it at all. On the first night I got taken for a date with one of the lads, Martin McKenna, and I was so tired I feel asleep in the back of the car. When I woke up I was absolutely gone. I was run down, delirious, exhausted and upset. I started crying and I couldn't stop. Then when I didn't feel like the situation was being dealt with properly I got belligerent. Some of the people on the show had never worked with me before and one of the production team fucking hated me. And to be fair, she was well within her rights. She must have thought I was an unprofessional idiot.

I was sat in the car sobbing with a sound guy and some of the crew who had all known me for a while. They were amazing and everything came spilling out and I sobbed and sobbed. I felt like as long as I was doing whatever people wanted they were happy, but now

I realised how much pressure I was under. As long as I was turning up for filming and getting my face in the magazines and arriving for PAs on time, apparently it was fine. My family hadn't seen me for weeks so they didn't know the kind of state I was in, otherwise they would have stepped in to help me.

I got driven to the crew villa and Joe, one of the crew and the world's nicest guy, laid on a bed and counted the ceiling tiles with me to calm me down. I will always be grateful to him for that because he saved me that night.

I was too scared to admit that I was having exactly the same feelings I did when I had my breakdown in *Geordie Shore*. I thought I could power through. I know if I'd told the girls at Mokkingbird how I was feeling they would have pulled me out of everything and given me a break, but in my head I thought if I could just get through *Ex* I had my holiday with my family to look forward to and everything would be OK.

I woke up the following morning in a shitload of trouble and the producers were incredibly pissed off with me. I was so apologetic and tried to explain, but as far as they were concerned I'd turned up, got drunk, been a nightmare, demanded to speak to the head of MTV and then had a massive meltdown. I knew I was in the wrong and I'd messed up their recording schedule, but I wanted a second chance. They told me I had two options; I could either walk into the house and have a huge row with Cami Li and go home that night, or suck it up and do what I'd been contracted to do. I didn't have it in my locker to argue with anyone – and I didn't want to fight with someone I didn't know – so I had no choice but to stay for the three days.

I was like a little lost sheep. Everyone had been expecting me to be Vicky Pattison from *Geordie Shore*, to come in wearing a massive sombrero and start kicking cactuses, but I didn't have it in me. I'd been broken by my own relentless pursuit of success. Kirk was really good to me and didn't leave my side that day. He made me a green tea and got me to phone my mam and slowly I started to feel a bit better.

There were whisperings amongst the crew that there was a guy in the house they thought was going to fancy me, and as soon as I saw Stephen Bear I thought 'what a fucking sort!' – I was attracted to him instantly! We went to do Mexican Wrestling that night and because I'd cut my foot on my glamorous exit from the sea I couldn't wrestle so I got made a team captain. For the sake of diplomacy I chose Cami Li to be on my team and I could tell she was less than enamoured with me. I got where she was coming from because she'd fallen in love with Kirk, come to the UK to move in with him, then moved back to Miami heartbroken when they split – and almost immediately after that she saw pictures of him and I out together. As far as she was concerned I'd stolen her lad, but that was never the case.

Cami told me that Chloe Goodman had said loads of stuff about me not being very nice, and I replied, 'That's fine because I don't like her either and there are two sides to every story. Are we going to have a problem, Cami? Because I came here to have a good time, meet some new people, drink a lot of tequila and probably make some bad decisions, but if you want drama I can't face it.' After that we clicked. I don't think either of us were what we expected, and weirdly she's since become one of my best friends. Once we bonded there was no looking back. She's an incredible girl, strong, feisty and fiercely loyal – I would like to think Cami will be a friend of mine for life and it's for reasons like that I will always love shows like *Ex on the Beach* and *Judge Geordie*. They bring people into your lives who otherwise you would have never met and quite often these amazing people change you for the better.

After that, the rest of my time in *Ex* turned out to be really good. Because I came in right near the end, despite being a total melt on the first night, I really lifted the villa. Up until then it had been very Megan McKenna-heavy. Now when Megan is sober she's a darling and I have a lot of time for her, but when she drinks she liked to get really drunk and storm around thinking she was queen bee, which didn't make for a great atmosphere. Everyone was getting really bogged down by the arguing so once I'd picked myself up it was a lot more fun for everyone.

The next day the producers said I could go home, but in order to do that I had to be evicted from the villa, and Ali was going to do it. Me and Ali had of course had a huge row the night before over what I would like to call 'nipple gate' – she'd let Bear lick her nipple on a date! I'm sure most of you have seen the explosive fall out of this but if you haven't let's just say it didn't go down well and both him and her received the full and comprehensive Volcano Vicky treatment. So Ali was more than willing to kick me out as we had history, to say the least. Everyone was crying when I left and people were so pissed off with Ali, but I didn't give a shit because I could finally go and have a good time with my family.

Bear played on my mind a bit while I was on that holiday and I wasn't sure if there was something between us or not. I fancied him and we definitely had fun together, but was a man really what I needed in my life right now? Nevertheless, I didn't neck off with anyone else while I away, and he messaged me and said he wanted to see if we could make a go of things. Even though a few people in the house had warned me off him, I decided to give him a chance and see what he was like away from the cameras.

I got back from a lovely holiday and finally felt pretty relaxed. It was *such* a relief. I had no idea even more drama was just around the corner.

Chapter 20

Hen Don't

In early May I went on my friend Yazmin's hen do in Marbella, and I knew I wanted to let my hair down a bit before I went back to work. We were in a club with a group of football lads I'd met on the flight over, but my friends were dead tired so they all decided to head home. I was having such a good time I decided to stay – stupid decision, I know, and a sober me would never have done it! But I was smashed and having fun and wanted one final hurrah before I got back to my gruelling schedule. I genuinely just wanted to forget for a weekend! I was doing Jägerbombs with strangers and having the time of my life. Before I knew it I was *beyond* mortal and in serious trouble.

I remember wandering out of the club but after that everything is very hazy. I was found passed out in the street by some people walking by who called the police, and they ended up taking me to hospital. My phone was missing and no one knew where I was apart from the *Sun* newspaper, because some holidaymakers had seen me lying on the floor and instead of helping me, they'd videoed me. There were journalists sniffing around trying to find out what I'd been doing and whether or not there were drugs involved, but there absolutely weren't.

I thought my life had been bad before with all the stress and pressure I'd been under, but it was nothing compared to this. I woke up in a hospital bed not knowing where I was or what had gone on and I'd lost my bloody phone. Someone from the *Sun* had phoned Gemma, my agent, so thankfully she sent a pap she knew out there to come and get me. There were so many photographers out the front of the hospital, and he managed to arrange for me to go out the service entrance at the back so I could avoid them. By this time Gemma had phoned my sister, who had phoned my friends; no one knew where the hell I was so they were all panicking. We headed back to the pap's hotel so I could hide out, and after I phoned everyone to let them know I was OK and I slept for nearly 48 hours. It was horrendous. I've learnt not to accept drinks off people I don't know now, but I learnt the hard way.

Everything felt very uncertain with my career, and I was still feeling very fragile after my adventures in Mexico and Marbella. I knew I was becoming more high profile and I couldn't act the way I used to – getting drunk and foolishly trusting everyone – but I wasn't ready comprehend all that! I was in limbo I suppose between thinking I was still ordinary Vicky Pattison who went out with her mates and sometimes acted like a bit of a helmet, and being the 'celebrity' Vicky Pattison. I was struggling with the transition and feeling strained. But there was light at the end of the tunnel, and that came in the form of an audition for *I'm a Celebrity ... Get Me Out of Here!*

When I signed with Gemma and Nadia they asked me to write a list of everything I wanted to achieve in the next year. Top of that was going on *I'm a Celebrity*. Gemma and Nadia both had good relationships with ITV and they put me forward. I think there was some hesitation at first but eventually they agreed to see me – I knew that all I needed was the chance to be in front of them. You can say no to the idea of me, but I was going to make it very hard for them to say no when they actually *met* me.

I went along to the meeting and I smashed it. You know when you know you've done well at a job interview don't you? And I knew. It was so intimidating – I felt like I was going on *The X Factor* when I walked in. They're all just sort of sat there in a row – all the big cheeses for *I'm a Celeb*, sitting there with your life in their hands. I could have easily let the pressure get to me – but I knew I had to relax and be myself. I knew I was right for it. Though at first I don't think they were very sure; there was a younger girl there called Micky who obviously really liked me, but I think the others were in two minds.

I wasn't giving them the answers they wanted to hear; I was saying what I truly believed. I swore, I made jokes, I had a laugh and I was totally honest. They asked me how I felt about falling in love in the jungle and I told them I fall in love everywhere I go – in fact I was pretty sure I'd just met 'the one' in the lift on the way up! I also told them I may be a bit of a girl with the trials but they would never hear me say, 'I'm a celebrity, get me out of here.' And I meant it. It's not in my nature to quit. We laughed a lot and it felt natural and easy and I felt *great*.

Later on in May I headed out to Spain to film an advert for *Ex*. I'd started properly seeing Bear by then – reality shows are the only way I get to meet men these days. They're my personal Tinder.

When we were filming the advert I was really shocked

by everyone's attitude. Cast members were turning up hungover or tired and being arsey to make-up artists and the MTV crew. I remember looking at them and thinking 'you think you've already made it and you really have no idea. Be nice to everyone on the way up because they'll kick you twice as hard on your way down and with the attitudes you've got that will come a lot sooner than you think'. But then in the midst of all that diva behaviour there was Bear. He was nice to everyone, he learnt everyone's names and he was respectful, and that's when I started to really fall for him. I wasn't in love with him or anything, but I knew I really liked him. He admitted he felt the same, but we kept it a secret because of *Ex*. It couldn't become public that we were seeing each other until the show came out. But stories started getting leaked left, right and centre and although I tried my best to act casual and I just said we were spending some time together, it wasn't long before the truth got out – I'm not very good at secrets. When we did the MTV press day it was very obvious we were together and there was no point in trying to hide it anymore. Megan and Jordan were allowed to say they were together, so we did too.

Bear was like a breath of fresh air. We had so much fun. We'd to go the zoo and get our faces painted like lions and tigers, and he'd take me to his local café for a full English. He had a great work ethic – Bear is a proper

East End boy who was a roofer before *Ex*, and he loved the gym like me. I didn't think he was trying to be something he wasn't. He was childlike and endearing and I loved spending time with him.

Everything was looking up. Filming *Judge* had come to an end, Bear and I were getting on amazingly and in June I got the best news I've ever had in my life. I went along to do a shoot and interview for the *Sun* and Gemma said that she wanted me to go and see these people she knew called the Speakmans, to help me sort out some of the stuff in my head. I was like 'what have I done now? I've been really well behaved!'. Then she said, 'I need you to be really strong because I'm going to be saying goodbye to you for a while at the end of the year.' I thought she was ditching me – that she'd finally had enough of all the trouble I seem to cause ... then she dropped the bombshell I was going into the jungle. I jumped up and screamed in the middle of the café we were in. I was so bloody happy. It was what I'd dreamt of for so long.

Bear and I booked a holiday to Ibiza together in August so we could spend some proper time together, and the first few days were incredible. We had romantic meals and drunken nights clubbing where we spent all evening telling each other how much we loved each other. We'd fall into bed together and sunbathe and drink cocktails and watch sunsets. We were talking about spending the rest of our lives together and I couldn't believe I'd only just met him. He was so proud of me and everything I did. I was so excited about the way his life was going to change due to *Ex* and about all the unreal times we were going to have together! In short, I was on cloud nine but of course that would never last.

About halfway through the holiday Bear's agent phoned and he took the call in another room. When he got back he told me about a Skype chat he'd done with a girl in America two years before. It had got pretty sexual and she'd just sold the pictures. Balls. I tried to see it rationally because obviously he didn't know he was going to meet me, he didn't know he was going to fall in love and most of all I suppose he didn't realise that the person he'd fall for would be in the public eye, but I was still fuming.

When the story came out the headlines in the press were saying things like 'Vicky's new beau's shame' and 'Will Vicky stand by her man?' Bear didn't embarrass himself; he embarrassed me. That was the beginning of the end really. I hadn't seen the pictures but I remember Cami phoning me and telling me how bad they were and I was horrified. Then things went from bad to worse.

When *Ex* started to air and I saw the first episode, Bear was talking about being in love with Megan McKenna. Then he went and kissed Amy. Then he lied about that and called her names, and *then* he shagged her the following week. Who the hell was this lad? Like, I knew he could be cheeky and a bit of a ladies' man but this disrespectful attitude to women and their feelings was something I had never seen before and certainly something I couldn't get on board with.

He was always getting funny with me about blokes and he hated any lads I'd ever been with. He even had a massive problem with Alex, and yet he thought it was OK to have done all of this stuff and, what's more, not told me about. Fine, we weren't together when it all happened, but a bit of warning would have been nice, mate.

The second episode of *Ex* aired the same night as the *Judge* wrap party, and all my friends in the crew were asking me about Bear. One of the sound men, who also worked on *Ex*, told me that he'd heard Bear speak about women in a way he found shocking and he really didn't think I should be with him. I didn't know what to do. Everywhere I turned people were telling me he was wrong for me.

Bear was trying to convince me that it was all in the past before we fell in love, and I *so* wanted to believe him. But every time another episode aired, there was more shit to deal with. One of the celebrity magazines ran a cover line that said 'How much heartache can Vicky handle?' and that crushed me. I was a strong, confident women and yet I was being mugged off by him.

One night I went up to do a PA in Aberdeen and Bear came along with me. Just before we went to sleep my phone beeped and I looked and saw I had a text from Alex. I knew Bear would go mad so I deleted it straight away. But of course he'd heard my phone go off and when he found out who it was we ended up having a massive row about it. Shouting, screaming, waking up the other guests – the whole embarrassing nine yards!

After that Bear told me that I had to block Alex from my phone and not be in contact with him unless we were working together. I think he knew Alex could see right through him and that I listened to what he said and trusted him, and Bear was scared he would be exposed for the dick that he was being.

On the flipside, Alex was telling me that if I stayed with Bear he could no longer be my friend because he couldn't sit by and watch me look stupid. I was in a right fucking pickle. But once the seeds of doubt were planted in my mind it became harder and harder to be with Bear. I'd finish with him one week and get back with him the next because I literally didn't know what to do. I got locked in this ridiculous cycle and it was having hugely a negative effect on my life. In the end, after a very rocky seven months, I walked away.

I knew it was the right thing to do but I missed Bear so badly. I knew I was being weak but I was hurting, so in October we arranged for him to come and see me in

Newcastle and meet my family so we could give it another go. Then just days before he was due to arrive I got a phone call from Zara at *New!* magazine, who I write my column with, telling me she'd seen the following week's *Ex* episode and that Bear kissed his ex-girlfriend Connie, who flew out to Mexico after I got back. What a tosser! I knew I had to get rid of him once and for all and I made the decision right there and then. Bear had promised me that from the minute I appeared on *Ex* and even after I had gone he was the epitome of a gentleman and didn't so much as look at another girl – I believed him . . . I was a mug. And there it was, concrete evidence that he was mugging me off – that he kissed people behind my back and lied to me. So I gave Zara a comment to add to my column, blocked him from everything and I basically finished with him via that. I didn't need to be used by him anymore.

I knew for certain I'd done the right thing breaking up with Bear when I was scrolling through Instagram one day and I saw a fan account from a girl who has always supported me. She'd written this massive rant about how she hated me and Bear being together and that if I got back with him she could no longer respect me. That really hit me hard. Whether I like it or not I have girls looking up to me now. They miss nothing, and this girl could see how destructive the relationship was. I felt like I was basically telling people that if it's OK for me to get treated like that, it's OK for them to get treated like that. And that made me stand up and really take notice – I can take an awful lot of pain and hurt but I won't see some innocent young girl follow in my footsteps because she thinks I've made it acceptable. No way.

Gemma was *still* on at me to see therapists and life coaches Nik and Eva Speakman before I went into the jungle but I had no idea how I could fit it in. And I'll be honest; I didn't love the idea of it. Gemma arranged for me to go but I'd had a big weekend out in Manchester and then loads of photo shoots, interviews and book signings, so the last thing I wanted to do was to go and talk to people who knew nothing about me when I could have a few extra hours in bed.

I arrived at their house near Manchester in a tracksuit and wrapped in my penguin blanket that came everywhere with me, not in the mood at all. I'd had to fill out a long form for them, and they said that they can usually gauge a lot from a person's form, but all they got from mine was that I was very angry. I can't argue with that, particularly as I didn't want to be there – I didn't see how these people could help me when there was nothing wrong with me? But then something crazy happened. Within an hour I went from being a total non-believer – tired, angry and frustrated – to being totally in love with both Nik and Eva. In fact, I was crying my eyes out, sobbing like a baby, because what they did for me was so amazing.

I'd been in the public eye for so long and read so many horrible things about myself that I'd started to believe them and lost sight of who I really was. I was thoroughly convinced I was a bad person. I thought I was the monster everyone said I was. I believed I had nice friends and that I was a good entertainer, but that was it. I knew I had good qualities somewhere, but I thought I had horrible boyfriends and people said horrible things about me because I *was* horrible. The Speakmans sat me down and worked back over my family history to figure out why I believed all of that.

I didn't even know I had things to deal with but they kept unravelling in front of me. I'd never really processed things before because I'd always bottled them up. I powered on through, got drunk and then let everything out in a ridiculously exaggerated way. I'm like my mam – she's always been the strong one that keeps it all together. She takes the weight of the world on her shoulders and will only stop when she's totally worn down. I've learnt from her that you keep going until you can't take any more, and I've mirrored it.

The Speakmans taught me I'm not a bad person. They made me realise that I'm a good person with good friends who does good things. It was like having a spring clean of my mind and they gave me so much clarity. I put on a brave face because that's what everyone wants to see, but I had so much going on inside of me all the time and they helped me to deal with all of that. They helped me stop going round in the same old bitter cycles. I finally tapped into my inner Beyoncé and realised that I genuinely am the strong woman I kept saying I was. It wasn't an act after all; I needed to make some changes and believe in myself. Nik and Eva cemented a lot of things Alex had been teaching me, and suddenly life started to make sense again.

I went to see Nik and Eva a couple of times again after that and I'm going to go again soon. I honestly don't think I could have handled going into the jungle in the headspace I was in before seeing them. I would have lost my temper or cried non-stop or been frustrated. Nik and Eva gave me a deeper understanding of everything and made me feel like I could take on the world. They put me in the perfect frame of mind for the next adventure. And for that, I will be eternally grateful and love them always.

Chapter 21

Welcome To The Jungle

I had to get all my ducks in a row before I flew over to Australia so I did my AW/15 shoot for my Honeyz range as well as shooting our first national advert with my Honeyz girls and friends Cally Jane, Danielle Armstrong and Jem Lucy. I got everything sorted with Mini V, filming cooking tutorials and workout videos so we were good to launch the company as a subscription model in January, something I'd been wanting to do for ages! And finally I finished up everything for my second novel, *A Christmas Kiss*, including doing a national book tour and loads of press. I had a massive leaving party with all my mates in Newcastle the week before I went, and all everyone kept asking me was how I felt about eating bugs. I just said, 'Have you seen some of my ex boyfriends? I've had worse things in my mouth. I should be fine.' I was so excited and ready for it. Nothing was going to get in my way.

I'd seen the line-up for the show and I couldn't wait to be in the jungle with Jorgi Porter because I'd fallen in love with her when she was on *First Dates*. I thought I'd definitely flirt with Spencer, and I'd pick Duncan Bannatyne's brain. I see myself as a little entrepreneur and he is like a business god to me. I wanted Tony Hadley to sing *Gold* to me, and I wanted to shadow box with Chris Eubank. I was well happy my new camp-mates. And then I found out about Ferne McCann going in and suddenly that excitement dissipated.

Ferne and I had bad blood because of that 'date' I'd gone on with Charlie. I'd seen her at a few events and it had been *OK*, but I knew it could go one of two ways. I told myself not to pre-judge her because I hate it when people do that to me, but I couldn't help getting wound up before we'd even spoken.

I was kept in lockdown for a week and then I found out I was going in later to everyone else with Ferne and Spencer. I didn't know how to feel. The producers swore blind it was a good thing because it meant I wasn't competing with as many people straight off, but I didn't really care about that! I cared about meeting my other campmates and bonding with everyone. I just wanted to get myself in there. I was desperate for the experience to start – I was certainly not playing hard to get with the jungle.

Walking into the jungle for the first time was just amazing. Yes, it was hot and there were creepy crawlies and it was muddy, but that didn't bother me one bit. I got dropped off by a helicopter wearing a maxi dress and heels, and as soon as I changed into my shorts and boots I was good to go on my jungle adventure – weirdly I just felt at home.

Spencer and I bonded straight away because we were both so excited to be there. We felt really lucky – like every reality TV tit in the country wanted to be in the jungle and here we were, the two luckiest tits in the UK! Then Ferne arrived and I was waiting for her to get on my nerves like she does on *TOWIE*. She's always arguing on there and it really bothers me. But she never did – not once! In fact, she was the complete opposite; she was the dream and I felt terrible for misjudging her. I couldn't believe I'd got her so wrong. She was just like me: yes, we can both be feisty and we can row, but that element of our personalities has been totally exploited by reality TV. It's all anyone had wanted to focus on, so much so our other *good* qualities had been ignored. We'd all been pigeonholed. Spencer was the top shagger,

Ferne was the troublemaker and I was the bitch. But we went into the jungle to smash those stereotypes and prove people wrong and I think it was this common goal that bonded us all instantly!

I was absolutely devastated when Spencer went. We weren't given any kind of explanation and I was gutted I didn't get a chance to say goodbye to him. We were told he'd left because of a medical condition but I knew he was as fit as a fiddle, so I didn't hear the whole story about the steroids until I got out. I only spent a couple of days with him but we couldn't stop smiling at each other. Would I have done a bit with Spencer? Probably. But then that would have changed who I was in there, so if anything I was stronger and showed more of myself because I was on my own and I can't argue that that was a good thing.

There was a story in the papers about Spencer trying to crack on to me once before, and I can confirm that was true. He tried to chat me up over Twitter and then he sent me a happy Christmas message. That led to him calling and telling me he was in 'some god-awful hotel waiting for his flight to the Caribbean'. I was sat in a bedsit in Dunfermline waiting to do a PA. He said he was spending New Year in St Bart's and I replied, 'That's funny, because I'll be in St Helen's!' I had thought I was being funny, comparing the Wigan nightspot and my next club PA location to his luxury

Caribbean hideaway but unfortunately it didn't go down well. I knew it was game over so I thought it would be funny to completely exaggerate my Geordie accent. He couldn't understand a bloody word I was saying and he made his excuses and hung up. Funnily enough we didn't go on a date.

My worst day in the jungle the entire time I was there was actually the first day Ferne and I arrived because it was so obvious the other campmates didn't want us there. I could feel it; it was palpable. Certain people were more obvious about it than others, namely Yvette, Susannah and Brian. They didn't think we understood the three days of 'struggle' they'd already been through. It was ridiculous. Hats off to Susannah because she admitted she had massive pre-conceptions about me and Ferne when we walked in and she hated our shows and everything they stood for. She's completely entitled to her opinion, and I'm pleased to say she also confided in us that by the time her experience was over she'd totally changed her mind but, still, for us to walk in and not feel welcome was horrible. People actually talked over me at times because they were so disinterested, but I wore them down eventually. I'm like a friendship ninja – I strike when you least expect it and make you love me! Duncan Bannatyne didn't know what hit him!

So many people have asked me what Lady C was like since I've been out and I'll be honest, I had mixed feelings about her before I went in. I'd heard a few whispers that she was a diva and a nightmare, but people also said she was very entertaining so I was intrigued by her.

To be fair to her, she was lovely to me and Ferne from the word go. She was so friendly and really the only one who properly opened her arms to us from the start. She wasn't a problem personally for me at all, but she did become toxic for the environment and when she eventually left the camp it felt like a dark cloud had lifted. I think Lady C's an amazing woman in a lot of respects – feisty, strong and formidable – but at the same time she went at the right time. Camp became fun again and Duncan and Tony were finally able to relax. Even if you don't want to get sucked into the arguments, you're in such a small area it's really hard not to, so we all felt like we were involved and it brought us down – that's not how I wanted to remember this experience!

The only person I argued with at all in the camp was Yvette, and that's because she accused me of pandering to Lacy C. I was livid. I don't think Yvette knew an awful lot about me before I went in the jungle and it was because of this I think she made that mistake. I told her she'd made a mistake in taking my kindness for weakness. I may not have agreed with everything Lady C was doing and saying but at the end of the day she was an older woman and I could have never argued with her – I was brought up to respect my elders. I knew I was right for standing up for myself but I really gave her what for, and as I walked off I thought 'I've just fucked myself there. That's going to look really bad'. I was worried people would think I was just like I had been portrayed on *Geordie Shore* and I was really beating myself up about it.

I bumped into Kieron and he told me I'd done the right thing, and then Yvette ran after me and apologised and it was forgotten. I don't agree with pack mentality – I wasn't going to follow the crowd just because everyone was slagging off Lady C, and Yvette picked on the wrong person. They didn't actually show the argument in the end, so maybe it wasn't as dramatic as I thought. Your mind can play tricks on you in the jungle as you've got too much time on your hands ... and maybe that was one of those instances.

Pretty much everyone in there was great once they got used to me and Ferne being there, but it took a little while. Tony Hadley was a darling and the dad of the camp, and I couldn't have done it without Duncan. What you see is what you get. Did I genuinely fancy him? No, it was just that there was no one else to look at. I could hardly put a shift in with George – I was more like his ma!

George and Jorgi were amazing, and I'm gutted more wasn't made out of my friendship with Jorgi because we spent so much time together. I think the producers liked the dynamic between me and Ferne so they wanted to concentrate on that but I think it's important that I let you all know that Jorgi and me got on and still do get on like a house on fire. She's a fun and hilarious little pocket rocket and I love her!

As for the others? Susannah was like my mam and Kieron was like my annoying big brother. Meeting Chris was surreal because I'd grown up with my parents spending £14.99 on pay-per-view to watch him fight. He was a true gent and not what I expected. He wasn't cut out for the jungle at all, bless him.

I will hold my hands up and say I did get narked off with Brian sometimes. He was very competitive and *really* wanted to win. He thought he had it in the bag. Brian's the only person you visibly see me get salty with because I overheard him saying he didn't like the change in camp when me and Ferne came in. He didn't know I was listening and I was fuming because we didn't *choose* to go in late. Did he think I wanted to look like the second act? I got confirmed back in June probably before any of they did, and I wanted nothing more than to swan in there like William large penis and own the jungle but instead I got dropped in late like an afterthought having to fight to get the campmates to see me as an equal! So I lost my temper and I moaned a lot to Ferne about him. Obvs.

Brian was a bit of a drama queen to be honest, and every time he came back from a trial it was like *War and Peace*. He had to describe everything in such great detail I felt like I'd done the fucking trial myself. He loves an audience and wanted it to be 'the Brian show' at all times. But I do like him and outside of the camp we get on a hell of a lot better! In the jungle everything is magnified and the smallest disagreement can seem monumental.

The boredom in camp did get to me sometimes. And the moaning. People would whinge about not having enough food or not getting Dingo dimes, and they would argue like petty children. I don't think everyone appreciated the amazing opportunity they'd been given. And I *knew* that some of them were being paid a bucket load more than me. Not that I minded because I got so much more out of it, but it did make me think 'stop your complaining!'. I got stuck into everything and tried to avoid moaning. I collected wood, I cleared up the mess and I even emptied the dunny – which was grim but having a purpose just made the time fly! It was also really nice to feel integral to the running of camp, like I was helping out my other campmates and I liked that.

When I was really bored I made my own entertainment. One day I took Lady C aside and played Snog, Marry, Avoid with her. After explaining the rules, I gave her Kieron, Chris and Duncan as options. She couldn't choose between Kieron and Chris, which I took to mean she'd have a threesome with them, and she said she'd avoid Duncan. No surprises there. In return she gave me Prince Harry, Prince William and Prince Charles, and I opted to snog William, marry Harry and avoid Charles, and she said she'd do the same. Strangely enough me and the big LC actually had a lot more in common than people would think and I salute her for making the series the success it was! Lady C has a wicked sense of humour. She was a real tinker.

The odd thing about the jungle is that you've got no clue how you or anyone else is coming across to the outside world. Even on *Geordie Shore* I could kind of guess what people thought, but in there I was clueless. I had no idea how I was being portrayed. Before I went in Jake Quickenden gave me some great advice which was 'be yourself, don't be a fanny in the trials, get stuck in in camp, don't sleep through the day, and choose your battles.' I managed all of those things apart from sleeping during the day sometimes. You do get surprisingly tired in there. Viewers just see you popping up in the trials like it was just next door to the camp or something but sometimes it was a 30–40 minute walk to get there, and the heat is exhausting.

The hunger didn't bother me because actually we ate pretty well. We had rice and beans for breakfast and lunch, but we got so many stars through the trials there was only one night when we had rice and beans for dinner too. I've always been quite adventurous with food and I'll try anything once so the weird stuff didn't bother me at all. I wasn't that keen on gnawing the meat off a crocodile leg when it still had feet, and when a wallaby turned up with its tail I didn't like the idea of eating Skippy, but I cracked on. No wonder I was the only person in the history of *I'm a Celebrity* to put *on* weight while I was in there. I am the true definition of a greedy little piglet.

On a normal day I'll have eggs and avocado for breakfast, a protein shake and salad for lunch and vegetables with chicken or fish for tea, so I only put on weight if I'm smashing the booze at Christmas or something. But in the jungle I was eating rice and beans every day and we weren't exactly struggling for food because of how brave we all were as a camp.

My big pre-Australia plan had been to take a month off and get down the gym every day so I was in really good shape. But, needless to say, I only ended up with three days off in total, so I wasn't in my best shape. I'd been so crazily busy all I got to do were two personal training sessions and a quick sunbed. I was hardly 'jungle ready'. As a result people started saying that all my images in magazines are photoshopped, but the pictures everyone were comparing me in the jungle to were the ones where I'd just done my fitness DVD and I was about eight stone. I weighed about nine stone ten when I went into the jungle and I never once pretended to be something I wasn't. I'll admit I've looked better at times, but life gets in the way of going to the gym twice a day and existing on raw carrots. I refuse to apologise for the fact I'm a normal busy woman and my body fluctuates. If anything I think people should apologise to *me* for being so narrow-minded and judgemental and that they only have one idea of beauty. I went into the jungle off the back of a really busy year and a lot of fun nights out with my mates. I'm not a fucking supermodel nor have I ever pretended to be! I wish people would give women a break. Beauty comes in all shapes and sizes.

I think as I get older I'm becoming more relaxed about my body and my weight. I don't mean I'm going to be complacent and act like a giant sloth; I just mean that if I spend Christmas with an IV drip of Baileys in my arm and I put on a few pounds, so be it. It's not the end of the world and I can always lose it again. I can just pick up where I left off. There are more important things in life – like actually living and enjoying yourself – and I don't beat myself up over it.

The biggest highlight of my time in the jungle were the trials. I loved them all! Though my favourite two were Badvent Calendar and Twisted tombola. It was weird when I did trials because something kind of took over. The physical element kind of switched off and all

I was thinking about was winning stars. I'd never realised it before but I must be an adrenalin junkie because I loved the buzz and the pressure. I thrive on doing things people think I can't. The bugs, height, animals ... Nothing affected me – I was just focused and determined.

I definitely would have done an eating trial, but the closest I got was Cocktails and Screams task where I had a Shlong Island Iced Tea, which was basically blended camel peen. To be fair it tasted better than some things I've drunk on holiday ...

The squirrel task was one of the best things that's ever happened to me in my life. I was literally praying George didn't want to do it. I don't actually think I would have let him. Flying through the jungle dressed as a giant squirrel with boy-band heartthrob George Shelley will forever be one of the highlights of my life!

Considering I like dressing up and being all glam, amazingly I loved the fact I didn't have to wear make-up in camp, and that I could roll out of bed each morning and wear the same thing I'd slept in. We were all allowed to request one luxury item to take in with us and mine was such a letdown. I asked for in a bottle of tequila or a lilo, but both were vetoed, so in the end I asked for a pillow so I could sleep well – thought I'd choose function over fun. But because Susannah had a pillow I ended up with a shit, bright pink fluffy cushion instead. Lady C had several pillows *and* her pearls and all I got was a hideous cushion.

Not surprisingly you do think about winning when you're in there and who you think is your biggest competition. No matter what anyone says, everyone is in it to win it. I was convinced Tony Hadley was going to win because I thought he'd get the housewives' votes. He was such a nice guy, but then he started to get down about missing his family and he got dragged into the Lady C drama. If you argued with her you were done for. When I realised it wasn't going to be Tony I thought it was Jorgi, but then she got exhausted and went really quiet. Then I thought it was George because of all his young fans, and everyone else in the camp thought so too. Literally no one thought it would be me. There was one day towards the end when Duncan took me aside and said he thought I'd got it, but I really didn't believe him. You just never knew. I didn't mind who won if it wasn't going to me, but I didn't want it to be anyone who had whinged. I wanted it to be someone who deserved it and I think if it had to have been anyone else I would have liked it to be Ferne!

I think some of the other campmates were surprised I won because they didn't 'get' my humour. I don't think knew what I was capable of doing on the jungle cam or in the trials. People loved to come back after a trial and wax lyrical about how amazing they were whereas I'd come back and just say, 'Nine stars. Smashed it.' They were more talk, I was more action, and I think that came across in the end. That's the only thing I can think won it for me. I found out afterwards that I got 70 per cent of the final votes, and I was top of the votes every night. I was stunned when I was told and to tell you the truth I still can't get my head around it.

When it was down to just me and George he was really diplomatic and said that he was happy just to have got to the final and didn't mind if he won. I thought 'fuck that! It's lovely of you to say that but I want to win!' And how did I feel the moment when I realised I'd actually won? I can't really explain how it felt. It's hard to put it into words. I had wanted it *so* badly. All I know is when my name was read out it was honestly the happiest moment of my entire life. The first things I thought were 'where's my mam? Where are my mates? Where's my phone? Where's my agent? Where are Ant and Dec? Oh, and fuck everyone who thought I couldn't do this!' I felt so thankful and grateful and humbled I suppose – what had I done to deserve this?

Making my mam proud was one of the best things about it for me. I hated that in the past I could disappoint her so much that she was embarrassed to be my mam. So to finally be able to do something she could be proud of was unbelievable. I felt the same way about my friends. They've had to defend me so much in the past and this may finally give them a fucking break. People who were close to me were sick of knowing that I was a good person, but having to stick up for me when people thought I was a nightmare or a monster. For once I didn't let them down. I silenced all of my critics in the best way possible – by being me and winning. That was the real win.

When I walked over the bridge and saw my mam at the end I didn't know what to do with myself. I was told to stand on this star to get my photo taken and I couldn't find it because I was flapping so much and being a fanny. All I wanted to do was hug my mam, and when she ran towards me and that was it. I just went. Bawled my tits off. Tears flying everywhere.

I had no idea what had been going on in the outside world and I didn't know that people like Cheryl Cole were rooting for me. Amanda Holden and Carl Fogarty had tweeted about me and I was beside myself when I found out. I kept saying to myself 'the nation doesn't hate you any more Vicky!' People had started saying things like, 'She's really nice actually!' as if it was a big shock, which was funny. At long bloody last I proved to myself that I really wasn't this awful person I'd told myself I was for so many years.

It was lovely hanging out with Ant and Dec at the wrap party when the show finished. They're so amazing – they took me aside at the wrap party and, after doing some tequila shots, told me they'd got into trouble because people thought they were showing me favouritism. I don't think they did at all. We just had good banter. But I suppose that's Geordies for you isn't it? We just get so excited when we met one of our own! Those lads are the nicest blokes in the industry and it was a true honour to work alongside them! I am in love with both of them.

One of the cameramen pulled me to one side at the wrap party and said he'd worked on the show for fifteen series and I was the best winner they'd ever had. When I asked him why he said it was because I knew his name. He said the crew were so pleased I'd won because I'd taken the time to get to know everyone. Then Matt, a great bloke who plans the trials, pretended to be really pissed off with me and said, 'Pattison I want a word with you! I work on those trials for a year and you came in and made them look too easy! You even beat some of my records!' We laughed and I got him a drink to ease the pain of being beaten by a girl.

The whole night was amazing. Everyone was coming up and congratulating me and I even offered to get Kiosk Keith a tequila. He said no – but I think it's because he thought I was trying to put a shift in with him. I had to be carried out of the wrap party by a particularly burly security guard at the end of the night, which I thought was my first duty as queen!

The one thing that really upset me when I came out of the jungle was the fact that Gaz had slagged me off, saying I was putting on an act and calling me bipolar, which is so disrespectful to anyone who suffers from that condition. I've never had a bad word to say about him in the press but the minute I got a bit of success he couldn't wait to stick the knife in. What he said was strong and hateful, but at the end of the day, it came from jealousy.

There are rumours that Gaz also had a meeting about going in to that series of *I'm a Celebrity*. If that's true then obviously he didn't get on the show and I did, so I reckon a lot of what he said could have been because he was bitter and jealous. He had the same chance as me, but the difference between us was that I was right for it and I was ready for it. The other big difference is that I would have backed him if he had got in. I would have voted for him and supported him, but he couldn't bring himself to do the same for me. Instead he flew out to Australia, started rumours he was going to be Spencer's replacement – which he never was – and then tried to stop me from winning.

But at the end of the day his comments weren't detrimental to me, they were detrimental to him. It's taken me a long time to realise it but when someone says horrible things about someone else it only hurts one person, and that's themselves.

I don't want people like Gary in my life. If I see him I'll say to him, 'Good luck to you Gaz. I'm sure you'll be successful and I'll never hate on that, but I don't want to be around negative people.' What he did was transparent and it was embarrassing and it showed him up for what he was.

I feel the same way about Marnie. She'll do anything to get press attention, and she gets that by talking about me. So to be honest, I don't want to give her the time of day.

Anyway, enough about them, let's get back to *me*! Touching back down in the UK was mad because there were about twenty photographers at the airport snapping away and I was there in my tracksuit with my messy bun on top of my head. The next couple of weeks were a whirlwind of interviews, TV appearances and a few cheeky nights out. Chris Eubank managed to get me ringside seats to the Anthony Joshua fight, and I went to the *The X Factor* final where Cheryl Cole got me up on stage and told me I was a Geordie queen. People say never meet your heroes? Well she is proof that statement is wrong – she blew me away! Stunningly beautiful, genuine and warm – I fangirled her so hard and even asked for a selfie. One of the highlights was doing a couple of signing events for my novel, *A Christmas Kiss*, where the turnout was insane; my homecoming signing in Newcastle was so special. None of it felt real.

I wasn't ready for everything that happened to me at all and things got overwhelming quite quickly. I had a night out with my agents just before Christmas and I was on Grimmy's Radio 1 show the following morning. I was so hungover and he was so lovely to me, but when I got in the car after the interview I burst into tears. Once again, everything was getting on top of me and I just wanted to go home. And, once again, it was my own fault because I still couldn't say no to anything. I was enjoying the buzz of everything but I was also scared that it would end and life would go back to the way it was before, so I kept on pushing myself. Gemma sent me home that night and I had an evening at home chilling on my sofa with my family, and that sorted me out.

My life has changed beyond all recognition in such an amazing way, but I know that I have to be careful not to let things run away with me again. I don't want to get burnt out and end up in the same place I've been in the past. I used to walk around and no one would know who I was. I might get the occasional double take, but now I can't even sit in the back of a taxi without the cabbie recognising me. I feel like I've won over a nation of grandmas and white van men and it's so brilliant, but also quite crazy at times.

I won't lie; as well as the post-Grimmy meltdown

there have been a couple of other times where there have been tears, just because I don't really know how to cope with the intense attention. I've gone from having loads of people hating me and having to be really defensive, to everyone wanting a picture and asking me to call their mam, and while it's lovely, it's a big thing to get my head around. I'm trying to stay humble and down to earth and nice in a world where it's very easy to become a tosser. It's a tricky transition period but it's very exciting.

I'm on cloud nine and I've got an amazing group of people around me now like Casey, Gavin, Alex and my family and friends from home. That's the most important thing to me. That, and not having a nervous breakdown. Some people I haven't seen for years have come crawling out of the woodwork and tried to be friendly again but I know now who I can and can't trust. It's horrible that I have to have that filter because once I'm friends with someone we're friends for life and I'm very loyal, but I have to be a bit mindful.

I had a really good chat with Rylan Clarke and Eamonn Holmes when I went on *Big Brother's Bit on the Side*, which helped me to understand things more clearly. Rylan said to me that no one had thought anything of him in the same way they didn't think anything of me, and then we both did big shows – me the jungle, him *Big Brother* – and we totally changed people's perceptions.

He admitted that it took him a while to get used to everyone being so nice. Eamonn gave me some amazing advice – that it's more important what I say 'no' to right now than what I say 'yes' to, and I've taken that on board. If anyone knows how it all works, it's those two. I'm meeting so many heroes of mine and successful people within the industry. I really do feel so lucky.

I've had some great meetings with ITV since I left the jungle, and they're trying to find where I fit in with them. Apparently when I did *Loose Women* before Christmas the ratings doubled, so I was really hoping that may become a regular thing. I absolutely love being on there and being around other strong, ballsy women. It doesn't feel like work – more a night out with the lasses.

I've been embraced into the bosom of ITV, and let me tell you, it is warm and it is safe and it is lovely. On top of that *Judge Geordie* is looking likely to be recommissioned – I love the fact I'm international talent with MTV. I'm also doing a lot of pilots for panel shows, and I've been talking about doing some documentaries. It's ridiculous when I think about how things have changed in a year, and they're still changing every day. I'm going to take every good opportunity that comes my way, but I'm also going to take holidays!

No matter how much things take off I have to remember that the reason I did so well on *I'm a Celebrity* is because I was myself. People got to see who I really am, and they liked it. And so do I. So I tell myself every day not to forget who I am and where I came from because you know I don't ever want to be anything other than me. The real me.

Acknowledgements

To my fantastic mother Caroll, to whom I owe every-thing – from my confidence to my eye colour. In these last couple years I have learnt so much more about you – not just as a mother but what you are capable of as a woman. You're my inspiration and my hero and I hope I continue to make you proud. Nothing I have achieved would have been possible without you. I can't thank you enough for your continued and unwavering support.

My lovable dad John, you are an amazing man and I don't think you realise how much I need you and how much you've given me – for starters your love of reading and passion for the written word is evidently alive in me too. It's been one of your greatest gifts to me and I can't THANK YOU enough. I love you.

My incredible sister, Laura. I do not know how people

survive without one – you are my support system, my sparring partner, my conscience, my partner-in-crime, the biggest pain in my arse and my best friend in the world … You have saved me so many times and no doubt will save me many more before we're through – I hope you know that without you I could not have achieved a fraction of what I have. I love you.

To all my incredible friends who I've shared so many memories with and basically this book would not be half as funny without! But with special mention to two people who I don't think I could live without, Alex Cannon and Gavin Foord – I don't measure our friendship on how long we've known each other but more how big of an impact you've had on my life. And you two lads have knocked me for six – you're the best. Please don't ever leave me.

To my hardworking and patient agents Gemma Wheatley and Nadia King – you have helped me achieve so many of my dreams and professionally I have never felt safer and more sure about anything than my decision to join Mokkingbird. On a personal level – I love you both dearly and can't THANK YOU enough for putting up with me and seeing something that many others didn't.

Steve Regan, Kerri Taylor, Craig Orr and everyone at MTV for giving me some incredible opportunities and this amazing platform to achieve my dreams!

Acknowledgements

The *I'm a Celeb* booking team – David and Micky and the producers Richard Cowles and Becca Walker – you helped me tick the biggest item off my bucket list and gave me the experience of a lifetime and for that I will be eternally grateful.

Sally Shelford, the fabulous *Loose Women* editor, THANK YOU for allowing me to get paid to be a mouthy cow.

The three musketeers over at ITV who have made so many of my dreams a reality: Angela Jain, Claire Zowlker and Peter Fincham.

Jordan Paramor – the best ghost-writer I could have hoped for, a talented writer, a great listener and just an all-round wonderful woman!

Hannah, Rhiannon, David, Manpreet, Jo and all of the team at Little, Brown. It's been a pleasure working with you all!

Brian Aris, Mikey Phillips and Tracey Winwood for the gorgeous cover.

David, Fiona and everyone at MBA Literary Agents – thank you for making this happen.

And to everyone else who has believed in me and supported me . . . Thank you x

Read on for an extract from Vicky's debut novel

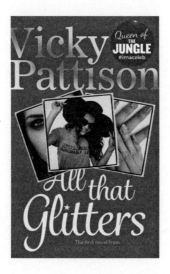

Out now

And look out for her second incredible novel,
A Christmas Kiss also out now!

Prologue

Issy Jones felt fat warm tears sliding down her cheeks. She grasped her dad's hand tightly; it felt cold and unfamiliar. She barely recognised the man lying in front of her on the hospital bed, multiple tubes and wires attached to him. He had the same familiar dark hair and even features she knew so well, but his face was pale and so, so still. She squeezed his hand tighter as the machines continued to bleep around them.

'I promise I will do anything, absolutely anything if you get better, Dad,' Issy whispered, unsure if he could hear her. 'And I'll never leave you again. Just be all right. Please, Dad. *Please.*'

Still holding her dad's hand, she slumped down in the hard, uncomfortable hospital chair next to him and rested her head on his arm, remembering how safe she used to feel when he hugged her as a child. She didn't want to let go, afraid if she did she would lose him forever, and she wouldn't be able to bear that. Even the thought of it brought tears to her eyes and Issy breathed deeply, trying not to despair.

It had all happened so suddenly. Only the day before she'd been working on an assignment at her hairdressing college in London, when she got a call from her brother, Zach, shakily telling her that their dad had suffered a heart attack. She'd dropped everything, rushed to the station and caught the first train she could home. A tear-filled three hours later, Zach had met her at Manchester station and had warned her that their dad was in a bad way. But nothing could have prepared her for seeing him look so frail.

The man in the hospital bed, wired up to machines, wasn't the gentle giant who had cared for her growing up. Issy's dad was a tall, handsome, muscular man, the years working in his garage had seen to that, but the figure in front of her seemed smaller and older than the man she knew.

The change in him had been so shocking her legs had almost given way when she'd first seen him. Zach had grabbed her to stop her from falling, and then held her while she cried. Her mum, Debs, who always had something to say, was silent as they stood together watching his chest rise and fall.

The three of them stayed by his bedside all night. At some point Zach had dropped off to sleep, and while he softly snored Issy and her mum had talked for hours, trying to keep each other's spirits up. But it hadn't worked. The fear was visible on their faces and in their trembling voices. Neither of them had wanted to think about what life would be like without the man who made them feel safe.

Issy took another deep breath, reminding herself to stay positive.

'Issy?' a husky voice said. She lifted her head off her dad's arm and tried to blink the tears away.

'Dad?' She wondered if she had imagined it. She felt a rush of hope as she saw his eyes flicker towards her.

'Isabelle, are you crying?' His voice was croaky and full of concern.

'Of course not,' Issy replied, brushing her cheeks. 'What's with the Isabelle? You only call me Isabelle when I've done something wrong.'

'I don't want you crying, kiddo. Help me out and find someone who can tell me what's really going on here, will you . . . ?'

'I'll call someone and get some help,' she said, getting up and reluctantly letting go of his hand.

She walked out into the corridor and took several long, deep breaths. A few hours after he'd been admitted the doctors had declared her dad 'stable', but she hadn't believed them. Not until now. This was what she'd been praying for, yet she still couldn't quite believe it.

After steadying herself, Issy grabbed the first nurse she saw, a young woman about her own age who looked perky enough to be early in her shift, so when Issy explained that her dad was awake she followed right after. She was the only member of the family left at the hospital and felt like a child, hopelessly out of her depth. Her brother had gone to check on the garage their dad owned and ran, while her mum had gone home for some rest. She wished they were both here.

When Issy followed the nurse back into the room, her dad had barely moved but his eyes were wide open and there was a sense of awareness about him. Relief flooded through her. He really was going to be all right.

'You gave us quite a fright, Mr Jones,' the nurse said sternly but with a smile.

'Yes you bloody well did,' Issy added, flashing him a beaming smile.

'Hey, love, sorry about the fright, but please, call me Kev.' He winked at the nurse.

'Really, Dad? One minute you're at death's door the next you're putting a shift in with a nurse!' Issy shook her head but she was still grinning.

Before he could reply the door to the ward burst open and her mum ran into the room clutching her yapping little dog, Princess Tiger-Lily, followed closely by Zach. She immediately launched herself on her husband, showering him with kisses.

'Debs!' Kev spluttered.

'You can't have dogs in here,' said the nurse sounding shocked and angry. 'We don't allow animals in the hospital and your husband is still *very* ill.'

'You shouldn't have brought her in here, love,' Kev said quietly. It was an effort to lift his hand but he gently stroked the side of Debs's face.

'I did try to stop her,' Zach said, turning his attention to the flustered nurse. He mouthed a silent 'sorry' at her and she visibly melted. Issy rolled her eyes. Her brother could charm his way into a nun's pants.

'Oh for God's sake, he's alive, that's all that matters. And surely you know how important pets are for patient rehabilitation?' Debs said, wagging a finger at the nurse.

'Just be careful. There are a lot of wires,' she simpered, eyes still fixed upon Zach. 'I'll go and see where the doctor's got to.'

'You do that, love,' Debs replied with a smile before carefully placing Princess at the foot of the bed and launching herself onto Kev again.

'Mum, you'll give him another heart attack carrying on like that,' Zach half-joked.

The nurse backed out of the room, her gaze firmly fixed on Zach, who had been pretending not to notice.

Issy stood in the small, grey hospital room surveying her family. She couldn't believe all their happiness had nearly been taken away from them. A rush of pure love filled her as she looked around at them all; her dad, her mum, Zach, even Princess Tiger-Lily, right now she'd even forgive all those times her barking interrupted a much-needed Saturday morning hangover lie-in.

It wasn't normal, it was quite far from normal, but they were hers and she loved everything about them. She meant what she had said before her dad had woken up; she would never leave them again.

Chapter One

'So, what are we doing today, Vi?' Issy asked, wielding a pair of scissors and standing behind Violet, one of her regulars. They were in A Cut Above, her mum's hairdressing salon in Salford, on the outskirts of Manchester. It was the most popular salon in the area but that was because most of the clients belonged to the blue rinse brigade. Although there were a few younger customers, it wasn't exactly what you'd call edgy, and Issy longed to get her creative hands on people who wanted more than a trim and tint. Issy had asked what Vi wanted, already knowing the answer. She'd known Vi and many of her mum's other clients since she was a little girl.

'I just want a little bit off, duck. Not too short, mind. I don't want to look like a poodle,' Vi replied. Issy nodded. With her tightly permed white hair, no matter what she did Vi *always* ended up looking like a poodle.

'Of course not, Vi, God forbid,' Issy said, smiling warmly at Violet in the mirror.

Issy got to work on Vi's hair when suddenly a wave of nostalgia hit and she was catapulted back to her days at The Hair Academy. It felt like a lifetime ago that she'd walked away from her course.

The Hair Academy was the most illustrious hairdressing college in the UK, and Issy had worked her arse off to get a place on one of their courses. They only took a handful of students each year so competition was fierce, but back then Issy was full of confidence – and had the talent to back it up. Prior to her dad's heart attack, she'd been so driven and ambitious. Whether she ended up styling hair for magazine shoots or working backstage at fashion shows – one way or another she had been determined to make a name for herself.

It was a far cry from where she was now.

Issy looked around the salon. She'd practically grown up here – hairdressing was in her blood. Her mum had started teaching her how to style hair when she was barely a teenager. She'd practised on dummy heads, swept up hair, made notes – whatever it took to learn the trade. As a young girl, it had amazed Issy that people could come into the salon looking pretty ordinary and leave feeling amazing. Hair was powerful, she truly believed that. Hairdressing was about more than just the physical, there was a psychology to it too. People poured their hearts out when they sat in the hairdresser's chair and Issy understood that she was much more than a pair of scissors to them, they put their trust into her when they sat down in her chair.

Issy shook her head to dispel her nostalgia and tuned back into Vi's chatter about her latest ailments. Issy missed the glamour and the creative challenges of The Hair Academy, but her mum's salon had heart and the clients were important to her. They needed her and so did her family. Readjusting to living at home again had been hard but Issy had never once doubted that leaving her course and coming back to Salford had been the right decision.

A melodic hum of chatter filled the air. A Cut Above was a medium-sized salon and as well as Issy and her mother, Karen and Brenda, two other stylists, also worked there. Alice, their trainee, completed their small team and though at the moment she was shampooing, sweeping up hair and making tea, she was bright and good with the clients so Issy knew it wouldn't be long before she had the skills and confidence to start tackling cuts on her own. It was how they'd all got their start.

'Thanks, Alice,' Issy said as Alice delivered a cup of milky tea to Violet. Alice smiled back at Issy and said hello to Vi, before going off with her broom.

There was a commotion as the door opened and Issy turned to see Zach walking through the salon. He'd clearly come from the garage – it was just around the corner so they were always popping in and out – as he was wearing his oil-covered overalls, and his cuffs were rolled up to reveal his full-sleeve tattoo. Since their dad's heart attack, Zach had taken charge of all the manual labour at the garage and Issy's dad had taken a step back and focused on the office work. Kev insisted that he didn't mind the change but Issy secretly thought that he did miss getting his hands dirty.

'Ooo,' Vi said, turning her head suddenly and almost losing an ear in the process. Issy pulled her scissors quickly out of harm's way, she knew how Vi could get around Zach, or any young man, in fact. 'Zach, hi!' Vi waved flirtatiously as Zach made his way over to them.

'Hey, gorgeous,' he said to Vi. She blushed like a girl a quarter of her age and Issy shook her head.

At six foot two, Zach shared the same dark hair as Issy and their dad. He was definitely a good-looking lad, and had been for as long as Issy could remember. She'd been one of the most popular girls in school simply because girls thought they could get close to Zach through Issy. And he was still one of the fittest lads in Salford – not that Issy would ever tell him that. Zach definitely didn't have confidence issues.

'What are you doing here?' Issy asked.

'I had a few minutes so I thought I'd pop in for a sunbed.'

'Are you going to be naked?' Vi asked hopefully.

Issy's eyes sparkled with amusement. 'Vi, you're old enough to be his nan,' she rebuked.

'I am not,' Vi replied indignantly.

'No, Vi, I wear boxers in there,' Zach said conspiratorially, lifting his T-shirt to snap at the waistband of his Calvin Kleins and exposing a strip of muscular stomach as he did so. 'Got to protect little Zach!'

Issy looked around the salon. Alice was almost the same colour as Issy's crimson nails, Vi was grinning from ear-to-ear and Karen couldn't keep her eyes off Zach's groin.

'Right, that's enough.' Debs shouted, coming out from the back fresh from cleaning the sunbeds. 'Zachary Jones, get into that sunbed and leave everyone else to cut hair.' Zach threw Vi a final cheeky wink and then disappeared.

Vi chatted non-stop about Zach for the rest of her haircut. Issy shared a smile with her mum who was sorting out accounts and manning reception. Zach had taken on the lion's share of the work at the garage for the last three years and she was proud of him – despite the fact that he flirted with old ladies. Although in fairness he flirted with everyone and everything – dogs, pot plants, a packet of chocolate digestives. Nothing and no one was immune to Zachary Jones's charms.

Issy was just finishing up with Vi when the salon door banged open again and her father appeared.

'Hello, gorgeous,' Debs said coming round from the reception desk to kiss her husband, wrapping her arms around him in a display of affection that made Issy feel like an awkward teenager.

'Hi, love.' Kev looked around the salon and smiled. 'Hi, ladies.'

'Two handsome men in one day,' Vi said. 'I shall never recover.' Issy thought, not for the first time, that despite her age, Vi was still a saucy old flirt.

'What other handsome man?' Kev asked, sounding perplexed.

'Your son, love. He's having a sunbed.'

'*That's* where the bugger got to. He said he had to pop out for teabags half an hour ago. I should have known where he'd be.' Kev looked annoyed but deep down he was more amused by Zach than angry. Father and son were like peas in a pod, but Zach was the new generation, for sure. He took care of himself in a way that Kev could never understand. Zach was a man's man, but a well-groomed one.

At that moment Zach reappeared, a few shades darker than when he'd come in.

'Bollocks!' he said on seeing his dad. He ducked down behind Vi's chair. 'Protect me, Vi.'

'Any time, love,' Vi said, a wicked glint in her eye.

Zach laughed. 'What are you doing here, Dad?' he asked, standing up but still keeping a good distance.

'Well, I was hoping for a word in private with our Issy,' he said, shuffling awkwardly from foot to foot.

'What about?' Debs asked.

'Yes, what about?' Vi repeated. Vi loved coming to the salon – it was better than an episode of *Coronation Street*.

Issy jumped in. Just because it was a family business didn't mean that everyone got to hear all their business. 'Give me five minutes and I'll come and see you – Vi's my last cut of the day.'

'Meet me at the café, I could murder a cuppa.' He shot his son a look. 'And Zach, get back to work.'

'Come on, Dad. At least I'm a lovely colour now,' Zach laughed.

'A lovely colour? You're starting to resemble a bloody tea bag, you big girl – now get back to the garage, will you?' Kev said, exasperated.

'Oh you really are a lovely colour,' Vi agreed. 'If only you'd show me your tan lines.'

'Bloody hell, Vi!' Debs shouted, but with a laugh. 'Boys – out, any more of this and Alice'll be sweeping up fainting pensioners instead of hair.'

Issy pulled her black cardigan around her as she walked toward the café. It was cold, but she didn't have far to go. She pushed open the door and saw her dad, sitting at a corner table, reading a newspaper, with two mugs of tea in front of him. She smiled at the woman behind the counter and made her way over.

'Hiya,' she said, sitting down and pointing at his mug. 'There better not be any sugar in that tea?'

'Course not,' Kev replied, looking guilty. Since his heart attack, Issy had been on a one-woman mission to make sure her dad stayed healthy. She resisted the urge to take a sip to check. He was pretty patient about her bossing him around but she didn't want to push her luck.

'So, what's going on?' Issy had a sudden thought. 'Is everything OK? Is it your heart?' However many years passed, Issy didn't think she'd ever stop worrying about her dad having another heart attack.

'No, it's nothing like that. I'm fit as a fiddle, promise.'

Issy relaxed back into her chair. 'Am I in trouble then?' She smiled at her dad the way she always did when she needed to get round him.

'No, you're not in trouble. I just ... well ... OK ... Look, there's something I wanted to talk to you about.' Kev looked awkward as he shuffled in his seat. 'The thing is, well, you've been back at home for three years now.'

Issy frowned. *What was this all about?*

Kev took a deep breath before continuing. 'Here's the thing. Three years ago you were in London, following your dream, full of ideas and ambition. We both know why you came home but I'm not sure I know why you're *still* here.'

'Dad, what are you getting at?' Sometimes her dad took for ever getting to the point. Cars, rather than conversation, were Kev's strong point.

'I just want to make sure that you're happy, you know, living at home and working at the salon. Is cutting old ladies hair really what you want?'

'There are worse jobs,' Issy said defensively.

'I know that, and your mum's salon is grand. But you've always wanted more. You've got your mum's talent but we always wanted more for you as well. Once me and your mum met it was all marriage, babies and bloody dogs. Wish I'd put me foot down and insisted we got a cat.'

'Dad. I have no idea what you're talking about. Is this about me or Princess?' Issy looked her father straight in the eye.

'Bloody hell, Issy. Can't I have a proper conversation with my daughter?'

'Sure.' Issy smiled sweetly. 'And if I knew what this was about then I could join in with that proper conversation.'

Kev looked cross at first and then started laughing. He should've known better – Issy always cut to the chase.

'Here's the thing. It's time for you to put yourself first,' Kev said gruffly. 'You kept this family together when I was ill. Now it's time I did something for you, and I have a plan.'

'A plan?'

'I saw an advert for a new reality TV show. It's a hairdressing competition and the production company is looking for contestants. The best thing is that it will be filmed in Manchester.'

'A TV show? Are you mad?' Issy loved watching reality TV, she was a hopeless addict, but that didn't mean she wanted to be on it. Of course the 'what if' had crossed her mind, but she couldn't see it. She'd never wanted to be famous.

'You're perfect for it,' Kev said. 'You have the talent for it and you'd still be nearby so you wouldn't even be leaving us really.'

'This show – what is it exactly?' Issy fiddled with a salt shaker as she tried to make sense of what her dad was saying. The idea of it had filled her with an uncharacteristic dread.

'All I know is that it's a competition for hairdressers, it's going to be on TV, and there's some big prize.'

'Well, that's not a lot to go on. It sounds all right but, Dad, a TV show? Come on. They probably wouldn't want me anyway.'

'The thing is ... that ... I sort of filled out the application form for you and it turns out they *do* want to speak to you.' Kev stared at the table as intently as if they were showing an episode of *Match of the Day* on there.

'You did *what*?!' Issy shrieked. 'Dad, have you gone mad?' Issy couldn't believe what she was hearing.

'Someone had to do something!' Kev looked annoyed until he saw the panicked look on Issy's face. He picked up his mug and then put it back down again. 'I only did it because I love you,' he said talking to the table again, a blush slowly creeping up his neck.

Issy was silent for a moment. *How am I meant to respond to that?* she thought.

'I love you too, Dad,' Issy said finally. 'But what's that got to do with some daft TV show?'

'The London thing . . . it was a big deal and you gave it up. For us, for me. I know you felt that you had to prop all of us up and we let you, but only because we thought you'd go back once everything was back to normal.' He smiled, back on more comfortable territory. 'It's time for you to get back to your life and stop living ours.'

'I'm not sure I have it in me anymore, it's been too long.' Issy felt confused. Of all the things she could have imagined her dad was going to say, this didn't come close. She didn't know how to react and it was bringing all her unacknowledged fears to the surface.

'Don't be so bloody dramatic, of course you have. You're only twenty-five. You've got your whole life ahead of you.'

'But Dad—'

'This show could open doors for you. Look, you're wasting your talents here and it's not on.' He looked stern and Issy wondered if she was still expected to do as she was told at her age.

'I'm scared, Dad,' she admitted, looking at the table herself now.

'There was a time when nothing scared you.' Kev reached for Issy's hand. 'Where's my brave daughter gone? The daughter who had bigger balls than most of the lads in my garage? Is she still in there?'

Issy laughed, despite herself. 'I don't know, Dad. I need to think about this properly. I'm a little bit blind-sided.'

'OK, love, but don't take too long. They won't wait forever.' Her dad looked her square in the eye for the first time since she'd come in. 'The only thing that matters to me is that you're happy. And I don't think you've been truly happy since you moved back home.'

Issy stood up and walked round the table so she could sit next to her dad. She enveloped him in a hug. Kev gave her a squeeze back.

The two mugs of tea were left undrunk.

Chapter Two

Issy stared at the rain thumping against the bus window. Her mind had been racing ever since she left her dad a few hours ago. She'd needed to chill out and the best way she knew how was a bit of retail therapy. She'd treated herself to a pair of black Kurt Geiger peep-toes, and, although they probably weren't going to be the most comfortable, she'd felt some of her old confidence returning when she'd tried them on in the shop. *What harm could come from meeting the producers?* she'd managed to convince herself. *They might not even like me so the decision is out of my hands, really.* As she'd looked at herself in the full-length mirror, she'd felt a small spark of excitement – the first real excitement for a long time. She was always amazed at how a beautiful pair of shoes could make her feel more confident, even powerful. As the bus jerked around the corner on the way back home, Issy smiled to herself. At the very least, she'd wear her new shoes on her next night out with the girls. Maybe she'd even meet a nice lad wearing them.

Since moving back to Salford Issy had had a couple of short relationships but nothing meaningful. She was a romantic through and through, and wanted to meet someone kind and lovely and who she could spend the rest of her life with – she wanted the kind of relationship her parents had. They'd met at fourteen and had been together ever since. Because of them, Issy wasn't going to settle for just anyone, and she was sure the perfect lad for her was out there somewhere. It was just that lately most of the lads she met thought that buying her a drink would also buy their way into her knickers. It would take more than a G & T and a bit of banter to get Issy's attention.

Mind, she was in Salford, not a Jennifer Aniston film. Maybe she was aiming too high with that level of romance.

Issy's thoughts snapped back to the TV show. Shopping had made her feel excited about the prospect for a while but now on the bus, with the shoes in her bag and another charge on her credit card, the confidence she'd felt in the shop had disappeared and she was left with a gnawing anxiety in the pit of her stomach. Her mum and Zach thought the show was a good idea so Issy had then called Molly, her best mate, for support. Molly had been on the same side as the rest of the Joneses, but Issy remained unconvinced. Was she cut out for reality

TV? Did she even *want* to be on a show that could make her a household name?

After the chat with her dad, it had all been a bit of a blur. They'd headed over to the garage office and he'd shown her the email from the TV company, presenting it to her as if it was a golden ticket. Issy had read the email over and over, unsure what to do, calling her mum again to talk it through and getting endless texts from Molly, along with Zach shouting through from the workshop every few minutes that she should 'just bloody get on with it' until eventually her dad had handed her the phone and *made* her call the producers.

And it had been fine. Good, in fact. They had talked about Issy's hairdressing background and her interests, and then they'd invited her in for a face-to-face meeting. Her dad had been standing right next to her, listening to every word, so she'd had no choice but to agree. That still didn't mean she was actually going to go though. Speaking to the researcher, whose name she now couldn't even remember she'd been so nervous, Issy had been full of excitement at the prospect of something new – the TV company sounded a million miles away from the blue rinse set – but she still couldn't shake her nervous feelings about the whole idea. She didn't know if she could put herself through it.

And she had so many questions. All the researcher had told her was that the show would be a competition and the contestants would have to live together some-where in Manchester. They wouldn't even tell her what the prize was. Issy felt conflicted and having so little information wasn't helping. Mostly she wanted to run a mile in her new shoes but there was a small part of her that thought, *screw it*. Maybe she should go for it. Plus, she could barely walk in her new shoes, let alone run.

Issy thought back to how she'd felt when she'd first arrived at The Hair Academy – confident and full of excitement about the future. She was a talented stylist and she'd stood out from the beginning. She hadn't wanted to give up her life in London but nearly losing her dad had changed everything. It had been a wake-up call and now all she wanted was to keep her dad in sight and make sure he didn't eat too many Mars Bars or drink too much beer. Had her ambition simply gone away?

'Get a grip, Issy,' she hissed to herself as she got off the bus. Her emotions were all over the shop, and that was far from a good thing. She had a decision to make.

Issy was still rolling thoughts around her head when she arrived home. She walked into the lounge ready to col-lapse on the sofa and watch some mind-numbing TV to calm her nerves. Fat chance. Her dad stood in the middle of the room, arms behind his back. Her mum was on her reclining chair, Princess on her lap. Zach was on the sofa and next to him was Molly.

They were all clearly waiting for her – it was an ambush. Issy resisted the urge to flee back into the rain and sat down next to Molly instead, stunned that they'd called her in for reinforcements. No one spoke. It was weird. Issy's family wasn't the silent type. As she looked around, Issy realised they were all staring expectantly at her.

'OK . . . What's going on?' Issy asked eventually.

'We thought we should have a family meeting,' her dad said, sounding serious.

'A family meeting?' Issy raised her eyebrows. *Who are we, the Kardashians? Bit dramatic, isn't it?* The last time they'd had a family meeting, she'd been fifteen. Zach had thrown a party, emptied their parents' spirits cabinet and refilled all the bottles with water and cold tea. *That had been fun*, she remembered, *as her brother had tried to blame it all on her.*

'Here, have a Hobnob.' Zach shoved a plate toward her.

'Now I know something's wrong. Zach, you never share the Hobnobs,' Issy tried to laugh but her throat was too dry.

'We want to talk to you about the show,' Zach said.

'Right . . . ' Issy said warily.

'You keep saying you don't know if you want to do it,' Molly's voice was firm. 'But we think, no, we *know*, that really, deep down, you do know. You want to go for it but something's holding you back.'

Issy looked at Molly. She was petite, blonde and had

gorgeous blue eyes. She and Issy couldn't have looked less alike if they tried, but in personality they weren't that different. They'd been joined at the hip since primary school, ever since Issy had chased away the playground bullies who'd made fun of Molly's stammer. The stammer had made Molly a quiet child but once she became friends with Issy, she'd come out of her shell. Now she barely stammered at all, only when she was upset or angry, and never when she was with Issy or the rest of the Jones family. She'd also become pretty good at standing up for herself and making herself heard. As she was proving right now. Molly looked determined, Zach steely, her parents concerned.

'Why are you all so keen that I should do it anyway?'

'Because it's perfect for you,' Kev said.

'Your dad's right, Issy,' Debs said. 'I love my salon – I wouldn't change a thing about it, but you're far too talented to be stuck doing shampoo and sets for the rest of your life.'

'It's good enough for you,' Issy protested.

'Issy, you're not me. All I've ever wanted is your dad, my small business, and you two. I'm lucky that my life turned out exactly as I hoped, but you used to have all these big dreams so it's time you started chasing them again.'

'Maybe I want what you have too,' Issy said quietly.

'Issy.' Molly put her arm around her friend. 'Before

you came back from London you were unstoppable. But that's not the case anymore.' Issy should've been offended but she knew Molly was right. Molly was always right.

'And anyway, you're single, so you can't have what Mum and Dad have,' Zach pointed out.

Issy knew he didn't mean to be cruel but Zach didn't do subtle. She punched him on the arm. 'So what you're saying is that I'm twenty-five, have no lad and no career?'

'Yeah, kind of,' Zach agreed, rubbing his arm. Issy was stronger than she looked. 'Listen, this show could change your life. You might even end up on the cover of one of those magazines you're always reading.'

'No daughter of mine is taking her clothes off,' Kev growled.

'He said the magazines *I* read, Dad, not the ones he does,' Issy protested. Princess yapped.

'Bloody hell Issy, why are you making this so hard?' Debs said, looking at Kev. 'Kev, can you talk some sense into her?' she asked seriously.

'It's not about sense. I'm scared,' Issy admitted.

'Oh, love,' Debs sighed.

I'm only twenty-five, Issy thought. *That doesn't make me old with no future, does it?* As soon as the thought crossed her mind, it became suddenly clear that she was the only person holding herself back. Her parents had confidence in her, so did Zach and Molly. Why didn't she feel it anymore? Her parents were happy with their lives, and

Zach was more than content working for their dad. But then she wasn't her brother, or her parents. Or even Molly, who loved her job as a teaching assistant at a local primary school. Issy had lost her way a bit, she had to admit that.

'Look, love, we just want you to start living your life again. And we think you may have forgotten how to do that.' Kev crouched down in front of Issy, like he used to when she was a child.

'Issy, what happened to your dad changed things for all of us. You gave up a lot to look after us, but we're OK now. You don't need to do that anymore,' Debs added.

'I know I have to make a decision but it's hard,' Issy said. She knew their hearts were in the right place but she was feeling pressured and that was making it harder.

'The last thing we want to do is make you feel ganged up on. It's just that the show is perfect for you, and we all care about you, Is,' Molly said. 'Of course it's your decision, but we all think you'll really regret it if you don't go for this now.'

Issy took a mental photo of them all. Her mum: Princess in her lap, all Dolly Parton hair and pink fluffy high-heeled slippers who always wore her heart on her sleeve. Zach: a softie underneath all the style and tattoos. Molly: with her core of steel, looking like butter wouldn't melt in her mouth – although Issy knew different. And her dad: striding around the living room like a general of this dysfunctional army. They might be bloody interfering but they were also annoyingly right.

'Argh, I feel so pressured!' Issy buried her head in Molly's shoulder.

'Calm down, Gwynnie. Stop being so dramatic. It's only an interview, they might not even bloody want you,' Kev said, patting her knee, but surreptitiously checking his watch. The United match was about to kick off.

Debs smacked Kev on the arm. 'Of course they'll want her! Is, we've got faith in you and we think you should do this. You have to *want* to do it too, though,' Debs added gently. 'Remember, if I was being selfish I'd want to keep you here. Good hairdressers are hard to find – and it doesn't hurt that you're quite handy to have round the house.' Debs stroked Princess and smiled.

'And I don't want you to move away either,' Molly added. 'I come over here all the time to get away from my mum and Pete rowing.' Molly's stepdad was always rowing with her mum, and Issy was always having to pick up the pieces when they upset Molly with one of their fights. It always made Issy even more grateful for her own parents. Zach looked at Molly in concern and handed her a Hobnob – this was as close to sympathy as Zach got.

'I'd probably be deep frying Mars Bars and sneak Guinness into my IV drip without you here,' Kev said.

'And who'd wax my eyebrows?' Zach said. Kev turned

sharply to look at him and shook his head. Zach had the decency to blush – but only slightly.

'So do you want me to do it or not?' Issy laughed.

'Not!' they all answered in unison. Zach rolled his eyes.

'And what if I *do* want to go to the audition?' Issy said, with a mischievous glint in her eye.

'So you'll go? Great! I've put a bottle of Prosecco in the fridge to celebrate. I'll go and get it,' Debs said, kissing Issy's head as she walked past. 'Zach, share out those Hobnobs, love, before you eat them all.'

'Hang on,' Issy said. 'You already had a bottle in the fridge? So you knew I'd say yes?'

'Of course not, love,' Kev said, with a wry smile as he reached for the remote. 'We had no idea.'